Protest at Midnight

Protest at Midnight

Ministry to a Nation Torn Apart

Peter Storey

FOREWORD BY
Will Willimon

EDITED BY
Sarah Musser

CASCADE *Books* • Eugene, Oregon

PROTEST AT MIDNIGHT
Ministry to a Nation Torn Apart

Copyright © 2022 Peter Storey. All rights reserved. Except for brief quotations in critical publications or reviews, no part of this book may be reproduced in any manner without prior written permission from the publisher. Write: Permissions, Wipf and Stock Publishers, 199 W. 8th Ave., Suite 3, Eugene, OR 97401.

Cascade Books
An Imprint of Wipf and Stock Publishers
199 W. 8th Ave., Suite 3
Eugene, OR 97401

www.wipfandstock.com

PAPERBACK ISBN: 978-1-7252-9356-4
HARDCOVER ISBN: 978-1-7252-9357-1
EBOOK ISBN: 978-1-7252-9358-8

Cataloguing-in-Publication data:

Names: Storey, Peter John, 1938–, author. | Musser, Sarah, editor. | Willimon, William H., foreword.

Title: Protest at midnight : ministry to a nation torn apart / by Peter Storey ; edited by Sarah Musser ; foreword by Will Willimon.

Description: Eugene, OR : Cascade Books, 2022

Identifiers: ISBN 978-1-7252-9356-4 (paperback) | ISBN 978-1-7252-9357-1 (hardcover) | ISBN 978-1-7252-9358-8 (ebook)

Subjects: LCSH: Storey, Peter John, 1938–. | Methodist Church of Southern Africa—Clergy—Biography. | Christianity and politics—South Africa. | Church and social problems—South Africa.

Classification: DT1927.S76 P67 2022 (print) | DT1927.S76 P67 (ebook)

01/03/22

All Scripture quotations, unless otherwise indicated, are taken from the New English Bible, copyright @ Cambridge University Press and Oxford University Press, 1961, 1970. All rights reserved.

Scripture quotations marked (NIV) are taken from the Holy Bible, New International Version®, NIV®. Copyright © 1973, 1978, 1984, 2011 by Biblica, Inc.® Used by permission of Zondervan. All rights reserved worldwide. www.zondervan.com The "NIV" and "New International Version" are trademarks registered in the United States Patent and Trademark Office by Biblica, Inc.®

Scripture quotations marked (GNT) are from the Good News Translation in Today's English Version- Second Edition Copyright © 1992 by American Bible Society. Used by Permission.

"This is no ordinary memoir that one reads with detached intellectual engagement. It is a complacency-shattering challenge to invest one's life on behalf of justice, compassion, truth-telling, and radical hospitality rooted in the 'kin-dom' of God. Here is a book of profound theological insight and vision that reads like a riveting novel. It is a must-read for anyone who wishes to be an agent of transformation in this dangerous world."

—**Kenneth Carder**, Duke Divinity School, emeritus

"*Protest at Midnight* is sure to become a classic of Christian conscience. . . . It emerges from the inside of South Africa's struggle against apartheid and from inside the soul of the courageous man of faith who helped lead it. On every page, one encounters the brutal truths of politics. And every page is suffused with the blood of the martyrs. We owe Peter Storey a debt of gratitude that can never be repaid."

—**Richard Lischer**, author of *Just Tell the Truth: A Call to Faith, Hope, and Courage*

"Peter Storey's long-awaited memoir of his extraordinary life and ministry in South Africa during the apartheid years is one of the most insightful and theologically rich accounts of the racial struggle of both nation and church that we now have in print. . . . Peter places us all in his debt with this powerful text, and it needs to be placed in the hands of everyone seriously committed to faithful Christian witness."

—**Willie James Jennings**, Yale Divinity School

"Bound to be a classic. *Protest at Midnight* is right up there with the greatest accounts of Christ's collision with a world in need of redemption."

—**Will Willimon**, Duke Divinity School

"While reading *Protest at Midnight*, I was overwhelmed with tears, because Storey not only tells his story but gives context to my own. As a Black girl growing up in the shadows of Jim Crow in Mississippi, Storey's memoir tells the parallel stories of two lands and one church's response to systemic racism. Storey dares us to look at the painful past, truthfully name the social and theological ills of today, and respond to God's clarion call for radical justice and freedom."

—**Theresa S. Thames**, Princeton University

"This awe-inspiring memoir chronicles a ministry ordered and orchestrated by God in the process of liberating South Africa from its brutal system of apartheid. It could provide the key to the character, courage, and convictions necessary to deliver America from its deadly scourge of racism and temptations toward autocratic government."

—**James A. Forbes Jr.**, Senior Minister emeritus, Riverside Church

With gratitude for
CLIFFORD KINGSLEY STOREY
my father for only twenty years,
too few by far,
yet long enough to show me
by his great heart and noble spirit
the face of Jesus
and the meaning of ministry

A candle-light is a protest at midnight,
It is a non-conformist.
It says to the darkness,
"I beg to differ."

SAMUEL RAYAN
Your Will Be Done (Singapore: CCA, 1984)

Contents

Foreword by Will Willimon | ix
Preface | xiii
Acknowledgments | xv
Abbreviations | xvii

Introduction: Prisoners of Venda | 1

1. The Island | 12
2. District Six | 19
3. Ocean in a Single Drop | 29
4. Then Came the Bulldozers | 36
5. Amateur Journo | 42
6. Young Church | 53
7. Widening World | 61
8. No Soft Landing | 68
9. Broken Open Church | 78
10. Ministry with a Whiff of Tear Gas | 89
11. Public Square Encounters | 102
12. Shadows of War | 112
13. Perfect Storm | 125
14. Bearing Witness | 135
15. National Leadership | 147
16. Among God's People | 156
17. Stress Fractures | 168
18. Winnie Crisis | 175
19. Confronting Expediency | 188
20. Soul Wounds | 193
21. Thin Orange Line | 203
22. Taking on the Guns | 214
23. Days of Grace | 222
24. Search for Healing | 231
25. America the Vulnerable | 239
26. A Church the World Might Take Seriously | 247
27. Postscript: Loss and Gratitude | 257

Foreword

IF YOU THINK THE best that Jesus has to offer is serene Sabbath rest, a well-balanced, placid, stress-free life, you need to read *Protest at Midnight*. Allow this South African Methodist to take you where he has been with Christ, journeying with him as he dares to walk with the oppressed in their darkest hours, and you are sure to see wonderfully disruptive light.

Hold on to your hats. Peter Storey invites you to take a fast-paced journey through the ending of one world and the dawning of a new. His memoir begins with the threat of a life-ending bang that could have ended the lives of Storey and Tutu and ends by delivering a Jesus-instigated blow to complacent, compromised American Christians who've bedded down with Trumpism as if it were Christian. What a ministry Peter Storey has had; what a God to have summoned a straight-talker like Peter to speak up and act out for God.

Having read dozens of clerical memoirs, having written one myself, I predict that this book is bound to be a classic. Peter's *Protest at Midnight* is right up there with the greatest accounts of Christ's collision with a world in need of redemption. Here's an inspiring story of a man who found himself cast by God into the crucible of the death of a wicked social order and the birth of a nation, a narrative of a preacher who, by word and deed, dared to live into God's future.

From the first, Peter risked allowing Christ to make Christian witness as dangerous, conflicted, and adventurous as Christ means it to be. Enlisted as a young man, partnering with vivacious, committed Elizabeth, the Storeys began their work in a culture in which racial apartheid affected everyone and everything in South Africa. As a new pastor, Peter was cast into situations where he experienced first-hand the ravages of apartheid. At the same time, Peter got a front row seat from which to witness black

Christians living courageously and (an heroic few) white Christians doing right at a time when it seemed the whole world was wrong.

Peter takes us to the front lines where the battle raged, introduces us to history-makers, good and bad, like Tutu, Mandela, Botha, and de Klerk, and to places where God was working in spite of it all, like Robben Island prison, a bullet-riddled church in Mozambique, Central Methodist Mission, and a simple but inviting kitchen in a basement in Cape Town's District Six.

Like our Lord, Peter never backed down from an argument, showed undue deference to tyrants, or refused to tell the truth as God had given it to him. Like all Holy Spirit–consecrated preachers, Peter has never been able to keep his mouth shut when somebody needed to speak up for justice and righteousness. From the first, he got into trouble for what he said and where he showed up. In spite of itself, Peter's church called him to lead, though there were many times when, if truth be told, the church regretted having Peter up front doing the talking. Accompany Peter as he mixes it up with the powerful and marvels at the witness of ordinary people doing their part in God's continuing program of truth and reconciliation; you will never again be able easily to dismiss us preachers and bishops as mere people-pleasing sycophants.

At Duke Divinity, I got to witness Peter equipping seminarians for ministry more demanding than congregational hand-holding and unctuous caregiving. I know many clergy today who are bored by the dreariness of keeping house in the church. They wouldn't be if they dared to follow Peter's vocational trajectory. In an age in which too many church leaders have exchanged fluffy spirituality and calming pastoral caregiving for bodacious truth-telling, I say read Peter's memoir and be reminded of the quest that Christian ministry is meant to be.

I wish you could have heard Peter preach on his first visit to Duke Chapel, an unforgettable sermon in which he testified about how joining Jesus in his apartheid-dismantling work in South Africa had led to a renewal of the church's sense of its God-given mission. When the front of the building where Peter worked with the South African Council of Churches was blown away, he said it exposed the mural of the risen Christ, arms outstretched as if to bless the work of South African Christians who were paying such a price laboring with Christ for the coming of his kingdom.

Then there's Peter's later sermon on repentance in which he spoke of his sadness at his friend Winnie Mandela's unwillingness to repent and atone for her sins against innocent victims shortly before the fall of the apartheid regime. My accommodated congregation gasped but listened in spite of themselves.

You would have also been thrilled if you could have seen Peter come up to me, after a service on Maundy Thursday, bristling with annoyance as he asked, "Do you think there's a chance that, before Holy Week ends, we might hear from the chapel pulpit some mention of the horrors being perpetrated by your country in Iraq at the moment?"

Like I said, don't listen to Peter if you are truth-averse. And don't read this book if you are squeamish about the truth being told straight. Throughout his life, Peter has steadfastly kept close to his conviction that Jesus Christ is not only the way, the life, but also the truth.

Not content to narrate what happened back then and over there, Peter, ever the prophetic preacher, in this book confronts us with the need for faithful witness here and now. All that's needed, for the principalities and powers to triumph, is for Christians vainly to try to make peace between prophet Jesus and the politics of whiteness.

I remember a conversation with Peter in which I lamented that Durham had set a record for deaths by handguns. "If Durham were South Africa," mused Peter, "they wouldn't call it a crime wave; your media would call it race war. What does that tell you?"

This book, like Peter's sermons, begins graciously and engagingly, but then ends with a wallop. How typical of Peter, before he finishes the story of his ministry, to refuse to leave us admiring what he did then and there and instead challenges us in our time and place.

After one of Peter's sermons, I made an innocuous comment about the surprising insights to be had by having a South African Christian comment on American racial, political, and ecclesial dilemmas. Peter—true to form—thanked me, but then said, "And what are you going to do about it, friend?"

Will Willimon
Duke Divinity School

Preface

PROTEST AT MIDNIGHT WAS born out of forty years of ministry forged in the crucible of the anti-apartheid struggle in South Africa. It began as an autobiography called *I Beg to Differ*, commissioned by Tafelberg Publishers and released in South Africa in 2018. By that time, I had long since retired as a Methodist and ecumenical leader and had completed a "second career" teaching on seminary campuses in the United States. I agreed to write about the years I had lived through, not because my life was particularly extraordinary, but because those years certainly were. There are only so many people who can say, "I lived in three South Africas: the hateful land of apartheid, the bright rainbow nation of Nelson Mandela, and the desperate years between."

I Beg to Differ had a positive reception in my homeland and made the list for Africa's prestigous Alan Paton literary prize. Some copies traveled across the Atlantic, where American friends in academe and church circles convinced me that it had relevance beyond South Africa. They believed that a story of costly Christian witness in a racist police state needed to be heard in an America grappling with systemic racism and growing right-wing populism. They also believed that the book offered a challenge to a large section of the American church seemingly unwilling to pay the price of standing prophetically in resistance to these evils.

This book is the result. Shed of material of exclusively local South African interest, it focuses primarily on the years between my first parish appointment in 1960 and my retirement as bishop of the Johannesburg-Soweto area in 1997. These years coincided exactly with the most intense decades of the liberation struggle beginning with the 1960 Sharpeville massacre and climaxing with the work of the Truth and Reconciliation Commission in a free, democratic South Africa.

During those fraught years, whether pastoring Nelson Mandela and other prisoners on Robben Island, sharing the tears of congregants losing their homes simply because of their skin color, praying with armed police in my pulpit trying to silence me, heading the SA Council of Churches with Bishop Desmond Tutu, or leading twenty-five thousand protesters marching against Johannesburg's secret police headquarters, my ministry was shaped by a simple question: *"What does it mean to obey Jesus in apartheid South Africa?"*

This book is about my attempts—alongside many others in the strange and wonderful community we call "church"—to live into that question.

The closing chapters of *Protest at Midnight* include thoughts about the current crises facing American society and the role of the church, for better or for worse, in either shaping or responding to them. They are offered with a deep sense of love for our "second home" and gratitude for the years my wife Elizabeth and I lived there, learning, teaching, preaching, and worshiping among its remarkable people.

Acknowledgments

I HAVE SO MUCH and so many to be thankful for: my parental home and family and especially my father, to whom this book is dedicated. He died when I was only twenty years old, but his mark on my life remains indelible. A beloved pastor and a preacher whose words and deeds witnessed to a Christ of "unutterable beauty,"[1] he loved me more than I deserved. The Jesus he preached was the Jesus I came to follow. In the early 1950s, he declared that the newly elected National Party government in South Africa, with its nostrum of enforced segregation, was driven by an idolatry of race and nation similar to that of the Nazism recently vanquished in Germany. He was the first church leader in the land to denounce the apartheid policy as a sin against God, earning the anger of its main architect, Prime Minister H. F. Verwoerd. As leader of the Methodist Church in South Africa, he continued this strong stand, but at age fifty-seven he died of heart disease. I wish he had lived longer, but his life and death taught me that depth of integrity, not length of years, is what counts most.

Australian preacher Dr. Alan Walker was another powerful influence who liberated the gospel from privatized piety without diluting its personal claim. I spent two years with him in Sydney's Central Methodist Mission to discover that my passion would be, like his, to minister among the gritty streets of the inner city. My colleagueship alongside then-Bishop Desmond Tutu threw us together at the sharp end of the church-state conflict when it was at its most fraught and dangerous. I honor him for his iron discipline of prayer and devotion, the spiritual center without which no prophet can be faithful. Others who touched my life at different times were Martin Niemöller, Donald Soper, Clarence Jordan—and through speeches and writings, Dietrich Bonhoeffer and Martin Luther King Jr.

---

1. *The Unutterable Beauty* is the title of a book of poems written by Rev. G. A. Studdert-Kenney in the trenches of WWI that my father used to quote often.

South Africa's own Beyers Naudé's example of courage under immense duress from the apartheid "system" reminded me through all the years of struggle that the cost of truth-telling could be high, but that nothing less was required of the followers of Jesus.

There is no way to fully express my gratitude for the fifty-four rich years of marriage with Elizabeth, whom I have loved since our schooldays, and for our four remarkable sons, their beloveds, and seven wonderful grandchildren. I also thank the Methodist Church of Southern Africa in whose bosom I was nurtured and with whom I have enjoyed a "lover's quarrel"[2] for most of my life. Then there is a God whose relentless patience with me is proof that none are rejected. I am indeed fortunate.

This book could never have happened without the encouragement of good friends at Duke University Divinity School. Professors Rick Lischer, Ellen Davis, Dean Greg Jones, and Jason Byassee, a former student and now a professor at Vancouver School of Theology, all lent their minds and hearts and helpful advice. I am indebted to Dr. Will Willimon for his lively Foreword, although I do not recall saying some of the impolite things he records with such relish.

My former commissioning editor Gill Moodie and Tafelberg Publishers deserve special appreciation for facilitating permissions and making all the illustrations used in the original book freely available for *Protest at Midnight*. I am also most grateful to Charlie Collier of Wipf and Stock Publishers for his willingness to take on the project and his ready advice and encouragement.

My final word must be to my former student, Dr. Sarah Musser, now my good friend and editorial mentor. With great skill, much grace, much patience, and a wonderful enthusiasm for the project, Sarah shouldered much of the sensitive task of reducing a 470-page volume down to its current size, correcting dozens of drafts, "Americanizing" language, and punctiliously checking detailed footnotes. I feel greatly blessed to have had her always positive collaboration throughout, because without her, *Protest at Midnight* would certainly not have happened.

Peter Storey

Cape Town, November 2021

---

2. The phrase is borrowed from great preacher William Sloane Coffin—former pastor of Riverside Church, New York City.

Abbreviations

ANC	African National Congress
CCMC	Civic Centre Methodist Church
CI	Christian Institute
CLC	Christian Leadership Center
CMC	Central Methodist Church
CMM	Central Methodist Mission
CO	Conscientious Objector
COSATU	Congress of SA Trade Unions
ECC	End Conscription Campaign
GFSA	Gun Free South Africa
GS	General Secretary
IEC	Independent Electoral Commission
IFP	Inkatha Freedom Party
IMSSA	Independent Mediation Services of South Africa
JOC	Joint Operational Center
LPC	Local Peace Committee
MCSA	Methodist Church of Southern Africa
MDM	Mass Democratic Movement
MK	*Umkhonto we Sizwe* (armed wing of ANC)
MOP	Methodist Order of Peacemakers
NIR	National Initiative for Reconciliation

NPA	National Peace Accord
PAC	Pan Africanist Congress
RENAMO	*Resistência Nacional Moçambicana*
RPC	Regional Peace Committee
SA	South Africa/n
SABC	South African Broadcasting Corporation
SACC	South African Council of Churches
SACP	South African Communist Party
SADF	South African Defense Force
SAGA	South African Gunowners' Association
SAIRR	South African Institute of Race Relations
SWAPO	South West Africa People's Organization
TRC	Truth and Reconciliation Commission
UMC	United Methodist Church
WCC	World Council of Churches
WPCC	Western Province Council of Churches

Introduction

Prisoners of Venda

IT WAS ON A hot summer's day in 1982 when Bishop Desmond Tutu and I were told we were going to be shot.

I was president of the South African Council of Churches (SACC) at the time, and Desmond was its general secretary.[1] The council we led stood in the forefront of the church struggle against South Africa's racist white rulers and their apartheid policy.[2] We had driven three hundred miles north from Johannesburg hoping to intervene in the imprisonment and torture of three Lutheran priests. They were being held in a police station in one of the puppet tribal "republics" set up by the regime as dumping grounds for people they called "surplus bantu."[3] It was called Venda, and its black proxy ruler was chosen for his ruthlessness and rewarded for his willingness to obey the white regime's instructions. It was well known that the SACC regarded "bantustans" like Venda as illegitimate, so our presence was doubly unwelcome.

After crossing Venda's "border," news of our coming went ahead of us, and when we arrived, the station commander met us: "So you want to visit prisoners? We have no prisoners here." We said that we believed he was holding some Lutheran priests, and we wanted to pray with them. What we didn't know was that one priest had already been tortured to death just days

---

1. The SACC represented some fourteen million Christians from most mainline denominations.

2. Apartheid stood for a systematized policy of racial discrimination and its ruthless implementation over forty-five years. It was declared a "crime against humanity" by the United Nations in 1966.

3. "Bantu" is a generic term referring to black Africans. Altogether, three million people were uprooted from their homes and forcibly moved to tribal "homelands" or "bantustans" like Venda.

before, and that the others were in no condition to be seen. We were told to wait while he "sorted things out." After an hour in a grim little room, during which time we could hear snippets of telephone conversations in Afrikaans, apparently with the white government in Pretoria, he came in and said, "You have been declared persona non grata in the Republic of Venda, and you will be deported immediately." A couple of nasty-looking militia men then entered the room. With berets and reflective dark glasses, low-slung trousers, and guns on their hips, they looked more like thuggish enforcers than disciplined soldiers. They escorted us outside to where Desmond's Toyota was now sandwiched between two military vehicles with more men touting sub-machine guns sprawling over them.

It was all very menacing.

We drove in convoy for a while, but instead of leading us to the "border" of their puppet republic, our escorts turned off onto a track leading into thick bush. A few minutes later, they stopped in a clearing and pulled us out of our car. Some began to push us around while others took articles out of the trunk and threw them to the ground. They were particularly angered when we couldn't produce passports—after all, they were an "independent republic," and we were therefore "foreigners"—so the threats and the waving and pointing of guns continued. "We are going to shoot you. You know we can kill you. No one will find your bodies. This isn't Jo'burg, nobody knows Tutu or Storey here." This went on for a while, and a cold fear gripped my innards, until, as if in obedience to some signal, it ended. We were ordered to pick up our stuff and get back into the car. Led back to the tarred road, we were soon at the "border," where our escorts peeled off and we continued south, deeply shaken.

If anyone doubts that prayer and life are inseparable for Desmond Tutu, I have scary proof. He was at the wheel as we drove in silence for a while, waiting for our hearts to slow. Then he spoke: "Peter, we nearly died back there. They could have shot us as easily as swatting a fly!"[4] I answered in a not-very-steady voice, "Yes, it was close." Desmond said, "We must thank God for preserving our lives," and immediately launched into an impassioned prayer of thanksgiving. I looked at him and saw that his eyes were tight shut. I grabbed the wheel and let him do the praying while I ensured that death didn't get a second shot at us.

---

4. We were fortunate to have been spared. The regime had secret assassination teams, including those who flew their victims out over the Atlantic, dropping their bodies into the depths. One team poisoned the clothing of Rev. Frank Chikane, Tutu's successor as SACC general secretary, who was traveling in the USA when he fell desperately ill. The FBI identified the poison, and he recovered.

Two decades later in a liberated South Africa, I was at a conference when a tall Afrikaner with a military bearing approached me.[5] He asked me if I remembered Venda. It was the first time this deeply repressed memory was jolted to the surface, and I felt anger and fright rush through my body. "Yes, I do remember Venda," I said. "That was where my wife was nearly widowed and my four sons orphaned." He said he needed to confess to me: he had been the South African Military Intelligence adviser attached to the Venda government at the time, and he had passed on the order from Pretoria that we should be eliminated. He still didn't know why it had not been carried out, but was glad it hadn't. Would I forgive him? I had been struggling to breathe as he spoke. My heart was thudding in my chest, and my throat was tight. Finally I muttered, "Of course, yes, I forgive you. I have to."

A Wider Challenge

These two events perhaps form appropriate bookends for the story recorded in this book: How did a white Methodist minister find himself facing death with a black Anglican bishop in the middle of the African bush? What kind of personal journey would lead someone to jeopardize the security of his South African whiteness in a life of struggle for racial justice—and then on to the hard work of forgiveness and reconciliation? The two encounters may also serve as a microcosm of the witness of the SACC and other Christians in first resisting the horrors and indignities of systemic racism and then helping a nation heal from its wounds.

However, the story behind these two moments in my life may also be more immediately pertinent because, while South Africa's "struggle years" are falling rapidly into the past, the issues we faced then are not: they are alive and more dangerously relevant than ever. At the height of the apartheid evil, South Africa was often referred to as the "last outpost" of organized racism, but current crises in the United States and elsewhere are proving the opposite. We are at risk of a global form of apartheid, with great democracies being taken over by government-driven prejudice and hate. We are witnessing a "re-fracturing" of humanity; a backward slide into the worship of the deathly idols of nationalism, pride, and fear; of walls and drawbridges; of the arrogance of whiteness and the fear of "otherness." We South Africans know these signs: we've been there! Please believe us: these withdrawals into apart-ness always signal much worse to come.

---

5. "Afrikaner" describes the descendants of the first white colonizers of the Southern tip of Africa. They were also known as "Boers" (farmers). The Afrikaans language is a derivative of the Dutch spoken by their ancestors.

My father used to say, "Everything begins in theology and ends in politics." It was theology, our biblical understanding of God and humankind, that thrust Desmond Tutu, myself, and many others into the public square to stand against the state. This is how it ought to be: if the gospel of Jesus has nothing to say about the outrages rulers perpetrate on our common humanity, then the gospel has nothing to say about anything. So too with the church: confronted by systemic evil, a silent church is no church at all.

In South Africa, some of the church refused to be silent, and I will always be grateful that it was that kind of church that challenged and nurtured me, changing me along the way. It is my hope that the story told in this book may yield some clues—unearthed slowly and painfully in my own journey—about the role of church, especially in cultures of systemic racism, oppression, and injustice, in witnessing to God's truth.

Bantu, Boer, and Briton

People like me are usually called English-speaking South Africans, as distinct from the Afrikaners whose Dutch ancestors were the first European colonists who arrived in 1652. The British came a century and a half later, finally wresting the Cape Colony from the Dutch in 1806. Of course, others were there first: the indigenous KhoiKhoi herders and San nomads were on the beach to meet these strange pale humans, while the taller, darker Xhosa clans were soon to be encountered not far to the northeast. Settler expansion was met with fierce Xhosa resistance. One hundred years of intermittent warfare steadily dispossessed the Xhosa of their territory. As part of a plan to stabilize the latest "frontier" they had created, the British government offered free passage and one hundred acres of land to any family wanting to begin a new life in South Africa. My English ancestors were among four thousand settlers delivered into the midst of that turmoil in 1820.

My great-great-great grandfather John Oates came with a group of largely Methodist families. He was a lay preacher whose faith must have carried an enduring gene, because I am the seventh Methodist minister in his family line, and one of my sons the eighth. The chaplain accompanying them, the Rev. William Shaw, was determined to reach out to the Xhosa too, and not least because he was such an enterprising and fearless missionary, the Methodist Church of Southern Africa (MCSA) was to become the largest multi-racial church on the sub-continent, with 85 percent of its two million adherents being black.

The 350 years of colonial South African history is peppered with conflict between Bantu, Boer, and Briton. When Britain abolished slavery in its territories in 1833, angry Boers opted out of the colony and trekked northwards in a "covered wagons" saga as voracious and violent as that of the American West. Their trek led to the final dispossession of most of the black tribes and the achievement of white hegemony over the sub-continent, with two Boer republics in the north and two British colonies in the south. As if ethnicity and land were not sufficient reasons to fight, the discovery of gold in one of the Boer republics made war with Queen Victoria's mineral-hungry Empire inevitable. Twice Boers and Brits clashed, with the Boers finally defeated after a bitter conflict marked by massive British casualties and enormous suffering amongst Boer families and their black retainers.[6] Both my grandfathers fought on the British side.

One of the more respectable reasons advanced by the British for the fight was the general mistreatment of blacks by their Boer "masters," and blacks under Boer control were hopeful that life in a British-ruled South Africa might lead to full citizenship. It was a forlorn hope: in the 1910 peace agreement establishing a union between the four segments of South Africa, Britain treated its defeated foes with magnanimity, returning all their rights (except independence from the Empire) but betrayed the Queen's darker subjects, who remained without citizenship or franchise. According to black writer Sol Plaatjie, they woke up the next day as "pariahs in the land of our birth," and two years later the oldest liberation movement in the world—to become known worldwide as Nelson Mandela's African National Congress (ANC)—was born.

In the years following 1910, South Africa stood loyally alongside Britain in two World Wars, but a significant number of Afrikaners had other ambitions. By the time I was born on the eve of World War II, many were openly pro-Hitler, hoping that a Nazi victory over Britain would free them to pursue their dream of a purely Afrikaner republic. While this was not to be, two important factors enabled them to win a narrow victory in the whites-only election of 1948. First, many returned soldiers voted for them in a protest against the government, which they felt had let them down after six years of fighting and sacrifice. Second was an obscure new word: *apartheid*. The Afrikaner Nationalists promised to enforce complete separation of the races and to preserve what they called *wit baaskap*—white dominance—guaranteeing that blacks would be kept in a subservient relationship by a raft of discriminatory laws.

6. Twenty-two thousand British soldiers were killed and seventy-five thousand were sent back to England sick or wounded. Only 6,189 Boer soldiers were killed, but twenty-six thousand of their women and children and twenty thousand African retainers died after being taken from their farms and herded into the first "concentration camps" the world had seen.

Thus, in May of 1948, when I was nine years old, the Afrikaner Nationalists took power and turned South Africa down the path of apartheid. I would be fifty-six years old before their rule ended.

Race

My father being the sixth Methodist minister among John Oates' descendants meant that my mother, my sister, and I saw the inside of a number of parsonages before dad was appointed as governor of one of the great black educational campuses that were the pride of Methodist missionary endeavor.[7] Located a few miles outside Pretoria, Kilnerton Institution consisted of a preparatory school with 700 children, a high school with 600 pupils, and a teachers' training college with 230 students. Even though Kilnerton was not without its colonial paternalism, by the fifties the institution had produced numbers of alumni who were making their mark opposing white dominance.

Living on this largely black campus was powerfully formative. It was at Kilnerton that I first encountered my own potential for racism. I was too young to engage meaningfully with South Africa's tortured politics of race, but even at Kilnerton being white could be good for privilege and bad for the soul. My father's witness was a powerful corrective, however. In the Sunday morning chapel services packed with students and staff, he spoke out strongly against the apartheid menace, attacking its roots and describing racism as a "disease of the heart, diagnosed in the look." Uninvited lessons about race hate were also taught by white vigilantes who burned our fields and fired shots into the mission property. Among the students were immensely talented young men and women bold enough to confront me. They helped me see attitudes within myself that I was blind to, and I began to relate to them in a different way, grateful for our relationship and sad that my white friends never had the same life-changing opportunity.

Call

After five years at Kilnerton, my father was appointed to a church in Cape Town, one thousand miles to the south, where I finished high school. I immediately took the first steps toward the career I had wanted ever since I had first set foot in a boat: becoming a naval officer. So I went to sea, revelling in

---

7. The Methodist Church at the time was educating 27.3 percent of all the black scholars in the land. Nelson Mandela attended another historic Methodist institution, known as Healdtown, in the Eastern Cape province.

doing the things I loved in ships and boats, but in the very week when I was to become a midshipman, God appeared to intervene in a rather startling way. I have often said that my call to the ordained ministry was like being ambushed. Alone on the cliffs overlooking the Naval Academy harbor, I experienced a clear and unexpected conviction that cut across everything I had wanted and worked for. Something spoke inside me, saying, "You will be a minister." It was as simple as that and almost as matter of fact as if a passing officer had barked an order, yet it came with more authority than anyone in uniform could muster. This was not what I wanted. I loved and admired my dad, whose preaching had always moved me, but while I wished I could emulate his fine character and moral example there was no conscious desire to follow his vocation. Having listened since to scores of stories from young candidates for ordination, I know beyond doubt that God "calls" people to serve in this way, but unlike most of them I felt more kidnapped than called. I loved the sea desperately, and it took a long time before God and I got to speaking terms about it.

The choice may not have been mine, but it was final, and I know it was right. I still often yearn for all that the sea meant to me, but in the years ahead the military was drawn ever more deeply into defending a ruthless regime. If I had remained in the navy, I would have spent my life on the wrong side of history.

I attended seminary at Rhodes University, where I was no more than an average scholar, still struggling with my amputation from the navy. However, there did come a moment in my second year when a new peace settled on me, and I could say to myself, "Yes, I do belong, I'm meant to be here," and to God, "You called me, so you're going to have to put up with me." Something was settled then for the rest of my life.

While I was there, Dad became the leader of the MCSA, and I was present when he made a powerful denunciation of the regime and its policies. Apartheid was slavery in another form, he declared, and when pushed to logical conclusions, it ran into theological conclusions: it was a sin against God. "The government's view is that while one white man and one black man are friends, apartheid will have failed; the Church's view is that while one white man and one black man are enemies, the Church will have failed." He warned that it might be necessary to disobey apartheid laws: "We will not put the Church at the disposal of the State."[8] I was proud of his stand but also shocked by the reaction of some of his colleagues.

---

8. Clifford K. Storey, "President's Address to the Annual Conference of the Methodist Church of Southern Africa," East London, October 1957.

While black Methodists warmly welcomed it, many white clergy were either lukewarm or openly hostile.

Dad (left) leading a 1957 church protest in Cape Town against the apartheid regime's ban on multi-racial worship

My own first act of public protest was in 1959. Rhodes faculty and students marched to protest a new law banning black students from registering at "white" universities. Little was I to know how many such marches—some of them much less dignified and far more dangerous—were to follow before the last great demonstrations four decades later. I also made a foray into student politics, being elected to the Student's Representative Council and sharing editorship of the student newspaper. Our greatest claim to fame was publishing an issue consisting of a dozen blank spaces showing how much content had been censored by the government. Oppressive regimes are humorless, so leaving blank spaces in newspapers soon became a punishable offense.

I was thinking that my father would not have an easy year in leadership, but it turned out that he would not have the year at all. A longstanding heart problem wore him down, and halfway through 1958 he had to travel to England for one of the earliest open-heart operations. It extended his life by eighteen months, but he died in August of 1959. The person I had most loved and admired was gone. There was little time to mourn because final exams were upon me. I managed to graduate and was grateful to be appointed to a young church in Cape Town, where I could be close to my newly widowed mother.

Then There Was Elizabeth

I could also further my relationship with Elizabeth Hardie, my teenage sweetheart. We had met when we were at school, and apart from her rosy Scottish complexion, ready smile, and bright blue eyes, what attracted me most was her steady, principled goodness and her quiet, unruffled, honest handling of anything that came at her, including me. So, while serving my new congregation in the clumsy way that inexperienced probationer ministers tend to do, I courted my future spouse.[9]

Young sweethearts: with Elizabeth in 1957

When I arrived at church with her on my motorbike, the youth group loved teasing us about the progress of our romance. It was a happy year with a congregation who were wonderfully patient with me as I learned the business of pastoring, and I soon discovered one of the first lessons of ministry:

9. Methodist trainee ministers were required to complete a three-year seminary degree and three years of "probation" in parishes before ordination.

our people may think that they draw their strength from our pastoring and preaching, but the real truth is that it is their faith that nourishes us.

Elizabeth and I made our marriage vows joyfully toward the end of my probation. It was the beginning of fifty-four years of marriage in which she was not only my strength and stay and the wonderful mother of four sons, but she carved out a remarkable ministry of her own.[10] Elizabeth refused to be stereotyped as the pastor's wife: "I am part of the body of Christ—the priesthood of all believers," she would say, and her ministry was a deeply personal one. She was the "great encourager," with a diary filled with the names of people who had shared some burden with her and for whom she prayed. She could empathize with people in all sorts of circumstances, and they knew instinctively that this person's concern was genuine and could be trusted.

More than that, though she never had the privilege of university education, her gifts and skills in the field of administration took her ultimately to the position of personal assistant to three general secretaries[11] of the SACC and later to the director of the nation's leading mediation and arbitration organization.[12] She saw this work as a vocation, saying, "My job is to set them free to do theirs." Above all, Elizabeth made me a better person. Wherever she may appear in the coming chapters, it will always be less prominently than she deserves, because any contribution I may have been permitted to make could not have happened without her.

Violence and Vows

We married in 1960, a year of massive political import in our land. A charismatic leader named Robert Sobukwe, whom I would soon meet under very different circumstances, called on his Pan Africanist Congress (PAC) followers to burn their "passbooks" and hand themselves in at police stations to be arrested.[13] These demonstrations took place all over the land, but in a black township called Sharpeville, when large numbers arrived demanding arrest, nervous police opened fire, killing sixty-nine people

---

10. John and Christopher, born 1962 and 1963, and David and Alan, born 1967 and 1968.

11. Mr. John Rees, Rev. John Thorne, and Bishop Desmond Tutu.

12. Independent Mediation Services of South Africa (IMSSA), responsible for training most of the black Trade Unionists and leaders in negotiation skills.

13. The "Passbook" or "Reference Book" was used by the regime to control the movements of all black people, who had to carry it with them at all times. In it were permits indicating which "white" areas they could enter and proof that they were employed. To be without it meant certain arrest, and it was a hated symbol of servitude.

and wounding many more. The world was outraged, and nine days later thirty thousand of Sobukwe's followers marched silently into Cape Town, filling the streets around Parliament. Deceived by false promises of a fair hearing by the government, they disbanded as quietly as they had come, but the next day the regime struck with lightning speed, declaring a State of Emergency. Soon eighteen thousand people, including Sobukwe and Nelson Mandela, had been detained. Both the PAC and ANC, together with the SA Communist Party, were declared illegal organizations. South Africa's slide into a deadly cycle of confrontation, repression, uprising, and more repression was beginning to take shape.

I was ordained two years later. There is something overwhelming about ordination. It is a moment made holy by its reminders of call and commitment, of love and service, of duty and sacrifice. Stern words are spoken, vows are made, prayers are prayed, and hands laid upon your head. You rise from your knees knowing that you have joined a two-millennia-old order—the "Ministry of Word and Sacrament"—and are wedded to it for the rest of your life. Feeling the crushing pressure of seven pairs of hands on my head was not a gentle benediction. It was a heavy, heavy transmission of gift and task. I specially missed my dad that day. He had been ordained exactly thirty years previously, and his had been a sadly truncated ministry. I knew that he had kept faith with his vows. Would I? When the presiding bishop prayed, "Father, send the Holy Spirit upon Peter," it was very much as if those pressing their hands upon me, aware that my frail soul needed a new measure of God, were willing it into me.

My second appointment was a two-point charge with the congregations separated by a few miles of Atlantic shoreline. Elizabeth and I settled into our first home, and during this time our first two sons were born. Elizabeth was a natural when it came to mothering, and our two little guys could not have had a more caring mom. I shuttled between the two congregations, one rather staid and the other a thriving new plant. I certainly spoke out about the dangerous road South Africa was following, and there were some objections, but most of my white congregation tolerated me. "You'll get over it," they said.

It was then that a simple happenstance became another life-changer: we heard that a new prison was being built on a featureless lump of land off the shores of Cape Town called Robben Island, and the Methodist Church was required to appoint a chaplain there. Still pining for the sea and realizing that this would at least get me onto the water regularly, I grabbed the opportunity and volunteered. At the time, we had no idea that this prison's primary purpose would be to incarcerate black political prisoners, nor could I know how significantly it would impact the course of my ministry.

1

The Island

It lies there like the just-visible hump of a submerged leviathan, barnacled with a sprinkling of ugly buildings and smelling of kelp and seagrowth. Just seven miles from the mainland city of Cape Town, it might as well be in the middle of the South Atlantic: Robben Island—South Africa's most notorious prison.

There is nothing beautiful about this place. Exposed to driving Atlantic gales in winter and the hot summer South Easters, the island is ringed by treacherous black rock shoals and thundering surf. Apart from a few gum trees, its vegetation consists mainly of the rapacious Port Jackson willow. It is traversed by old military roads made of a blinding mixture of crushed shells and white limestone. A rutted landing strip is located at one end. At the other, a small harbor provides the only safe approach from the sea.

Ever since Europeans came to the Cape of Good Hope, the island has symbolized white domination and been chaptered with human suffering. Variously a leper colony, a place of exile, a mental asylum, naval garrison, and prison, it has always offered cold comfort.

By the time I set foot on its shores in 1962, the regime had already turned Robben Island into their most feared political prison.

Nelson Mandela arrived in mid-1964 to begin his life-sentence, though he had previously been held for a brief time on the island awaiting trial for treason. His first arrival had been via the degrading route that introduced most Robben Island prisoners to their new home, the prison boat *Dias*. Seasick and desperately trying to keep their balance while shackled to one another in the stinking, rolling hold, prisoners often endured white prison guards urinating on them through the skylight above. Within months, Mandela was taken back to Pretoria to join the rest of the Rivonia treason trialists, so-named because they were netted by a Security Police swoop on the ANC's secret headquarters in the Johannesburg suburb of Rivonia. Those captured included most of the leaders of the fledgling armed wing of the ANC. The day after their sentencing in mid-1964, Mandela and his colleagues were secretly flown to the island airstrip to begin the incarceration that was to make the island notorious throughout the world. They had narrowly escaped the hangman's noose, and when they asked what their sentence of life imprisonment actually meant, the answer was, "You will be here until you die."

As the first Methodist chaplain there, I was also the first minister to visit them. That exposure was to have a huge impact on me. It dramatized the great gulf between white and black realities in our land. Each crossing in the *Dias* transported me between worlds that could not have been more different. Newly ordained, my primary appointment was to two white congregations in seaside Cape Town suburbs where I was expected to preach, teach, and minister to their needs within the context of a comfortable faith. The adults worked in banks, insurance companies, and other "normal businesses," and their children spent the carefree after-school hours surfing the breakers that rolled in from the west. A few miles out into that same ocean was a different universe, a bleak and hellish prison-house prepared for those who dared to challenge the *status quo* upon which every comfortable white suburb rested.

When I first arrived, the new maximum-security cell block was being completed by common law prisoners, and this is where the Rivonia trialists ended up, becoming the most prominent of thousands of political prisoners to experience the horrors of the island over the next thirty years. Looking back, it seems absurd—even irresponsible—that someone as inexperienced as I should have been entrusted with the sensitive responsibility of being their minister. What could a kid in his twenties do for people of this caliber, and in such straits?

On my first visit, I was met at the small dock by a warrant officer in a pick-up truck and driven through the entrance archway crudely painted with the Prison Service's motto, "We Serve with Pride." I wondered if this officer or his fellow guards saw the similarity to another arched gateway in Poland, where the mocking words *"Arbeit macht frei"*[1] greeted the train-loads of victims herded there by other claimants to a master-race ideology.

The white limestone road led to the Church of the Good Shepherd, also known as the Leper Church. Built in the leper-colony days, it is a church of beautiful proportions, but its lovely stone exterior belied the emptiness within. It had been stripped of altar, font, and pulpit, as if not

---

1. "Work sets you free," the slogan greeting prisoners arriving at Auschwitz and other Nazi concentration camps.

one symbol of the grace of God should be permitted to penetrate the lives of the inmates. Nor were there any pews: the groups of common-law prisoners, together with some of the less prominent "politicals" marched from their nearby cells, had to sit on the cold floor. The absence of service books was less of a problem because Christian hymns were widely known by black South Africans, learned by heart when they were children. The singing was soulful and the sermons simple. I tried to offer homilies on the love of God for these men, and God's care for their far-away families. In spite of my inadequacies, the words were always received with appreciation and with many sighs and exclamations, as if this strange young white man, this hour of rough and ready worship, and the words spoken in God's name let a tiny crack of light into their shadowed lives.

On that first day, between morning and afternoon services, I was offered lunch in the mess hall used by the Afrikaner warders. It was an isolating experience. Their remarks about the prisoners were crudely racist, and I was stung and shamed by their assumption that because I was white I would share their prejudices. Their world had no space for whites with a different view. It was frightening to see how unquestioningly they assumed superiority over their charges and how they relished the power conferred on them by this brutal job. Our conversation soon stumbled. I didn't have the courage to take them on alone, so I shrank into a cocoon of silence, seeking inner distance from them. I determined never to eat there again, and after that day Elizabeth provided sandwiches for my lunches.

Each visit over the next two years was a deeply lonely affair, but I was given one early gift. The warrant officer had pointed out a small, south-facing wooden bungalow. It was there that Robert Mangaliso Sobukwe, the charismatic leader of the Pan Africanist Congress, had begun his lonely exile after arriving the year before.[2]

He had just completed a three-year prison sentence for leading the "pass-burning" campaign that climaxed in the Sharpeville massacre, and instead of being released at the end of 1963, he remained incarcerated by parliamentary decree, utterly isolated for as long as the apartheid regime chose to keep him there. Justice Minister John Vorster liked to call him "public enemy number one." Only his guards were permitted near him, and they were not supposed to speak to him. Sobukwe had been a Methodist lay preacher, so I asked to see him. I was refused at first, but some persistence revealed that the authorities were legally obliged to give me access.

---

2. It was only later that Sobukwe was relocated to the house now displayed to tourists as his prison residence.

For every visit, however, I had first to get written authority from the Chief Magistrate of Cape Town.

By the time I visited him, Sobukwe had long since earned the grudging respect of his gaolers. My driver remarked that none of the baiting by bored young guards had succeeded in provoking him. "Every morning, this man comes out of his house dressed as if he is going off to work," he said. "He is very dignified."

As we approached the weathered hut, I wondered what kind of welcome I would receive. The media had portrayed Sobukwe as a dangerous black nationalist with a hatred of whites. Would he want to see me, a young white minister?

When he met me on the steps of his bungalow, I was immediately struck by his handsome chiseled features and patrician bearing. Tall and wiry and dressed in neat slacks, a white shirt, and tie, he offered me a guarded but polite welcome, inviting me inside as if this was his home and I was a guest coming for tea. The room we entered served as both bedroom and living space, with a neatly made bed, a simple bedside cabinet, a table and chair, and a small bookcase. It was spartan but adequate. Sobukwe gestured to the only chair and sat on the edge of the bed. Conversation was desultory at first. I knew he was sizing me up and didn't blame him. I said that many Methodists would be excited to know that one of our ministers had got to see him. We swapped names of mutual acquaintances and stories of Healdtown, the Methodist college both he and Nelson Mandela had attended.

Our conversation soon warmed, and after that, each time I came to the island, we were able to have about thirty minutes together. He had a consistent aura of calm about him, sucking contentedly on his pipe while we talked. He chose his words carefully, spoke quietly, and had a gentle sense of humor. Our discussions were perforce circumscribed, always in the presence of the guard, who stood near the door pretending to be uninterested. Even so, it was possible to engage something of the depth and breadth of his thinking. His Christian faith was informed by wide reading, and it was clear that he saw his political activism as an extension of his spirituality.

Robert Sobukwe impacted me very powerfully. For all my contact with black South Africans, for the first time I was engaging with somebody risking all for the liberation of his people. The caliber of this man, the cruel waste of his gifts, and the silence of most South African Christians around his incarceration touched me to anger. He always expressed genuine appreciation of our times together, but even though I was one of the only people ever permitted to visit him, I sensed that he would never put too much trust in me. Why should he have faith in this white man, any more than any other? Once, when leaving him, I expressed shame that I could depart the island so freely, leaving him a prisoner. His response was quick. Gesturing toward Cape Town, with its Parliament occupied by his tormentors, he said, "I'm not the prisoner, Peter—they are."

I was also the first chaplain to Nelson Mandela and his fellow Rivonia trialists. When they arrived in mid-1964, they entered a period of extreme hardship and very tough manual labor in the island's lime quarry. I saw nothing of this because Sunday was their one day of rest. They were incarcerated in the squat Maximum Security B Section, with its ugly watchtowers, cold grey passages, and grey-painted barred doors. The whole place had a makeshift look about it, as if thrown together in a hurry, using the cheapest materials—all except for the frontage, built of finely pointed stone. It was a hateful place, and it struck me just how little it cost to oppress people. Stone walls, crude iron bars and doors, a mix of concrete and barbed wire, and a few miles of icy ocean were all that was needed. Robben Island terrorized not only its inmates but was a bleak and forbidding warning to all considering defiance of the apartheid state.

Services of worship for Mandela's group were an exercise in ingenuity. I was not permitted into their cells, and in those early days of their incarceration they were not allowed out of them, even for church. Each cell in the now-famous narrow hallway in B Section had two doors: an inner iron grill, which was kept locked, and a wooden door, left open. I had to lead worship walking up and down the long passage, pausing at each door to make eye contact with the prisoner within. I was touched by the way each returned my glance very intentionally and by the friendliness on most of their faces. At each end of the passage stood a stony-eyed warder who preferred to fix his gaze on the middle distance until I turned around to retrace my steps. The forty-six-year-old Nelson Mandela was in the prime of his life, strong and robust, with a feisty look in his eye, and a ready twinkle, too. In those days he gave the impression of a coiled spring—much more the prize-fighter than the father figure who later became beloved around the world.

Obviously, this was a poor substitute for community worship. While we got the singing of hymns right very quickly, and the harmonies were as good as any, the reading of Scripture and the preaching had to come piecemeal to each person as I passed. This led to my developing a series of "sound-bites" (the phrase had not been invented yet) to leave with each one, a style that may have become part of my preaching.

I began to agitate for a better deal, demanding that the Rivonia group be given the same minimal privileges of worship as others on the island. My requests fell on deaf ears until, on one particularly cold day, I pleaded with the senior warder for the service to at least be held in a sunny corner of the exercise yard adjacent to the cells. To my surprise, he agreed, and we all crowded into that one warm spot, using a few wooden benches for pews. The singing was hearty, the smiles much in evidence, and I couldn't resist choosing an appropriate text from John's Gospel, "If then the Son sets you free, you will indeed be free" (John 8:36). As they basked in the welcome sunshine, I said that they could spell "Son" any way they wanted. Mandela and the group had no difficulty seeing the pun, and it added to the high spirits of the moment. I was struck by the poise and strength of these men. Being their first years there, my time visiting the island coincided with the worst and most degrading cruelties they were to suffer, yet they had a collective energy about them, an obvious solidarity with each other and, yes, a *confidence* that was remarkable.

There can be few instances in the world where such a remarkable group, of such moral stature, have been gathered in one place of shared suffering. Here were leaders of their people and future leaders of South Africa in short trousers, canvas jackets, sleeping in those early years with nothing but thin floor mats between their bodies and cold concrete, and regularly subjected to dreadful indignities. None of them was permitted more than two letters and two family visits each year. The story of their victory over these humiliating circumstances has been told and retold as a triumph of the human spirit.

Robben Island introduced me to the most remarkable of South Africa's future leaders, but it also stamped on me a deep aversion for the apparatchiks of apartheid and a lifelong inability to make polite small talk with fellow whites who supported this system. It affected my preaching in the comfortable white enclave where I served and would distance Elizabeth and me from some friends and family, too. Like most whites, they preferred not to hear about such unpleasant things, while I found it impossible to be silent about them. It was not something I could control. It was a reaction to the grotesque contrast between life for those prisoners and the life that went on for the rest of us just a few miles over the water. I remember conducting a family wedding around that time and struggling to get through it because a prominent National Party diplomat was present. For me there could be no easy conversations with the kind of people who needed a Robben Island to support their civilization, yet there was also the uneasy awareness that I and "my people" were complicit too.

Late in 1964, a letter arrived from the Prisons Department indicating that my security clearance had been withdrawn and that I could no longer visit the island. No reasons were given.

I did not realize just how deeply the pain of that place had seared my own psyche until the turn of the century, when I found myself escorting two American friends on what is now an obligatory pilgrimage for visitors to Cape Town. It was my first return to the island in thirty-seven years, and I had not prepared myself for this sudden encounter with long-buried memories and emotions. In the tourist bus, I suffered an unexpected and embarrassing breakdown. It happened outside Robert Sobukwe's house, where I had volunteered some extra information about him. The guide was overwhelmed at meeting somebody who had actually been with Sobukwe, and she and the driver, whom I recognized as an ex-prisoner from those dreadful years, both joined me in a flood of tears. When we got to the lime quarry, the three of us had to walk off some distance to have our weep, with a busload of bemused foreign tourists looking on and probably wondering whether people bawling on each other's shoulders was *de rigueur* for such visits. Fortunately, this is not the case; the island is today a shining example of reconciliation, with former prisoners and former guards sharing responsibility for its management. Nevertheless, as another former inmate, Anglican Archbishop Njongonkulu Ndungane, says, "Don't romanticize the island. It was a hellhole."[3]

---

3. As a young man, Ndungane served a three-year sentence on Robben Island. Much later he succeeded Archbishop Desmond Tutu as Anglican Archbishop of Cape Town.

2

District Six

THE THIRD SUNDAY OF January 1967, I am standing for the first time in the mahogany pulpit of Buitenkant Street Methodist Church, on the edge of Cape Town's District Six.

Two years have passed since my removal from the Robben Island chaplaincy, years spent in Sydney working with the Australian preacher/prophet Alan Walker. In a visit to South Africa in 1963, he had shocked many by combining evangelistic preaching with stinging denunciations of our nation's apartheid policies. Because he determined to liberate the gospel from privatized piety, his preaching was met with anger and opposition among the privileged, but it brought great hope to the oppressed. I was convinced that here was the kind of proclamation South Africa needed, and I was anxious to learn more.

Walker also headed up what many regarded as the most effective city church in world Methodism. Sydney's massive Central Methodist Mission had pioneered a number of unique urban ministries, the latest of which was the world's first twenty-four-hour telephone counseling ministry, known as Life Line. I had been sensing a growing call toward the inner city and knew I would benefit greatly from first-hand experience with Walker. A conversation with him had brought an invitation to join his staff, and I was now free to take it up in 1965. Elizabeth and I, together with our first two sons, John (3) and Christopher (1), took the steamship to Australia for a two-year stay.

It was another life-changing experience, not least because the time away gave me perspective. It became clear to me that in the coming years a new kind of church would need to be born in my homeland. Like that which had emerged in Nazi Germany, it would have to be a church "under the cross," willing to suffer. Preparing for our return, I had been asking myself what guidelines might help me stay faithful in the land of apartheid. I settled on four. I may have refined them since, but they are essentially the same today as they were when I formulated them in 1966.

The first was to be a gospel truth-teller, which would involve exposing the great lie of apartheid and offering God's alternative vision for our land; the second was to bind up the broken, standing with the victims of injustice and the hurting wherever I found them; the third was to shape congregations that would "live the alternative"—be visible contradictions of apartheid by "living God's future in the now"; the fourth was to join Jesus in working nonviolently to end our evil system and bring in a new dispensation of justice, equity, and peace.

Newly arrived from Australia and inspired by these four principles for my future ministry, I looked out from my new pulpit. This church on the edge of District Six[1] was once a Dutch wine-store, converted for worship for freed slaves in 1883. Its gracious interior imitates England's nineteenth-century Methodist chapels: in addition to seating five hundred people in the nave, a U-shaped gallery supported by delicate cast-iron columns accommodates another three hundred. The pulpit is elevated, lifting me halfway between the people below and those in the gallery. Sunlight streaming through the golden north window gleams softly on polished woodwork.

A service in the District Six Methodist Church in 1970

1. Early Cape Town was divided into numbered "Districts." In later years, they became named suburbs—except for District Six, which stuck stubbornly to its original label.

Today the church is full. It is a hot Cape Town morning, but everyone is in their Sunday best: men in suits, ties, and burnished shoes, and women in bright dresses with their heads covered either by hats or headscarves. The only hatless woman in the church is Elizabeth. Children are everywhere, let off Sunday school to come and inspect the new minister. Our two little paleface kids on each side of Elizabeth are sizing up the situation with wide eyes.

I'm both nervous and excited. Excited because I'm back in what we Methodists call "Circuit ministry"—preaching, teaching, and pastoring in my first city church. I am also nervous because most of the people facing me know that under the government's Group Areas Act, they and the rest of the area's sixty thousand mostly mixed-race inhabitants are to be ruthlessly cast out of the city and forced to live beyond its boundaries.[2] The only reason given is that they are people of color. Those making this decision needed no other authority than that they are white. Why should this congregation, forced to face dislocation and heartbreak by people like me, have any regard for this white preacher—and what hope is there that I might win their trust?

While we were still in Sydney, the leaders of what was then known as the "Cape Town Coloured Circuit" had invited me to become their superintendent minister. Their invitation helped our decision to return to South Africa because it meant that we would at least be serving people who were experiencing the pain, rather than the privileges, of apartheid. With the congregation soon to be exiled to the bleak Cape Flats,[3] my bishop warned that this would be an appointment without a future, but I had asked for just one assurance. "Promise me," I said, "that you won't entertain any moves to close it down, and I'll do the rest." He agreed.

District Six was a tightly packed inner city community occupying the lower slopes of Devil's Peak, which flanked Cape Town's iconic Table Mountain. It was the most multi-racial piece of real estate in South Africa, where "coloureds," Indians, Africans, and whites had lived in harmony for a century. "Coloured" (mixed-race) people made up the majority, with Muslims and Christians more or less equally divided, the former descended mainly from the Dutch East India Company's slaves and the latter either from Khoi roots, or the many interracial unions of the Cape's earlier history. Better-off classes—teachers and business-people—lived up the slope, while

---

2. On February 11, 1966, the government had declared District Six to be a "White Group Area."

3. "Cape Flats" was the name given to the low sand flats stretching some fifteen miles south-east of Cape Town, used as a dumping ground for people of color removed from their homes in areas declared "white" under the Group Areas Act. New arrivals found mile after mile of two-room, breeze-block houses with asbestos roofs, no ceilings, and no internal doors perched on the white sea-sand.

poorer residents lived below in tenement housing dating back to the late Dutch and early British occupations. Many homes, despite their occupants' limited means, were carefully tended, but half the tenements were owned by white slumlords and were badly neglected, their exteriors unpainted, with crumbling masonry, rusting balconies, and chipped steps.

Narrow cobbled streets were alive with bustling activity. Children darted everywhere, playing hopscotch, street soccer, or some form of catch. With most menfolk at work, the streets were commanded by the women— no-nonsense matriarchs who chatted across washing lines or while tending to various other chores. All of them mothered all the children around, equally quick to kiss a grazed knee or dish out a hefty smack. They were the cement in the community. Males were mainly artisans and laborers, and too many of them, rubbing up against the indignities of apartheid every day, relied on alcohol to dull their frustrations.

To outsiders, District Six was a slum, and though houses were dilapidated and overcrowded, the interiors of most belied their ruinous facades. The house-proud matrons saw to that. Neat linoleum covered the floors. Living rooms had an Edwardian parlor feel about them, with lace curtains, sepia family portraits, old-fashioned furniture, a radiogram, and often a fern in the corner.[4] Kitchens were the family's usual gathering places, with the warm after-scent of curry and other spices hanging in the air. Bedrooms were small, and it was unusual for a child to have a bed to him or herself. There were no bathrooms. The single outside toilet required a trek to the end of the narrow back yard.

Manners and customs had a period feel too, reminding me of my grandparents' era. Family discipline was firmly pre-Spock, with a cast-iron respect for elders, and children expected to be available at all times to run errands. Few homes were equipped with telephones, so barefoot kids were the usual means of local messaging, most often to the corner store where the Jewish or Muslim shopkeeper was always ready to arrange short-term credit. As older youths moved into employment, they were expected to "work for their parents" for two years before thinking of courting or regarding their wages as their own. District Six had its own economy tailored to the needs of people living close to poverty. There was the inevitable gang culture found on the mean streets of poor communities, yet the district was rich in cultural, religious, and sporting activities: people banded together not only to survive, but also to overcome their circumstances.

---

4. Television was resisted by the apartheid regime for fear that foreign content would spread "liberal" ideas. It was only introduced unwillingly to South Africa in 1976.

I arrived brimming with ideas about how to make a city church relevant, not only to its traditional membership, but also to the wider community and to the workers who poured into the city each weekday. But first, Elizabeth and I needed to feel the heartbeat of the District Six people. She had no idea that by simply turning up with the children on Sundays, she was already breaking new ground. Among our predecessors, the white minister's spouse and family had belonged to a "white" congregation elsewhere. With two small boys on her hands and a third child on the way, she had limited opportunity, but typically she focused on building one-on-one relationships with individuals. The best way for me to get close to the people was to visit them in their homes, yet I found that the circuit superintendency carried an enormous administrative load. Apart from some six hundred members at Buitenkant Street, there were three other congregations in "coloured" communities around the city and one fifty miles away. Each had day schools attached, with all the complications of teachers' appointments, staff disputes, and above all—toilets. I calculated that I now superintended over one hundred ancient school toilets, with at least one or two springing a leak daily.

Keeping afloat financially seemed to be the priority in this circuit. At least two evenings a week found me sitting in the cramped vestry waiting for class leaders to see me. One of John Wesley's great innovations had been the class meeting—a dozen or so members, meeting each week for spiritual guidance, prayer, and mutual encouragement. Each also brought a penny to support the general work and the poor. My congregations were still divided into classes, but the spiritual function had long since faded. Class leaders did little else than collect the "church dues" that they then delivered to me. As we went through their books, I recorded the $0.75[5] monthly offerings of each person, and they updated me about those who were sick or in trouble to guide my visitation in the next week, but money ruled us. The books of all five congregations were my responsibility, and each Monday was spent laboriously counting and banking hundreds of coins and the few banknotes that came in at Sunday services. I couldn't believe the paternalism and mistrust implied by requiring that these functions be kept in the hands of the white superintendent. If real ministry was to happen, things had to change.

I put out the word asking for suggestions of a possible volunteer assistant. A school principal offered the name of a young teacher named Jane Abrahams. "You should ask Janie," he said. "She is very bright." She volunteered to sit in the church and handle the monies, freeing me to discuss pastoral issues with the class leaders who began to get the message that from

---

5. All dollar amounts are based on what the SA Rand/US-dollar exchange rate was at the time.

now on ministry would be more important than money. I soon found that Jane had an encyclopedic knowledge of the congregation, a love for people, and a passion to see new things happen in this old church. I warmed to her sharp intelligence and feisty spirit and began to look for ways in which she could share the ministry and be my bridge into the community. After deductions, she was earning $90 per month in a school about to be shut down by the Coloured Education Department. If I could match that amount from somewhere, would she be willing to come on board rather than take another teaching post? When she said yes, I approached a generous Methodist who agreed to match her present salary for eighteen months—time enough for us to transform the financial picture. I had to think up a title for her because no appointment quite like this had happened before anywhere in the MCSA. She became my pastoral assistant.

With Jane Abrahams in 1966

We faced daunting challenges. District Six should not be romanticized. Its people triumphed over much, but racial trauma, poverty, and an unhealthy religiosity wove a destructive web in their lives. While the "coloured" community may have had it somewhat better than Africans, they too had internalized the stigma that racism inflicts on all people of color. Its indignities, beginning with race classification, insinuated themselves into people's sense of humanness.[6] Desmond Tutu identified the worst thing about apartheid as "when

---

6. The Nuremburg-like Population Registration Act of 1950 provided the foundation

they call you a non-European, a non-this, you might think it isn't working on you. But in fact, it is corrosive of your self-image. You end up wondering whether you are actually as human as those others. You wonder 'Does God actually love me, black, as he loves a white child?'"[7]

I was first shocked into awareness of this at our Sunday school's annual presentation in front of the congregation. Looking at the lovely children something seemed amiss, until I realized that the lighter skinned, more straight-haired children were in the front rows, with all the dark-skinned, more crinkly-haired kids relegated to the back. The person in charge of them was himself a person of color, a school principal by profession, proud of his education and university degree; yet when lining up these precious children, he had unapologetically enthroned "whiteness" as the measure of who should be more visible. The racial criteria used by the Race Classification Board—examining people's head and body hair, complexion, and facial features—had become imprinted on his unconscious.

Another heartbreaking example was when parents urged their more "European-looking" children to "try for white." If they could convince the Race Classification Board that they were white in looks and complexion—or that they were "generally accepted as a white person" even if "not in appearance obviously a white person"—then the doors to a better life would open to them. But the price was high: it meant an end to contact with their darker parents and siblings. During some funerals, I wanted to weep as I watched family members standing around the grave, united awkwardly in grief but still constrained from reaching out to each other by years of separation. In all those years they had never dared even to greet if they bumped into each other in a public place. Habit had made them guilty strangers.

Living under racism also turned people on each other. I was shaken in an early meeting when the most senior of our lay preachers launched a bitter attack on me for what seemed no reason at all. When I asked what I had done to offend, his answer was, "Nothing, Reverend, nothing. But today I was pushed off a bus by one of you whites, and I'm so angry. I had to take it out on someone." There were not many whites they could do that to, so resentments turned inward. Smallest slights led to destructive quarrels, and I found myself refereeing absurd spats in which one family decided that they were "not speaking" to another. All Christian teaching about forgiveness

---

for the entire apartheid edifice, requiring all South Africans to be classified by race. The initial categories of White, Coloured, and Bantu were later expanded to include Cape Coloured, Malay, Griqua, Chinese, Indian, and—just in case any person of color had been missed—Other Coloured.

7. Desmond Tutu, interview by Bill Moyers, *Bill Moyers Journal*, PBS, April 27, 1999, https://www.pbs.org/moyers/journal/archives/watch-tutu.html.

was forgotten until the approach of Easter or Christmas perhaps nudged them toward reconciliation.

Poverty was the second challenge. The poorer parts of District Six had families living from hand to mouth in often desperately crowded conditions. I once was called late at night to a home where an old man was "very sick," only to find him already dead. To move his body, we had first to wake the two children sleeping in the same bed. They had slept unknowing through his last hours. White landlords neglected their properties but never brooked late payment of rent. When one of my lay leaders contracted tuberculosis, exacerbated because of the damp in his tenement house, the uncaring landlord turned out to be the same respected gynecologist who had brought Elizabeth into the world. "The doctor who gave life to me," she said, "is making people sick here."

Poverty sucks the oxygen out of people's lives, but ironically there are few more rewarding places for a minister to be than with the poor. Perhaps I could do nothing about "big picture" systemic poverty, but it took very little to change the circumstances of an individual family. I often found myself arranging last-minute rescues for people facing eviction until we were able to launch a small revolving credit scheme to help tide people over these crises. Wonderfully, there were no defaulters. No matter how long it took, the poorest of the poor were punctilious in repaying their loans. Even amid all the pain, there was deep satisfaction going to bed knowing that somebody's family had a roof over their heads and a meal in their stomachs because the church was there for them.

Yet there was more to it than that. I was beginning to understand that if Jesus had a home address in this world, it was among the poor. The Jewish carpenter became much more real to me in District Six, and it was people like Mr. and Mrs. May who did it. They lived in a tiny two-room cellar not far from the church. A paraplegic for twenty-seven years, Mr. May was wheeled down into the city center each day to sell matches. When he was back in his bed, Mrs. May, a tiny woman with a badly twisted spine, used a crutch to hop around as she cared for him. The first time I visited them, I wrote, "A strange glow on a rainy day in that room." Their tender love for each other and the quiet gratitude with which they welcomed each day touched me deeply, and I used to take Holy Communion to them more often than necessary, not for their sake but for mine. And they were not alone: I found I was being changed by the poorest of the people I had come to serve.

Conversely, the Christianity of the more well-off in District Six often had a different face. As I struggled through my first months there I found little of the beautiful joy and freedom Jesus declared. A Calvinistic religiosity held too many of my congregation in thrall. They lived as if faith was all about sin and retribution, with the "Reverend" the apparent arbiter. My first leaders' meeting had an agenda item titled "Punishment."[8] It seemed that this was for disciplining unmarried girls who had fallen pregnant and suspending them from membership. It was redolent of the most straitlaced nineteenth-century legalism. This was not the liberating Methodism I knew, and I announced that this item would never again appear on the agenda. Much more than that had to happen: I had to introduce the congregation to a different Jesus and God than the one they seemed to fear more than love. I also had to be a different kind of minister, one who would be with, rather than over, the people. But how?

By happenstance, a primary school attached to our sanctuary was about to be closed, offering an opportunity to do something new and different with the property. In January 1968, I invited younger church members to join me each Saturday morning in transforming the two-floor former school. For six months we slaved away, sanding, sawing, remodeling, and painting, until there emerged an attractive upstairs community center and restaurant called the Carpenter's House. On the wall in the coffee bar was an impression of Jesus at his workbench with this prayer:

> O Master Carpenter of Nazareth,
> Who at the last with wood and nails
> purchased man's whole salvation,
> Wield well Thy tools in this Thy workshop,
> That we who come to Thy bench rough-hewn,
> May be fashioned to a truer beauty by Thy hand.[9]

But something more than reshaping a building was happening: we were beginning to reshape the lives of a remarkable group of young adults. They had quickly bought into the Carpenter's House vision but had also found themselves on level ground—hammer and nails in hand—with their white minister. A deepening bond was forming, and as we worked, they began to share about their lives. We decided to meet on Friday evenings too, calling ourselves the Seekers. Soon we were exploring issues of faith and life together. We talked of the "inner journey" of spiritual disciplines and the "outward journey" of engagement with society. There emerged a deepening honesty among us. Elizabeth and I knew that we could expect no transformation

---

8. In SA Methodism, the leaders' meeting is the body that gives direction to a congregation. It is chaired by the minister and consists of lay members with any kind of leadership responsibility in that congregation.

9. Various versions of this prayer are attributed to St. Basil of Caesarea; I found this version in my father's collection of prayers.

unless we were willing to expose our own vulnerabilities. She played a crucial role especially among the young women in the group, and there came a symbolic moment of liberation when they decided to attend church with hair uncovered. Because of the role hair texture played in the racialization and stratification of women in this community, this was a massive step toward self-acceptance. It was humbling for us to be part of a miracle: Jesus was working the kind of healing that invited these young women to stand up and reclaim their dignity and freedom. This new strength was echoed in the whole group, too: now that they were open about their discomfort when interacting with whites, they set up occasions when contact could not be avoided. Then, afterwards, they analyzed their behavior and feelings, all the time growing confident in their own self-worth.

3

Ocean in a Single Drop

THE SEEKERS CHANGED EVERYTHING. Soon they were challenging older members to get on board with the new directions in which we were moving. After-church coffee in the Carpenter's House had Seekers at each table stimulating discussion of the evening's sermon. My sermons didn't fixate exclusively on political oppression, but I made a point of showing that no matter the subject, the gospel had both personal and social implications, and the consistent thread in all of them was this thing Christians call "grace"—being loved for who we are as dignified children of God and loving others unconditionally and without exception. One Sunday night, the Seekers replaced the altar with a trestle-table loaded with food and proceeded outside to invite homeless people and passersby to a sit-down meal upfront, reminding the congregation about who Jesus regarded as most important. Church members were shocked out of their belief that faith was about being respectable and began to learn that it was about extravagant compassion and hospitality instead.

We launched Youth Cabaret with more than two hundred kids dancing to live bands on Saturday nights. It was a risky undertaking because of District Six's flourishing gang culture, but Cabaret was so popular that tough teenagers seeking entrance meekly submitted to body searches when Jane and her team suspected they were carrying knives or drugs—which they sometimes were. In the middle of Cabaret, the kids, Christian and Muslim, would pause with remarkable attentiveness while the Seekers presented a simple reenactment of a Jesus parable or I said a few words. Then the band would assault our eardrums once more. We had sanded off a fair bit of the gnarled floor they were dancing on, and I had some anxious moments as it bounced up and down under four hundred feet, but it held. Fifty years later, I still meet people who loved Youth Cabaret, "where we could enjoy ourselves without getting into trouble."

During weekdays, the Carpenter's House was a lunch club for workers. Simple meals were on sale for $0.75, and billiards, darts, and "kerem"[1] boards were available; but more significant was that people of color could sit down in dignity in a city where they were refused such service anywhere else. On Wednesdays, workers were invited to eat their sandwiches in the church while I offered a brief Christian perspective on current affairs and then took questions. Questioners were not slow in coming forward. Silenced people were finding their voice.

We deracialized the circuit's name to the "Inner City Mission" with the focus being on serving the community rather than simply pastoring a congregation. Word spread that my sermons were about real life and were not afraid to tackle political issues. One person still likes to remind me that as a teenager she used to get beatings for sneaking out of her house on Sunday evenings to come to our services. Her Catholic parents beat her, not for listening to a non-Catholic, but to "that Communist." When a young sex worker began to worship with us and found a new purpose for her life, extracting her from the brothel where she worked with two or three other girls was not a simple matter. She wanted to break free from sex work, but her friends needed her contribution to food and rent, so we paid the average amount she would normally have earned and took our new convert onto our staff to pursue her real passion of working with little children. The arrangement worked, and her children's club was a hit. This powerful parable of transformation was not lost on the District Six community.

When *Jesus Christ Superstar* took the music world by storm, it was unsurprisingly banned by South Africa's grim censors as "blasphemous." We felt that the rock opera had value as a contemporary portrayal of the Jesus message, so we decided to use Holy Week to stage a "listen in." Huge speakers were installed for the occasion, and eight hundred people packed the darkened church while Webber and Rice's work held them enthralled. It was a gamble, but I figured that the police would think twice before arresting me for playing music about Jesus in Holy Week.

The congregation's public profile grew. In June 1967, prominent anti-apartheid theologian Rev. Beyers Naudé came to promote his Christian Institute (CI) Bible Study groups in Cape Town.[2] The first meeting was held in our home, and Beyers preached in our pulpit. Another guest was Clarence Jordan, who had founded the multi-racial Koinonia community

---

1. "Kerem" was similar to billiards but played on a smaller board with puck-shaped discs instead of balls.

2. Beyers Naudé was a Dutch Reformed minister who rebelled against his church's pro-apartheid stance. Expelled from their ministry, he became the most prominent white cleric in the anti-apartheid struggle.

in Georgia and authored *The Cotton Patch* series of New Testament translations. His story of endurance in the face of Ku Klux Klan attacks and other intimidation inspired us. Veteran ANC activist Dr. William Nkomo became the first black African to meet with the Seekers and encourage them in their interracial forays.

I had been profoundly moved by Dr. Martin Luther King Jr.'s nonviolent witness to racial justice, and we had played banned recordings of his speeches at Seekers meetings. When he was assassinated in April 1968, we decided to hold a public memorial service to coincide with his funeral in Atlanta. It turned out to be the only one anywhere in South Africa. I was shocked when the American ambassador and his staff refused our invitation to attend, but it seems that they were waiting for the White House to tell them whether King was to be ignored as a rabble-rouser or mourned as a martyr. The decision must have come through just a few hours before the service because I suddenly got a request to reserve a whole bunch of seats for the ambassador and his entourage.

The church was also a venue to a number of protests against the District Six removals and the 90-Day Detention Act.[3] In those days such meetings were fairly polite affairs, but some fifteen years after my time, the venerable old building was to house much more risky protests involving tear gas with armored vehicles backed up against its doors to cut off escape. My priorities were trying to ameliorate immediate suffering caused by apartheid's cruelty. Because of the laws against interracial relationships and marriage, couples falling in love across the color-line became criminals.[4] If they wanted to stay together, their only hope was emigration, and for this I needed international help. The Australian consul general smoothed the way for a number of couples to obtain entry to his country where they could be together without fear of arrest, and Canada was also helpful.

In September 1969, Abdullah Haron, Imam of a prominent mosque, was tortured to death while being detained without trial in a Cape Town police station. The Security Police claimed that the human rights activist had "fallen down the stairs," but wounds on his body told another story. An Anglican priest named Bernie Wrankmore was so incensed by the callous official cover-up that he climbed Signal Hill—adjacent to Table Mountain—and vowed to fast until Prime Minister B. J. Vorster agreed to a judicial inquiry.

3. This act empowered the regime to detain anyone for up to ninety days without charge or trial. It was later extended to 180 days, and finally without limit. Detainees were usually kept in solitary confinement.

4. Section 6 of the Immorality Act and the Mixed Marriages Act prohibited any sexual contact or marriages between persons of different races.

I decided to spend some time with him each day if possible, and we became friends. I also met his spouse Valerie and their young children, and as he began to waste away, she became increasingly anxious. With Vorster ignoring him, Bernie announced that he would mark the fortieth day of his fast by preaching a sermon. Hundreds of Capetonians climbed the hill to listen to what became known as Bernie's "Sermon on the Mount." We hoped he would announce that he was calling it off, but he had nothing of the sort in mind. In spite of his weakened state, he preached for nearly an hour, mainly about his spiritual discoveries during the fast, then announced that he would continue until the Prime Minister relented. With Val's anxiety deepening, I determined to get her to see the Prime Minister. We approached Leader of the Opposition Sir de Villiers Graaff, who had little sympathy with Bernie's stand but helped persuade the PM to open his door. On October 4, 1971, Val and I flew to Pretoria for the appointment at the Union Buildings. Vorster was courteous but stone-faced while Val pleaded for some action that might convince her spouse to end his fast. He was adamant that torture was not tolerated under his watch but promised nothing.[5] He did indicate, however, that "his door was open" if Bernie himself wanted to see him. With this tiny shred of hope, we returned to Cape Town. Bernie did make a secret trip to Pretoria but never got to see Vorster. His fast continued to an incredible sixty-seven days before he finally gave up. We crowded into their little flat and watched as he sat down with a beatific smile and ate his first meal—a poached egg.

A sprinkling of white people began to appear in our pews on Sundays, offering new opportunities. I had been arguing that unless the MCSA congregations became more inclusive, our challenge to the apartheid government would always lack credibility. A Presbyterian minister in the Eastern Cape had launched an "intentional" integrated congregation, convinced that "you can't talk people out of apartheid, you have to mix them out of it."[6] In 1969, I visited him to learn more and then wrote a critique of the MCSA for "conforming to the very 'South African way of life' that it officially condemns." Arguing that integration would never happen "naturally" in the South African context, I laid out a three-year intentional plan for local congregations. Reversing apartheid on "the broad fronts of national life" might be the ultimate goal, I wrote, but meanwhile "the mere existence of any inclusive group offers a challenge to the basic premise of apartheid."[7]

---

5. Torture of detainees was in fact commonplace at the hands of the Security Police and certain military units.

6. Rev. Rob Robertson later moved to Johannesburg to pastor a second intentional inclusive congregation known as St. Anthony's.

7. Peter Storey, "Towards Racially Inclusive Congregations," proposal to the MCSA Renewal Commission, September 3, 1970.

Traveling to national church meetings in the 1960s offered further experiences of the humiliations apartheid brought. Tom Hanmer, a brilliant educator, joined me for the six-hundred-mile flight to East London. Tom was nervous because he had never flown before. When we got to the check-in desk, his boarding pass indicated the rear row of seats, while mine was somewhere toward the front. "There must be some mistake," I protested. "Mr. Hanmer and I are traveling together." The agent looked at Tom coldly and said, "There is no mistake. This man is classified 'Coloured,' you may not sit together." I was flushed with anger and shame but fortunately the plane was not full, and as soon as we were airborne I could walk back and join Tom. There are no words for what he must have felt, nor for my shame.

The MCSA leadership thanked me for my paper and referred the matter to the next meeting, but at Buitenkant Street we were already testing my thesis. I had written that integration would come about "not by pretending an absence of prejudice, but by consciously identifying and confronting our prejudice and wrestling with it every step of the way."[8] Thus the whites who wanted to join us had to be willing to move through a process called "My Brother and Me."[9] This consisted of weekly interracial encounters in which participants unpacked the meaning of racism and privilege. Today, "diversity training" is common, but in the 1960s it was revolutionary. Beginning with a polite welcome and some theoretical input on prejudice, it soon moved into more robust exchanges and role-plays. By the third week, the well-meaning whites arrived to discover that they were to be treated as "non-whites" for the evening. They could only look on and listen while people of color discussed them—their opinion neither sought nor permitted. They were not allowed to use the usual toilets and at the break had to go into the street to get their coffee or tea served through a window. There were more bruising evenings with responses varying from defensiveness to deep anguish before signs of transformation emerged. For the whites, it was nothing less than a conversion in which they had to recognize and confess their deep-rooted racism—and the guilt that came with it—for the first time. Some quit, but those who stuck it out found themselves becoming more humble and sensitized people, ready to be welcomed into their first multi-racial congregation. For the "coloureds," there was challenge too: Could they overcome their ingrained inferiorities, and in many cases, bitterness, sufficiently both to challenge and ultimately welcome white members? Typical was Kate Brown, who had spent her life in the master-servant

---

8. Storey, "Towards Racially Inclusive Congregations," Renewal Commission, September 1970, 3.

9. We were not yet sensitized to sexist language. My Brother and Me courses involved both women and men.

world of a domestic worker, and who found it desperately difficult to address whites as equals. When she finally did so, she spoke of being set free from an internal prison she had lived in all her life. I fretted to an American Methodist visitor that this effort at racial reconciliation was a mere "drop in the ocean," but he expressed amazement to find something like this in South Africa. "Never forget," he said, "that the whole ocean is present in every single drop." Ever since, I've tried to remember that when we live out even the smallest manifestations of what Jesus envisioned, his new world of justice and peace becomes present amongst us.

One of the whites coming to worship came to see me confessing embarrassment at the amount of money he was earning each month. He was looking for a meaningful way to put his wealth to work, and I suggested he invest in a small "coloured" community where we had a church and school and where 1,600 inhabitants lived with all the social problems associated with poverty. Anxious to avoid any kind of paternalism, he came up with a remarkable plan: using his high salary, he employed a social worker to visit the homes of the people and both research and engage with their needs. They then worked together seeking to meet those needs. Nobody ever knew that he was financing the project.

I had long been concerned at how few "coloured" youth could afford to go beyond school to enroll in university as they were expected to begin contributing to their parents' income. This being so, I believed that the church should at least be empowering young workers to be informed activists in the factories and other workplaces. When the apartheid regime forced the closure of another of our primary schools, we were able to renovate it and transform it into a fine preschool for local children as well as a space where we could train youthful Christian activists. We named the preschool Gateway. It opened with ninety children and a waiting list of one hundred fifty. The new Christian Leadership Center (CLC) consisted of lecture rooms and accommodations to offer three-month courses for twelve young workers per course. They would live in community for the duration, going to work by day and attending classes in the evenings. In addition to solid grounding in theology and biblical studies, they learned about leadership, worker-organizing skills, and how to contextualize their faith.

Later, Jane, who had meanwhile spent eighteen months in the USA gaining further experience of urban ministry, returned to become the second director of the CLC. Fired by the growing impatience of the US civil rights movement, she injected a more militant activism into the training. She and fellow Seeker graduate Gilbert Lawrence had become engaged to be married. With the help of a Methodist scholarship, Gilbert studied medicine at the "liberal" University of Cape Town, but he and the small handful of other non-white medical students did not escape discrimination: when the time came to dissect cadavers they were not only forbidden to work on white cadavers, but were also segregated into a separate room so as not even to see them. At their wedding in 1973, Jane and Gilbert left the church with a CLC guard of honor throwing the power salute with black-gloved fists. I conducted the wedding, and Elizabeth proposed the toast to the bride and groom. A deep friendship across lines of color had been sealed between the four of us. It survived the worst apartheid could do and would persevere unbroken for more than forty years until the night when we would hold hands around Elizabeth's hospital bed and Gilbert would say the last prayer she heard on earth.[10]

10. Dr. Gilbert Lawrence later studied community medicine, became superintendent of major hospitals in Cape Town, rose to become director-general of Health in the Western Cape and ultimately director-general of the province itself, retiring in 2016. Jane Lawrence later returned to education, earning a number of degrees, including an MEd. She was detained without trial for two weeks in 1985 and has spent the rest of her life helping form better teachers. They are both still active in the Central Methodist Mission in Cape Town.

4

Then Came the Bulldozers

ALL THE WHILE, A single-minded regime was proceeding to tear the heart out of District Six. Every week more families would report visits by the government. If they owned their property, they would also be told the meager compensation they would receive. They would be given approximate eviction dates, but only a rough idea of where they would end up on the vast Cape Flats.

The rituals of dispossession tended to be sadly similar, but for me the picture of the Abrahams family's dread "moving day" comes most painfully to mind. They gathered for the last time in the bare living room, with worn-out linoleums of long ago exposed once more. Ma Abrahams, sitting on an old box and asking in her gentle voice, "Why, Reverend Peter, what did we do wrong?" and me with no words—just hot tears of anger and shame. Then holding hands and praying, some crying, others standing in numb silence, remembering the generations for whom this humble tenement had been home. Then blessing the house for one last time, and the family filing through the front door to be met by a crowd of neighbors waiting to bid them farewell. Then Ma getting into the waiting car with her daughters and the men mounting the truck behind, loaded with their worldly goods. Ma giving a brave smile and a little wave and the sad procession of pain moving off down the street while old friends waved handkerchiefs and dabbed their eyes.

This gut-wrenching ritual was repeated over and over, in street after street, closely followed by the government demolition teams. It was as if a brutal regime could not wait to wipe out every remembrance of this one community in all of South Africa whose existence proved their race phobias to be nonsense.

Nobody will ever measure the pain of the District Six removals. My senior lay leader had just been relocated when we had an evening meeting at the church. I offered him a ride home. When we got out among the rows of identical matchbox houses perched on the sandy Cape Flats, he couldn't find his. We had to go to the railway station so he could retrace his daily walk back to what was now his home. In District Six, he had paid eight dollars per month for two bedrooms, dining room, lounge, and kitchen and walked to work each day. Now, his rent for two rooms plus a kitchen and bathroom—none with doors or ceilings—was almost exactly double. Train rides to town cost another three dollars each month. They were now thirteen miles from his work, and the nearest shop was more than a mile away. Another more elderly member who landed on the Cape Flats came to me after less than a month there, asking me to bury his spouse. Tears streaming down his face, he said, "She died of a broken heart." A few weeks later, he too died. It was not only the loss of their homes, but the destruction of community solidarity that broke hearts. The movers made no attempt to keep friends and relatives together. "In District Six," said one victim, "Muslims and Christians used to wish each other well for their holy days and share each other's feasts; our first Christmas on the Flats nobody knocked on our door to wish us. We were so sad." The price for the dumping of people into apartheid ghettos is still being paid. More than two decades into democracy, they are the most violent, gang-ruled, and drug-ridden localities in South Africa.

Out on the Cape Flats where the South Easter–blown sand found its way into every cranny in the matchbox houses, the church once more attempted to offer some small comfort to those forced to live there. My "coloured" colleague Rev. Abel Hendricks and his spouse Freda were sent there to begin a ministry. They were told, "You will start with nothing—do what you can for the people." Like everyone else, they lined up at the housing authority. Like everyone else, they began life on the Flats in a matchbox house where Abel's only office was his car. They ultimately became a legend, responsible for founding the Cape Flats Methodist Mission and building churches and preschools across the Cape Flats. In a few short years, they were caring for five thousand people. After our arrival in District Six, we had come to know them as deep and dear friends. My bond with Abel was sealed in—of all places—New York City when he was on study leave there in 1969 and I was passing through. We arranged to meet and walked into a restaurant together. Suddenly realizing what had happened, we both stopped, then broke down in tears, hugged each other and danced a small jig. It was the first time we had ever ordered a meal together in a public place. "There was liberation from years of conditioning, just in that small experience," Abel recalled.[1] In a very real sense it was true for me, too. Elizabeth and I drew some encouragement from the knowledge that when our dispossessed members got to their new dwellings, Abel and Freda were there to ease their arrival.

Sadly, our time in District Six was coming to an end. After five years, Elizabeth and I felt a belonging among these remarkable people that we had never known before. Our lives had been changed by them in deep and indelible ways. Two more sons, David and Alan, had been born there in 1967 and 1968, completing our family. Our children had the inestimable privilege of living their earliest years among South Africans of all shades. I felt that I had at least been able to touch the fringes of their pain, sufficient perhaps to witness to it with them.

But I was worn out.

Before I left Australia, Life Line International had tasked me with establishing the telephone counseling movement in South Africa, and this had consumed much spare energy. Just three months after returning home, I had met with a small team to plan Africa's first Life Line center in Cape Town. Later in the year, I got the ball rolling in Johannesburg by addressing a large promotional gathering there. The Cape Town center opened in November 1968 with five hundred calls received in the first three months. Life Line centers spread across the country through the early 1970s. Setting up the national body was stressful and time consuming.

Then, in 1970, there was added the task of editing the MCSA's new monthly newspaper, *Dimension*.[2] It was too heavy a load, and in mid-1971 my health broke down. The powers that be suggested I leave pastoral work altogether and take over the MCSA Publishing House, where I would administer the Methodist bookshops across South Africa and be able to edit *Dimension* undisturbed. Feeling very low, I briefly accepted the idea but soon decided that to give up serving a congregation would deny my calling. Unsure what to do, I left things in the hands of God and the upcoming Methodist Conference, hoping that their ideas might coincide. Driving the eight hundred miles to Durban to cover the conference sessions for *Dimension*, I had to stop twice to get treatment for awful flu. By the time Elizabeth and I arrived in Durban, our fate had been sealed. Somebody asked me how I liked my new appointment: "What appointment?" I asked. "Sorry, I thought you knew, the Stationing Committee has moved you to Clifton Church in Jo'burg." Though we often doubt it, Methodists are

---

1. Alan Walker, ed., *See How They Grow: The Story of Twelve Growing Churches around the World* (Glasgow: Collins Fount Paperbacks, 1979), 86.
2. See chapter 5.

encouraged to believe that the voice of the conference can sometimes be the voice of God. Elizabeth wasn't at all convinced this time, but we went home to pack our bags.

The people of District Six deserved one final salute. The cruelty, sadness, faith, and courage that we had seen needed to be memorialized, and I felt that that none should pass by our church without being reminded of it. I wrote some words to that effect and asked the best-known engraving firm in Cape Town to inscribe them on a bronze plaque. Fearful of the Security Police, they refused. Other smaller firms also refused. I finally had to get the plaque made in Johannesburg, promising not to reveal the engraver's name. It read:

> ALL WHO PASS BY
> Remember with shame the many thousands
> of people who lived for generations
> in District Six and other parts of
> this city and were forced by law to
> leave their homes because of the
> colour of their skins.
> FATHER, FORGIVE US . . .

On November 21, 1971, we dedicated the "Plaque of Conscience"—the very first public memorial to the horrors of apartheid anywhere in South Africa—and then affixed it to the front wall of the church. Preaching that day I said, "We come in sadness and shame that compassion has been blinded and that the gods of racial purity are more worshipped than the God who makes us all one family." I said that nothing could shut out the cry that a monstrous evil was being perpetrated and warned that white Capetonians would pay a price in their souls: "As whites place those we hurt beyond our city walls where they are no longer visible, we are cutting ourselves off from our consciences and sealing ourselves into our own ghetto of indifference. Let none become comfortable in the presence of this terrible thing. Let none pretend it didn't happen. *All who pass by—remember with shame!*"

The Plaque of Conscience: South Africa's first memorial to the shame of apartheid

But there was need to speak also of hope: "We meet in pain and anger, but not in defeat. We meet here in confidence because God will not allow apartheid to live forever. The wall of partition being so cruelly built at this time will be broken down by our Christ. The tears that so many shed today will one day be wiped dry." I pleaded that whatever happened to the homes of the district, "let us commit ourselves to preserve this place. Let it stand as a shrine of hope, as one small part of District Six that none can take away from its people—and as a promise that they will return." Until then, I said, "Let this plaque be a judgment on those destroying this community and an offence to those who let it happen."

The plaque did stand, but not without a struggle. With police headquarters directly opposite the church, that was to be expected. In the dead of night exactly one month after its unveiling, the plaque was crowbarred off the wall only to be replaced and ripped off once more. A smaller version was made and firmly cemented in place. Despite being defaced often, it survives to this day. Twenty-one years after, in an almost-free South Africa, I was invited to preach again under the Plaque of Conscience, this time celebrating that the people of District Six could begin to return and rebuild. Now I could quote happier lines from a song about a different city:

The light of God was on its streets,

> The gates were open wide;
> And all who would might enter,
> And no one was denied.
> No need for moon or stars by night,
> Or sun to shine by day;
> It was the New Jerusalem,
> That would not pass away![3]

In the intervening years, white Capetonians did feel shame. The bulldozed slopes above the city, set aside for their occupation, was prime land, yet apart from occupying a few renovated apartment blocks, nobody seemed willing to buy. It was as if the wasteland that was District Six was hallowed ground. Only the government's new University of Technology and a couple of hotel chains were brash enough to desecrate it. The rest stood bare as mute testimony to inhuman cruelty and human pain—as if waiting for its sons and daughters to return.

By the time freedom came, the remnants of the Buitenkant Street congregation, having refused in spite of much pressure and intimidation for twenty-two years to leave their church, responded with incredible grace to a cry from the grand old (white) "mother church of Methodism" right in the center of the city. By joining them, they integrated that congregation, lending it new strength and leadership. It is now known as the Central Methodist Mission, and by one of God's strange "coincidences," our youngest son, Alan, is Superintendent Minister. Buitenkant Street Church is now the District Six Museum, the most visited in Cape Town. The museum was launched by placing a giant map of District Six on the floor of the old church and inviting ex-residents to come and identify where they had lived and "write themselves back" into the district by leaving messages on it. For the sixty thousand people who lost their homes, it is a guardian of both grateful nostalgia and painful memory. For those few who have begun to return, it represents a promise fulfilled. For others yet waiting, it must remain a shrine of hope.

---

3. Michael Maybrick [Stephen Adams], "The Holy City" (1892). Lyrics by Frederic E. Weatherly based on Rev 21:25: "The gates of the city shall never be shut by day—and there will be no night."

5

Amateur Journo

IN 1968, I WAS drawn seriously into journalism. The context was a struggle for change within the MCSA initiated in 1964 by a group of younger ministers—unoriginally dubbed the "Young Turks." We felt that our church's public witness had become inconsistent and timid and that it needed to be much more robustly engaged in social issues, especially the anti-apartheid struggle. Its internal structures were still largely segregated and thoroughly out of date. Christianity worldwide seemed to be under siege, its theology out of touch, its ethics under question, and its practices increasingly irrelevant to the poor of the earth. In South Africa and the American South, there was the added issue of entrenched, legalized racism, brazenly upheld by conservative Christians in both countries.

Yet, in the midst of this depressing scenario were signs of new life. In the USA, churches were breaking out of their staid patterns and moving into experimental ministries in the inner cities. The civil rights movement, rooted firmly in the American black church and led by Baptist preacher Martin Luther King Jr., was demonstrating how relevant the church could be in confronting segregation. Among younger progressives in the MCSA was the belief that perhaps this creaking institution called "church" might be ready to embrace a different future. In 1965, a Commission for the Renewal of the Church was launched.

The Renewal Commission set about its work with a will. We called on the church to rediscover its mission in the world and presented a new structural architecture that looked outward rather than inward. Local congregations were to be governed by a much more participatory system, and experimental multi-racial congregations were to be established in the inner cities. Methodist Circuits—largely segregated at the time—were to be replaced by geographic entities that disregarded race. We called for an end to the tradition of an all-male ministry and to the racially segregated synod sessions still held in some areas. In the face of complaints that structural change should wait until "hearts were changed," we said that hearts were taking too long and needed a good shove in the right direction—that only when church members were made to change their behavior would their hearts follow.

The commission also proposed a revamped communication strategy involving the birth of a lively monthly newspaper. Being the only Young Turk with a smidgen of journalistic experience, my name was put forward at the 1969 Methodist Conference, and after a spirited debate, I found myself the part-time, unpaid editor of an unborn Methodist newspaper, soon to be named *Dimension*.

A room attached to the garage of our home became my studio. Hot-lead typesetting was still the norm. The resulting galley-proofs had to be cut into columns, passed through a messy hot-wax machine, and fixed to dummy pages on the light table. I soon learned how to estimate word counts and space but fell woefully short with the first issue. As the first rays of deadline day peeked into the studio, I had filled only seven pages, leaving one empty and staring mockingly at me. Panic gripped me: it was too late to write anything, and I needed to be at the printers. Desperate measures were called for. This first issue focused on Easter, so I grabbed a black marker pen and arched an enormous sweeping crucifix diagonally across the whole page, with the hanging figure of Christ in silhouette. Then I wrote in the shape of a cross, "*My Dear Children, there was once, a long, long time ago, once upon a time, many, many, many, years and months and hours ago—a man. Amen.*" I titled it *The Death of a Man* and raced for the printers.

Reactions to the first issue were a parable of this strange creature called "church." Some traditionalists thought their worst fears justified; they wrote scathing notes especially critical of *The Death of a Man*, hoping that this was not the blasphemous harbinger of low standards to come. But others enthused over it. A Jo'burg minister even elevated it to philosophical greatness, saying it had evoked the "fantastically releasing theologies of Bonhoeffer, Kierkegaard, and Tillich." About the rest of the first edition, battle lines were already being drawn. Some welcomed the mix of news, political, and spiritual content; others protested coverage given to a twelve-point Election Manifesto signed by seventy ministers and laypersons. Most hoped the new paper would "steer clear of politics." Thus was the church divided, but either way, *Dimension* was on the map.

Presenting Vol. 1, No. 1 of *Dimension* to the President of
the Methodist Church Rev. Derrick Timm in 1970

The second issue coincided with the 1970 general election and plunged directly into the public square. It carried a message from the MCSA President, calling for the all-white electorate to reject self-interest, love of power, race, and class. A full page highlighted the MCSA's history of opposition to apartheid reinforced by a cartoon showing a white voter casting his ballot while excluded blacks peer in through a window. Of course the paper carried plenty of in-house church news, too. White Methodists enjoyed reading about their local churches and personalities, but many were angered by *Dimension*'s political forays. Black readers welcomed our new engagement with public issues but, being deeply conservative about how they ran their churches, were suspicious of some of the renewal goals. An early editorial summed it up. Christians, it said, too often divided into "pietists" and "activists." The former thought the faith was all about personal salvation and the road to heaven, ignoring the need to transform the hells we made on earth. The latter tended to be so focused on bringing justice to the oppressed that they often neglected the inner spiritual life and forgot how to say their prayers. *Dimension*, I wrote, stood for a marriage of the two—"the Gospel of personal salvation is supremely irrelevant unless it is preached from a platform of active social concern; the Gospel of social righteousness is utopian unless it is buttressed by the changed life." As far as I was concerned, this "double thrust" was why I was a Methodist—and why my readers should be too.[1] The coming years were to prove that many disagreed, but *Dimension* was to remain unshaken.

In its first years, while circulation figures rose to eight thousand, my only staff person was a part-time secretary managing circulation and accounts. I was editorial writer, editor, cartoonist, illustrator, and layout artist. I asked Rev. Stanley Mogoba, ex-Robben Islander and now a faculty member at the Federal Theological Seminary, to be an assistant editor. His column, called Blackground, offered a black perspective on events in a church that still assumed a white Western character.

It didn't take long to discover the power of the Fourth Estate. The printed word, even in a newborn babe like *Dimension*, carried some clout. Our sixth issue front-paged a story about the food crisis in the new Transkei Bantustan, where four out of ten children were dying before they reached age ten. The South African Council of Churches was desperately trying to meet the need with no help from this puppet government. Our story got picked up by the national press, and they suddenly "found" more than one million dollars earmarked for the purpose, which they said had been "mislaid." The money was released and children fed.

We covered the first of what became a non-stop catalogue of church-state crises. The World Council of Churches (WCC) announced large grants to liberation movements involved in "armed struggle," including the ANC and PAC, and a firestorm followed. Prime Minister Vorster demanded that South African member churches denounce the WCC and resign from it. Town councils threatened to revoke member churches' tax-free status unless they did. White church members fulminated about resigning. Emergency meetings called by the SACC brought forth a church response

---

1. Peter Storey, "Transkei Food Crisis—Churches Battle to Meet Need," *Dimension* 1, no. 4 (June 1970).

"dissociating" from the WCC's implied support of the use of violence but also refusing to leave the world body.

Dimension's editorial "regretted and challenged" the WCC decision but acknowledged the failure of SA churches to address "Christian reconciliation and the overcoming of racism." I pointed out that if the WCC was to be condemned for implicitly supporting violence, the majority of white South Africans stood under a similar condemnation for supporting "the daily acts of violence against human dignity carried out in the name of apartheid."

Black Methodists were significantly silent. They held their peace until the Methodist Annual Conference a month later. The debate began with white delegates fiercely denouncing the grants and demanding that the MCSA leave the WCC. Some whites differed, but the real shift came when the first black voice spoke and accused whites of "regarding black people in their hearts as less than men," reminding them that his people had to move apologetically through the country of their birth, being "daily subjected to intimidation, violence and terrorism far greater than anything the guerrillas had yet done." Even if the guerrillas were doing the wrong thing, he said, "I will pray for them until I die."

This rebuke came with a confidence and conviction not heard from black delegates before, and even though the final resolution was something of a compromise, I knew I was witnessing the beginnings of a shift in the MCSA's center of gravity. The conference decided to remain a member of the world body, though its membership subscriptions would be held in suspense pending the outcome of consultations with the WCC leadership. More importantly, for the first time the Methodist Church confessed its "shortcomings in seeking a solution to the problems of racism," opening the door for a much more penetrating self-examination.

Dimension carried a blow-by-blow account and pictures of the conference debate—but not without a fight. The all-powerful secretary of the conference, who had clashed often with the Young Turks, told me that while "the press" were welcome at public events, they had never been allowed to cover actual debates, and nor would I. With hindsight, the idea of an institution banning its own newspaper from its deliberations is absurd, but we were still emerging from a very different era. His prohibition made me all the more determined, and after calling some sympathetic heavyweights to my aid, I finally got in on condition that I sat in one spot in the gallery and didn't move. I also secured agreement for the secular media to do the same. In spite of my enforced immobility, I had scoured Jo'burg for a long camera lens and managed to get candid pictures of delegates in debate—or in one case, asleep. Later, I had to stifle a guffaw when, in the tense WCC debate, it was the secretary who resisted a resolution to exclude the press: "The world should know that there is freedom of expression in the Methodist Church," he declared piously. Thus did press freedom finally come to the MCSA Conference.

In the next few years, the Renewal Commission was to discover just how stubborn and immovable a huge institution like the MCSA could be. The eighty-seven monthly *Dimensions* I edited show that some of the reforms mooted in the very first issue had only begun to take hold by the time I handed the job over eight years later. But other renewal objectives were achieved. The WCC crisis had pressured member churches, including the MCSA, into accelerating internal change. Countrywide "Justice and Reconciliation" task groups had ensured that racial nomenclature was removed from Methodist structures, and the last segregated synods were abolished. Multi-racial in-service training courses for ministers became routine, and with the launch of an equalization fund, inroads began to be made into our worst internal injustice—the inequality of ministers' stipends. The administration of local congregations was radically democratized, and the first woman was ordained in 1976. In all these internal changes, *Dimension* played a significant role in pushing the conversation forward.

But there was a bigger stage. Our little newspaper's story was being played out against a countrywide scenario of steadily increasing repression. What emerges from those early *Dimension* pages is the ruthless determination with which the government sought to bend the churches to its racial ideology. Confronting the state, often over objections from white readers, *Dimension* covered one crisis after another—all emanating from apartheid actions. Many of the battles were lost, some few were won, but each gave opportunity through the paper's reporting and trenchant editorials to witness to our deeply different understandings of right and wrong.

In 1972, a secretive government commission investigated progressive Christian leaders, leading to criminal charges in some cases. State agents harassed numbers of clergy, and some Methodist prison chaplains were axed—as I had been in 1964—without explanation. Informers were everywhere. One troubled black minister reported to me that he had just been dined by two security branch men at a posh Johannesburg hotel. They offered him $240 a month to inform on me. It was an enormous amount in those days, and I jokingly advised him to take it. I might have had a growing public profile as *Dimension* editor, but I had nothing to hide.

Time and again, *Dimension* took on the apartheid beast. It editorialized that if you were black, there was no such thing as "petty apartheid" because it carved deep wounds into the dignity of men and women.[2] In the same issue,

---

2. "Petty" apartheid referred to Jim Crow-type daily indignities, as contrasted with

I tackled whether ordained ministers should enter party politics. In April of 1974, my editorials dealt with the church's role in flood relief and with the South African Broadcasting Corporation's fostering of the right-wing Christian League.[3] That September, *Dimension* denounced the Defence Further Amendment Bill as an attack on the freedom of religion that Christians would be "unable to obey." The editorials for October 1975 hit out at the Terrorism Act, accusing the authorities of taking powers "disallowed by any Christian understanding of government" and "sowing the seeds of tyranny." A second editorial bemoaned the fact that 73 percent of whites still believed it was "not our business as Church" to confront such evils.[4] As state violence and black rebellion spread across the land, *Dimension* called the government's massive firepower "a form of powerlessness" and called for the real power "that grows out of consultation and respect."[5]

When June 16, 1976, broke upon the nation with the horrific police shooting of scores of Soweto schoolchildren, we led with the iconic pieta-like picture of Mbuyisa Makhubu carrying the dying Hector Pieterson away from the killing ground. That issue of *Dimension* was promptly banned.[6]

By the October Conference of 1976, feelings in the MCSA were at a boiling point. I had editorialized:

> The focus of this time must inevitably be the wider situation of unrest in South Africa and its implications for the Church's witness and conduct. With many Methodists bereaved through police shootings and others detained in the giant security sweeps, with Black ministers caught helplessly in the conflict, deeply concerned as to their role, it is obvious that Methodism's response to this situation will be the priority.[7]

But it took leadership from the Black Methodist Consultation to make sure that happened as they disrupted the opening session of conference, demanding that the agenda be suspended to discuss the nation's crisis and threatening a black walk-out. Wisdom prevailed, and the agenda was set aside.

"grand" apartheid, the large-scale forced removals of thousands of people and creation of bantustans.

3. "Editoral," *Dimension* 5, no. 3 (April 1974) 2.
4. "Editoral," *Dimension* 6, no. 9 (October 1975) 2.
5. "Editoral," *Dimension* 7, no. 8 (September 1976) 2.
6. "Editoral," *Dimension* 7, no. 6 (July 1976) 1.
7. "Editoral," *Dimension* 7, no. 9 (October 1976) 2.

The banned July 1976 issue of *Dimension*: "Cry, the Beloved Country!"

That December, speaking of the pall that events since the Soweto uprising in June had cast over the Christmas season, I wrote that "Bethlehem may be a far cry from Soweto, but the cries of men have changed very little and Jesus, whose life was saved only by being taken over the border into another country, would understand why many will observe this season in a spirit of pain."[8] The same issue called 1976 a turning point for our land. I called on Prime Minister Vorster to withdraw riot police from the townships, release truthful casualty reports, provide counseling centers for the

---

8. Many of the young people who escaped police bullets after June 1976 crossed SA's northern borders to join the liberation movements in exile.

bereaved, offer a Christmas amnesty to all detained youths, allow them to take their exams late, and set up a task force to deal with grievances. He should also sack his intransigent education ministers with a mandate to their successors that "Bantu Education" be scrapped.[9]

Meanwhile, our circulation had risen to fourteen thousand, and our little church paper was quoted from time to time in the secular press in South Africa. I was excited when *Time* and *The Washington Post* did the same.

After an anti-apartheid activist crashed through a sixth-floor window where he was being interrogated by the Security Police, *Dimension* took aim at deaths in detention: "the detention system is barbaric because it is designed to break people. Any form of imprisonment which can ... lead to suicide is inhuman and abhorrent. If 'suicide' is a euphemism for something else then we are back in the law of the jungle." I said that if government leaders didn't like us calling South Africa a "police state," they could deal with it by the stroke of a pen, "simply by putting the power over people's lives back where it belongs, out in the open and under our judiciary."[10]

Just before my time as editor ended in 1977, a small news story in *Dimension's* conference issue ignited the MCSA's biggest ever internal crisis. The puppet president of the Transkei Bantustan was outraged because the MCSA Conference refused to recognize such apartheid creations and would not include him among other Southern African leaders to receive greetings.[11] In return, he promptly declared the MCSA to be an illegal organization in his fiefdom. One might dismiss this action as the bizarre hubris of a tinpot ruler, but to the 200,000 Methodists living in Transkei, it was only too real. He proclaimed the establishment of a new tribally based "United Methodist Church of the Transkei," and his police moved to occupy the MCSA buildings. Some ministers buckled under the brutal pressure to change loyalties, while others heroically refused and were "deported." This was not the kind of impact I had planned for my penultimate issue of *Dimension*—but it made one heck of a story.

It took a military coup ten years later to ensure that Transkei's "president" was removed and its "independence" myth crumbled, restoring the MCSA to its traditional place along with its properties. Our exile from the region ended, clergy could return, and rank-and-file members who had never lost their loyalty to their mother church brought their MCSA banners out of hiding and celebrated.

9. "Editoral," *Dimension* 7, no. 11 (December 1976) 2.

10. Storey, "It's Been Fun," 2. "Bantu Education" was a policy designed to educate black children for subservience.

11. "No More Greetings," *Dimension* 8, no. 10 (November 1977).

I had carried *Dimension* with me from Cape Town's District Six to Central Methodist Church, Johannesburg. I'd had eight years of working impossible hours and was now deputy to our district bishop and a vice-president of the SACC. I was finding it difficult to report impartially on events that I was increasingly helping to shape.

It was time to go.

Putting my last issue to bed was a bittersweet experience. In a farewell article, I said editing *Dimension* had been like having a baby every month. "All the classic stages of pregnancy have been there," I wrote, "without having nine months to negotiate them . . . and there were always complications at delivery."[12] I talked about the file I kept, labelled "The Good, the Bad and the Ugly," which carried some of the more memorable bouquets and stinkbombs directed at us over the years—some quite unprintable in a church newspaper. "We have been accused of being unwitting tools of the Communists, the Progressive Party at prayer, and other epithets, some with accompanying threats to the health of the editor," I recalled.[13]

The unredeemed racism of many white Methodists had shamed me. Our letter pages consistently carried vituperative complaints about *Dimension*'s political bias and motives, and one wondered what these people had been hearing from our pulpits over the years. But at least there was a forum where Methodists could speak and listen to each other. They never stopped criticizing the paper, but surprising numbers of them did read it. Some apparently bought it for other purposes, as evidenced by one letter asking, "Has anybody ever told you that your paper is most uninteresting? I find nothing in it that I can read. I am enclosing my subs all the same."[14]

Looking back at the monthly late-hour stints that got *Dimension* published, it was a miracle that we stayed clear of any major bloopers, but one typo raised a few eyebrows: we had Rupert Stoutt, the famous choirmaster of Jo'burg's Central Methodist Church stating with conviction that "the standard of sinning [in his choir] has been made possible by the dedicated sacrificial service of hosts of past and present choristers."[15]

The big argument of course was always about *Dimension*'s editorial stance. Although political content seldom reached more than 15 percent of each issue, we were told repeatedly that without it we would have won many more readers. That is surely true, but I was clear that we couldn't worship

---

12. Peter Storey, "It's Been Fun—Editor Peter Storey Looks Back," *Dimension* 8, no. 11 (December 1977) 7.
13. Storey, "It's Been Fun," 7.
14. Storey, "It's Been Fun," 7.
15. Storey, "It's Been Fun," 7.

God and our circulation figures at the same time. I had no regrets and no repentance about *Dimension*'s unequivocal resistance to the philosophy and expression of apartheid and all its evil bedfellows. "Once allow this indefensible nostrum to find a place in your thinking," I wrote, "and all else becomes tainted with it ... racism and the whole security system by which it is enforced, stinks in the nostrils of God, and South Africa will never be clean until it becomes a forgotten memory."[16] As if to underline this conviction, my farewell article appeared alongside another story, a list of forty-four names, headlined "Requiem: They Died in Custody."[17]

To the oft-made charge that *Dimension* was not "spiritual" enough, I replied that being spiritual was to illuminate everyday reality with the mind of Christ. That is what the incarnation was all about: it was when we allowed our humanness to be touched by Christ's divinity that we were given a new citizenship by which all others had to be judged.[18] The good news of Jesus will always come as bad news to the doers of evil, but to others it offers the breath of new life. As one editorial had indicated, "The glorious mission of the church is to bring people out of the limbo that lies between Good Friday and Easter morning, telling the joyful truth that humanity's verdict [death] has been overshadowed by God's."

The MCSA Conference has no system to honor its servants, apparently trusting such rewards to heaven, but occasionally it places a "Special Resolution" in its minutes. After I presented *Dimension*'s report for the last time, such a resolution was carried by standing vote. Among other things, it noted my "pioneering work in establishing a very high standard of Christian journalism," and the conference gave thanks to God "for the pen of Peter Storey."[19]

What amateur journo could ask for more?

---

16. Storey, "It's Been Fun," 7.

17. Peter Storey, "Requiem: They Died in Custody," *Dimension* 8, no. 11 (December 1977) 6.

18. Storey, "It's Been Fun," 7.

19. Minutes of Conference, Methodist Church of Southern Africa (1977), 201–02.

6

Young Church

WE ARRIVED AT CLIFTON Church in Jo'burg on a hot Saturday in January 1972, having driven the one thousand miles from Cape Town through the night. The welcoming committee got to see us at our worst: two travel-worn parents with four rowdy boys aged ten, eight, five, and four released at last from captivity, shouting excitedly as they explored their new home. I was relieved to have been rescued from being sent to the Methodist Publishing House and was excited about pursuing urban ministry in South Africa's largest, most dynamic city. Elizabeth struggled at first with the idea of living in Jo'burg with its thin air, red soil, and dusty mine-dumps, but we ended up spending twenty-five fruitful and happy years there, during which she built a significant career.

With our boys in the year we arrived in Johannesburg:
John, David, Christopher, and Alan

After the excitement of the day, we got the boys down and collapsed into bed ourselves, only to be startled awake the next morning by what sounded like a giant gong booming in our heads. Leaping out of bed, I discovered that the Dutch Reformed Church over the road was tolling its mighty bell, announcing Sunday worship. When it finally fell silent, I went searching for a shower and located it oddly positioned on the back porch. I was luxuriating under the stream of warm water when the door opened and an elderly lady in black stood before me, wide-eyed. I grabbed for a towel and missed, but the second attempt covered what I thought was important. I should have remembered the Oxford don in a similar predicament who covered his face instead, explaining later that he prided himself in being better known for his face than his genitals. Then I said the only thing that came to mind: "Good morning!" Without a word my visitor retreated and closed the door. I was not to know that the addition on the back porch of our home also provided the only toilet for people coming to the old Methodist church next door. Nor was it the end of the story. A few days later when being introduced to the church women's group, I found we were face to—well—face once more. I shook her hand and decided to brazen it out: "I believe we've met before," I said cheerfully. To her credit she looked me straight in the eye: "Nice to meet you too, Reverend," she replied. Three years later, she died and sitting next to the undertaker on our way to the cemetery, I recounted how we had first met. I'm not sure what other motorists thought seeing a hearse with two men laughing hysterically up front of the coffin.

Clifton Methodist stood on the edge of the most densely populated square mile in South Africa.[1] It was the oldest church building still in use in Johannesburg, but its congregation was probably the youngest. I inherited chaplaincies at South Africa's largest university and two other colleges and the vital young students who went with them. Their youthfulness was a tonic, although I struggled with inevitable comparisons between these privileged white youngsters and those whom I had left in District Six. The old stone church building had reached the end of its life and was about to be demolished, while an exciting new complex had begun to rise right below Johannesburg's mayoral and city government offices. I had been sent to complete the building project and prepare the congregation for this new chapter.

Two events helped move us in a new direction: the first was a training weekend and the second a cry of need. Most members felt that their church was "doing fine, thank you," and wondered why new training was needed. A simple experiment made them think again. I sent someone armed with a tape recorder out into the busy streets around us, stopping passersby with

---

1. Called "Hillbrow," it is a tightly packed inner city high-rise area.

two simple questions: "What do you know about Clifton Methodist Church and what do you think of it?" Members were surprised to discover that hardly anyone interviewed was aware that they existed—such was the minimal impact they were making on our immediate surrounds. At the training, I shared the priorities that should drive our approach to city ministry. Essentially, we would focus on four: to *tell* the story of God's love affair with the world; *teach* its implications for every aspect of our lives—personal and public; *demonstrate the meaning of true community* in our life together; and *serve* Jesus in the suffering, pain, oppression, and need of "the least of his sisters and brothers" in the city. If we could be faithful to these priorities, we would be doing all God required.

The issue was whether a church congregation was a club obsessed with numerical growth and preoccupied with entertaining its members, or whether it existed primarily for those outside its membership. It is my conviction that a congregation is only truly church when engaging with the needs of the world. When congregations commit to caring about these needs—"acting justly and loving mercy" (Mic 6:8 NIV)—their members become less obsessed with getting to heaven and more passionate about bringing heaven to earth, which is what Jesus taught us to pray and work for. Only then do they find new life themselves. These were not my ideas, of course. They come straight out of Scripture, but many congregations had lost sight of them.

We also looked at how a congregation could learn to discern "calls" from God. If a conviction began to speak inside any of us, we should be free to bring it to the community for rigorous testing. If we discerned together that it was a ministry God was calling us to take on—and provided a small group was prepared to "own" it—then the body would recognize it and ensure that it was resourced.[2]

Immediately following the training weekend, a local teacher came to see me. She raised concerns about the number of "latchkey children" in the local primary school where she was teaching. These small kids came to school with keys hung around their necks so that they could make their way home through the teeming Hillbrow streets each afternoon, to wait alone in some high-rise flat until a parent returned from work. "I can't get these children off

---

2. The concept of "call" rather than institutional "programming" deciding the shape of a congregation's ministries belongs primarily to the famous Church of the Savior in Washington, DC. I visited this remarkable community in November 1966 and a number of times thereafter. It was the most authentic church community I had ever known. The New Testament principles inspiring its life are described in Elizabeth O'Connor, *Call to Commitment: The Story of the Church of the Saviour* (New York: Harper & Row, 1963).

my heart," she said. "I wonder if we are being called to care for them?" This was exactly the kind of call I had been talking about, so we started the discernment process with a series of tough practical questions. A second test would be whether members of the church would similarly feel themselves called—not pressured—to this ministry. Sure enough, a small group responded, and the vision of Careways Children's Center was born.

Helen Muller, a gifted young Methodist who had trained as a teacher, took on this project, and with a small staff and thirty volunteers, Careways opened in May 1973. Every weekday, twenty-six children between six and ten years began to make our premises their after-school home until parents fetched them around 5:30 PM. Incredibly, Careways was the first specialized after-school care center we knew of anywhere in South Africa. More than that, we were pioneering a new kind of children's community. "Not a homework center, nor a Sunday school, nor a recreation center," Helen told a local journalist. "Careways is a program designed to provide opportunities and experiences which will enable these children to grow into 'whole' happy people." I used to be astounded when dropping in to "Council," for instance, to see the elected "Mayor"—all of nine years old—mediating a conflict between two younger kids with helpful suggestions from the rest of them, and adult staff gently steering things with minimal intervention. Listening in on "Thinking Day," I was again often touched by the sheer wisdom and inner strength of these children, many of whom were living in challenging circumstances. I marveled at the infectious sense of love and life that Helen and her team evoked each day. At first, children were walked from the local school, but the principal was so impressed by the change in their lives that he soon lent us the school's minibus to ferry more of them. The numbers doubled, and Careways touched about one hundred parents, who attended monthly Family Evenings with growing enthusiasm, supporting the center and—more importantly—each other. Careways became officially registered for training social work and education students, many of whom spoke about it as a life-changing placement. Soon, other churches were inviting our team to share the Careways story, and after-school centers began to spread. As I contemplated the widening impact of obedience to just one "call," I began to understand Jesus' reference to a single mustard seed growing into a broad tree offering shelter to many birds (Matt 13:31–32).

My university work drew me into an ecumenical group of Catholic, Anglican, Presbyterian, and Methodist chaplains who shared an office on the campus. The political climate required some unusual activities for student chaplains. In February 1973, we led services of protest following the banning of black and white student leaders. I spoke of a South Africa "riddled with the idolatry of race, power, and nation," and of the need to be confident that truth, right, and justice would prevail. When open warfare broke out between protesting students and the police, I found myself with others trying to act as a buffer between them and to lower the temperature of the confrontation. We reckoned ourselves successful if students got home without bruised heads. Being close by, our church became a sanctuary for some of those who needed to go into hiding.

Word spread through students and Careways volunteers that the church up the road had something different to offer and was eager to engage with their concerns. When we moved into the brand-new sanctuary in June 1973, it was a full house from the start. The newly named Civic Centre Methodist Church (CCMC) included a coffee bar and lounge and offered hospitable spaces for building community. In the afternoons, Careways kids thronged most of the building; the evenings saw students and others dropping in for coffee and a chat and the weekly School for Christian Living program. An annual academic service sealed our close relationship with the surrounding campuses. The work was fulfilling and joyful.

Three months into 1972, a stranger in his sixties had come into my office with a surprise request: he had been married in the old church, and as a sign of gratitude for a "specially blessed life," he wanted to donate a stained glass window for the new sanctuary. My response was careful. First, he needed to see the sanctuary: because it was designed for one ten-foot high window running its entire length, the cost would be enormous. Second, whoever the artist, we would need veto power over the design. Third—and I wasn't sure how he would take this—whatever the cost, I felt he would need to double it so we could use the balance for serving the poor. I quoted the ancient saying: "If you have two loaves of bread, sell one and buy a hyacinth for your soul,"[3] suggesting that the reverse was equally true: for every gift of beauty to God and for our souls, we needed to give to those who had nothing and whose stomachs were empty. To my joy, he saw the point immediately and agreed, then added a condition of his own: the stained-glass artist would need to be his son. "Oh Lord!" I thought. "That could be a deal-breaker!" But I needn't have worried. When I met with his remarkable twenty-four-year-old—today the widely known artist Paul Blomkamp—we warmed to each other immediately. We spoke about God's commitment to the concrete world in which we live, about how the story of humankind may have begun in a garden but Jesus' battle with evil was fought in a city, and how the Bible ends with God reclaiming the city as a place of justice and peace. I left Paul to meditate over a hymn by Frank Mason North, "Where cross the crowded ways of life,

3. "If of thy mortal goods, thou art bereft, and from thy slender store two loaves alone to thee are left, sell one and from the dole, buy hyacinths to feed the soul."—Muslihuddin Sadi, thirteenth-century Persian poet.

where sound the cries of race and clan, above the noise of selfish strife, we hear thy voice, O Son of Man."[4]

Soon he was back with a design for *Christ in the City*—it still hangs in my study. Dominated by a rich but somber blue, it spans the story of humanity's pretentious Babylons, trapped in the serpentine coils of evil and lost in conflict and gloom. Then, in a flood of red and gold that can only be described as "glorious," it has God's grace breaking into our world, not in triumph, but in love and service. The central focus is Christ crucified at the crossroads of the city, releasing new life into the world and leading to the beginnings of a new community. It was a breathtaking vision. In the months that followed, I watched the window take shape, praying that its theme would always remind us that God's concern was more about bringing heaven's *shalom* to this world than getting souls to heaven. And yes, Paul's dad honored his promise to fund the needs we struggled with on the city streets; all I had to do was lift the phone and his generosity did the rest.

Soon after our opening, the Group Areas Act struck again, this time taking aim at black congregations in the city. The Braamfontein Methodist Church not far from the university was told it had to shut down. Sad as this was, it offered an opportunity to address the historic separation of white and black Methodist congregations. We invited its members to make CCMC their home, fully sharing the new facilities.

Our usual services were beginning to integrate, too. A handful of black worshippers were joining us, especially in the mornings. An incident reminded me just how deeply rooted racism was in some whites. I was called to a nearby apartment where an older Afrikaans couple lived. He was in the last stages of emphysema, and I was able to journey with him through the days of his dying and conduct his funeral. Their past links had been with the Dutch Reformed Church, but his widow began to worship at CCMC and seemed to find sustenance from our community. Then one Sunday, she was sitting alone in a pew when a group of black latecomers moved in beside her. As more arrived, she finally found herself shunted up against the side wall, for the first time in such close proximity to people of color. I could see that she was distressed, and at the close of the service, instead of shaking my hand, she rushed past me in tears. When I visited her, she upbraided me for permitting what had happened: black people were not supposed to sit with whites. "Find your Bible," I said. "I think it's time for some Bible study." And for the next hour or so we went on a journey through the Scriptures, beginning with the Genesis story where God creates all living creatures "according

---

4. Frank Mason North, "Where Cross the Crowded Ways of Life," *Hymns and Psalms: A Methodist and Ecumenical Hymn Book* (London: Methodist, 1983), no. 431.

to their kind"—all except for humans, who are all made instead in one image: "the image of God" (Gen 1:1–27). Then all the way through Simon Peter's discovery that "God has no favorites" (Acts 10:34), to Paul's great statement that in Christ there is "no such thing as Jew and Greek, slave and freeman, male and female" (Gal 3:28). For a long time, my listener was silent, then in Afrikaans she said angrily, "I went to church most of my life and this is the first time I hear these things. Why did my pastor not tell me?" Another long pause before she said quietly, "It's a tall fence, but if it's in the Bible, I'll have to learn to jump over it." The encounter inspired me to resurrect the My Brother and Me courses that had been so effective in District Six. One of them was to play a significant role in events leading up to the 1976 youth uprising in Soweto, but that lay in the future.

Further ministries were launched out of CCMC, including an ecumenical ministry to lonely elderly people and a typing college for black women. In spite of being told that "no one would employ blacks" and banks refusing to do so on the grounds that their customers "wouldn't accept them," the college was able to place each of the graduates into employment, breaking yet another taboo.

At the end of 1974, the unexpected happened. I had been looking forward to a lengthy stay at CCMC when a group of lay leaders from the Central Methodist Church downtown requested a meeting. When they asked if I would consider moving to Central at the beginning of 1976, I swallowed hard. At one level, the question was a no-brainer: CMC was the most influential Methodist pulpit in the country, known far beyond Methodist circles for famous preachers, as well as its popular radio broadcasts and magnificent choir. It also had an emotional significance for me because in the 1920s my dad, as a young engineering apprentice, had been converted in that very congregation and had become Central's first candidate for the ministry. For someone only thirty-six years old, it would be an astounding appointment.

On the other hand, I knew the current CMC well because my present church was in the same circuit. The CMC congregation had a conservative reputation. All white, it boasted of having given the city a number of mayors over the decades and had a distinctly "United Party" flavor, with many World War II veterans and British immigrants among its members.[5] Unlike the days of the old Methodist Central Hall, which had focused strongly on inner city needs and the poor, the congregation had changed its name to the more dignified Central Methodist Church and now occupied a new cathedral-like sanctuary. My concern was its "suburban" character. I had

---

5. The United Party, now defunct, was the official opposition in the white Parliament at that time, opposed to the worst excesses of the apartheid regime, but only a shade less white supremacist.

preached there on occasion and sensed that its key people were not from the inner city; nor were its programs much different than those one would find in any white suburban church, focusing more on the needs of its commuting suburban worshippers than on the city itself.

So I thanked my visitors sincerely, but in fairness to them I needed to be up front with my thoughts. If I came, I would want to turn the church in at least three new directions, none of which would be easy for the congregation. "My first priority would be to work toward integrating Central," I said. The nation needed working models of God's future for our land, of blacks and whites finding one another. I had come to the conclusion that one couldn't preach the gospel with integrity in South Africa to a segregated congregation. If they were unhappy with that, they should not invite me. Then there was the need to turn the congregation away from itself and toward the needs of the city. This would mean profound changes—a whole new set of priorities—in the life of the church. Finally, "I believe passionately in the power of preaching," I said, "and I respect the CMC pulpit enormously, but I must preach the whole gospel, both personal and public. You will find me to be a faithful evangelist, but I can never be silent about apartheid and what's going on in our country. I would use the Central pulpit to engage injustice, and you must know that will not always be comfortable."

There was a long silence as the four grey-haired men glanced at each other. Then one spoke up: "Thank you for being so straight with us. Can we let you know in a week?" And we parted.

A week later, the formal invitation arrived.

7

Widening World

THE FOUR YEARS AT Civic Centre Church had been a time when my world began to widen. In the mid-seventies, I had my first experience of the body that was to play a pivotal role in my life. The MCSA asked me to attend the National Conference of the South African Council of Churches (SACC). It was my first exposure to national-level ecumenical relations. Here were the leaders of the major Christian denominations of South Africa worshipping and consulting together and reminding me very importantly that God was not a Methodist. Great church denominations were free to rise above parish-pump concerns and address the larger issues shaping people's lives in the nation. I recall very little else from that first encounter, except that the young general secretary, John Rees, who I knew through the MCSA's Renewal Commission, was determined to inject an entirely new activism into what had been something of an ecclesiastical talk-shop. The SACC churches were beginning to strengthen their opposition to the apartheid regime.

March 1973 saw a brave attempt by Rees on one hand, and Michael Cassidy of African Enterprise on the other, to bridge the gulf between the more liberal SACC churches and the conservative-evangelicals and Pentecostals, who tended to eschew any engagement with political issues.[1] They convened a Congress on Mission and Evangelism in a hotel in Durban. Getting the seven hundred delegates of all races under one roof was a miracle in itself, requiring agonizing negotiations with multiple government departments, every one of which initially refused permission.[2] For many blacks and whites, it was a "first" to share rooms and other facilities. It was certainly

---

1. African Enterprise was a parachurch organization headed by Cassidy. A dynamic but politically cautious evangelical Anglican, he had credibility in conservative-evangelical and some Dutch Reformed circles.

2. Very soon after, as church-state relations became more strained, the churches would have rejected outright any notion of seeking government permission for such a gathering.

the first time any South African hotel had accommodated black and white South Africans together. At a personal level, many bridges were built, and the experience of togetherness was initially both euphoric and surreal, but, as I wrote later in *Dimension*, every single session was reminded "of the great divide which wounds the body politic and the body of Christ in our land," and too many whites seemed tone-deaf to black concerns.[3] Ultimately, frustrated black delegates shocked the rest by demanding a separate session to caucus. When they rejoined us, they offered a number of critiques of the congress and then "spoke in love" to the white Christians: "For us to leave here with just words of repentance will be futility... you must do something to lift the foot on our necks."[4]

My contribution was a paper hammering home my conviction that the battle lines for the Christian faith ran through the great cities, not the sleepy suburbs of the world. After more about serving the city, I said that the one great, overriding challenge from God in our time and place was that of racial reconciliation. "Any evangelism which ignores the gaping, bleeding wound of racism is preaching in a cuckoo-land of unreality. Any message or any agent offering no healing for this wound is simply not speaking to the South African situation."[5] This last sentence was not an accident: I was speaking just a day or so before Billy Graham was to make his first appearance in South Africa. With many others, I had questioned the wisdom of inviting him to the congress—we feared that the hullabaloo around his coming would distract from the real issues that needed thrashing out between Christians of different stripes. John Rees confided to me that agreeing to a Billy Graham rally was the price paid to get conservative evangelicals on board for the congress. Now that he was coming and would preach to a massive rally that Sunday, a small group of us determined to engage him about our main concern.

When the great man arrived, there was hullabaloo indeed, but five of us managed to get him alone late one evening. I have to admit that we were fairly blunt: "Dr. Graham, we are here to tell you that unless you denounce apartheid on Sunday you will be harming the gospel, and it would be better if you went home now." We knew that Graham had preached in countries with ugly human rights records and always refused to comment on these issues. "Maybe the Christians there asked you to be silent," we said, "but we are asking you to speak out, otherwise your silence will shatter the hopes of black

---

3. Peter Storey, "Congress Touches Heart of God's Cross in SA," *Dimension* 4, no. 4 (April 1973), 1.

4. Peter Storey, "Split Was Misunderstood," *Dimension* 4, no. 4 (April 1973), 2.

5. Michael Cassidy, *Prisoners of Hope: The Story of South African Christians at a Crossroads* (Pietermaritzburg: Africa Enterprise, 1974), 79.

South Africans and give encouragement to an evil system." Billy was clearly taken aback, but he listened courteously and then spent some time explaining why he felt called to preach only the "simple gospel of salvation." He assured us that among the people who had been converted at his rallies there were those who later did see the need to work for human rights and justice. "Then why not tell people up front?" we countered. "On Sunday you will be inviting people to confess their sin. Why not declare that in this land the most widespread sin to confess is prejudice—that you can't follow Jesus and hate your neighbor?" Our discussion went on for a while, and Billy was gracious to the end. He said he would think and pray about our words.

On Sunday, facing a multi-racial crowd of forty-five thousand people, Billy preached one of his standard "simple gospel" sermons to great effect, but with one difference. For the first time ever, he crossed his self-imposed line and made a cautious and oblique reference to our nation's original sin: "If we don't become brothers—and become brothers fast—we will destroy ourselves in a worldwide racial conflagration." He went on hastily to diffuse what might be seen as an attack on South Africans alone: "This is not just a South African problem, this is a worldwide problem . . . the problem is deeper than the law. The problem is in the human heart. We all need a new heart."[6] As hundreds of people streamed forward to make their commitments, I breathed a not-very-happy prayer to God. This man who back in North Carolina still opposed interracial marriages had at least said something, but his timidity was pathetic. This was no prophet: people in power, no matter how evil, had little to fear from Billy Graham.

My work overseeing the growth of South Africa's Life Line centers was not all plain sailing. There were pressures from the state around our ignoring of apartheid's racial strictures and inner tensions about the movement's Christian roots. On the day we opened our first center in Cape Town, the government threatened to close us down unless we agreed to use only "professionals" and serve "persons of the white race only," absurdities we flatly refused to obey. Conflict with them continued for years. The movement's "Christian basis" got us into trouble from both secularists and religious extremists. Life Line was never about pushing faith or proselytizing on the telephones—our counselors were trained to be strictly non-directive—but we were unapologetic about our roots and argued that when it came to human healing, the insights of Jesus were as relevant as any trained psychologist. From the get-go, our Johannesburg center wanted nothing of this basis. The most strident opposition came not

---

6. Lewis V. Baldwin, *Toward the Beloved Community: Martin Luther King Jr. and South Africa* (Cleveland: Pilgrim, 1995), 83.

from Jews or Muslims, but from secularists eschewing any kind of spiritual emphasis. As Life Line International's sole Africa representative, I needed to honor its declared Christian ethos, but I believed we could do so while at the same time freely welcoming volunteers of any or no faith as long as they understood and respected our origins. A Jewish counselor in our Johannesburg center, whom I will call "Sam," lost patience with them: "Life Line has never asked me to compromise my Jewish faith," he said. "Neither has Life Line ever implied that I have less to contribute than anyone else here. All it has asked of me is to take seriously the insights of this man Jesus, about life, people, and relationships—things that can make me a better counselor. I've learned from Carl Rogers, and I've learned even more from Jesus." Then he went on: "My Scriptures talk about 'how the Gentiles rage.' I think some of you Gentiles are transferring your own doubt onto those of other faiths. I think I respect your Jesus more than you do."

I could not have said it better.

Years later, "Sam" came to see me. He was suffering from terminal cancer and would die soon. "I've never forgotten what I learned in Life Line," he told me. "I'd like you to pray with me." Then he smiled. "I'm still a Jew, of course, but anyone who could care as much as Jesus could be of help right now."

At the other end of the spectrum, the *Sunday Times* announced one day that an Afrikaans religious group was launching a Life Line center open to "white evangelical Christians" only. With friends like that, we didn't need enemies. I gave them short shrift, denying them the use of our name, and we never heard of them again.

We ultimately achieved the birth of Life Line Southern Africa, affiliated to the movement's worldwide network of twenty-four-hour telephone-counseling centers. After ten years of intensive commitment, I felt my work was done. I was grateful to have played a part in bringing this "mantle of safety"[7] to the cities of my own country but was increasingly uncomfortable about the—albeit unintentional—"whiteness" of the movement. In the sixties and seventies, the black community had extremely limited access to telephones, private or public, so it was understandable that interest was mainly among whites. Walk-in Life Line centers were set up in some black townships with limited success. At the 1989 conference of Life Line Southern Africa, I stepped back, and the movement honored

---

7. Life Line founder Dr. Alan Walker of Sydney, Australia, was inspired by this phrase describing the impact of the famous Flying Doctor Service on Australia's isolated "Outback." He established Life Line's international twenty-four-hour telephone counseling ministry to perform the same service to the cities of the world.

my founding role by naming me Honorary Life President. By 1996, there were twenty-four centers in our region.

As I write, Life Line has been serving South African cities for more than a half-century. Since we answered the first call in Cape Town with the words, "This is Life Line, can I help you?" thousands of lives have been saved and millions of South Africans helped and healed. More recently, however, the internet, smartphones, and social media platforms have eclipsed the simple technology that we used so effectively in the past. Everyone can talk to anyone now—simply by reaching into their pockets. Yet the longing for real human contact is arguably even more desperate, and the cries of the lonely, depressed, alienated, and soul-damaged as urgent as ever. The question is how and whether the movement can find new ways of penetrating and humanizing this different world with the same innovation, courage, and faith that the early Life Liners showed in the mid-twentieth century.

The year 1975 saw the WCC hold its first assembly on the African continent in Nairobi. I was among the South African delegates, but decided to go early to discuss launching Life Line in Kenya. The WCC had negotiated with the Kenyan government to temporarily relax their ban on South Africans,[8] and my early arrival made me the first to test their hospitality. Arriving at the Nairobi airport, it appeared that the good news had not reached the immigration gate, and I was held there until dark while the higher-ups decided my fate. A group of curious immigration officers gathered round me, pumping this white South African with questions about his homeland. It was all very friendly, and I was finally released. This was but the beginning of my Kenyan saga, however. A couple of days later, we received news from John Rees in Johannesburg. The Kenyans had reneged on their agreement: no South Africans would be allowed into the country after all, and I needed to know that Kenyan police were looking for me.

Staying in at my WCC-allocated hotel would have meant immediate deportation, so I decided to throw myself on the mercy of some trusted WCC friends and bunk down with them. My hope was to keep a low profile and stay at the WCC assembly as long as I could before being kicked out of the country. I found myself in a four-bed hotel room, sleeping on the floor with borrowed bedding and a thin mattress. There were only three companions when I went to bed, but they said the other bed was awaiting a late arrival from the UK. I woke at about 4 AM, and in the half-light was mildly alarmed to see a ghostly white apparition on the other side of the room. Then I discerned that it was a person covering himself

---

8. During the apartheid years, Kenya, with most other African nations, refused entry to white South Africans.

with a sheet while he knelt at prayer. Later, when I introduced myself and mentioned the fright he had given me, he let out a delighted chuckle and apologized without any sincerity at all: "I'm Desmond Tutu," he said, and we shook hands, beginning a friendship that remains sacred to this day. To its credit, the WCC, regularly vilified in South Africa as "communist" and "anti-South African," leaned very hard on the Kenyans. They threatened to abandon Nairobi and take their assembly to London unless all delegates—including South Africans—were allowed into the country. After another couple of days, I found I was "legal" again and could joyfully join the other South Africans when they arrived.

Two memories from Nairobi stand out for me. The first was meeting with a group of South African refugees who had been marooned in the Kenyan capital for some years, living in a limbo of poverty and rejection. They had left South Africa to join the ANC's armed wing but had fallen out with the organization. Now unwanted in Nairobi, they couldn't return home for fear of prison. It was heartbreaking to hear their homesick questions about the Jo'burg skyline and receive into my hands pathetic letters to take home to their families. The second memory was the furor over Canon Burgess Carr's provocative and frankly absurd statement that Christ, by dying on the cross, had "sanctified violence."[9] It would not be the last argument I would hear justifying "armed struggle," but it was certainly the most bizarre.

For some time, both in Cape Town and at CCMC, I had occasionally broadcast devotions on the radio. The SABC had already been co-opted by the state, and we called the public broadcaster "His Master's Voice," but I determined that I would continue until and unless they interfered with anything I said. Television went live in South Africa on January 5, 1976, and two days later, by accident rather than design, the beautiful sanctuary at CCMC was the venue for the very first televised church service in South Africa. I was asked if the SABC could use our church to telecast the special "prayers for the nation" called for by Prime Minister Vorster. The circumstances were very unclear, but there had been serious military encounters and loss of life involving South African and Angolan armies in the border area.[10] I didn't believe that prime ministers should be telling the church

---

9. "In accepting the violence of the cross, God, in Jesus Christ, sanctified violence into a redemptive instrument for bringing into being a fuller human life." Address by Canon Burgess Carr at WCC Assembly, Nairobi, 1975.

10. In October 1975, disguised South African troops, initially with the support of the American CIA, mounted a secret invasion of Angola called Operation Savannah. By mid-December, they were nearing the capital city Luanda when news of it began to leak out. The CIA abandoned the South Africans and international pressure forced Prime Minister Vorster to order a retreat. The South African public had been kept entirely in the dark.

when to pray, but I saw an opportunity and acceded on condition that the service went out in its entirety—no cuts at all. To my surprise, they agreed. As TV cameras and endless cabling cluttered our sanctuary for the first time, I began by telling viewers that I would not allow the telecast to "serve any interests in conflict with the Christian gospel"—that we could pray for those in danger, but there was no evidence in the New Testament that God sanctioned armed might, nor that God had favorites: "God grant that we be saved from false patriotism this day."

I went on to pray for all in danger and for their families, whether friend or foe, and for the bereaved, and that "the horrors of war may drive us to seek more ardently for peace." I pleaded also that we may be saved from hate and that we were commanded to love our enemies, respecting people "of whatever race, nationality, or ideology." We needed to acknowledge that "the use of arms would never bring permanent solutions to human crises—and that those who lived by the sword would die by the sword."

Then I prayed for South Africa: "Let us pray for that higher patriotism which, rather than being blind to all that is wrong in our land, will root it out: to love South Africa in such a way that she may not only be defended, but changed; that all that is evil may perish from our nation and all that is true and just and right and loving and merciful may flourish."

There followed a time of penitence, and the service was over. I have no idea how many viewers there were, but messages I received affirmed my decision to proceed. Most were appreciative, and some came from parents whose sons had been mysteriously called up in October, and from whom they had heard nothing. A few were predictably hostile and racist, accusing me of putting the black enemy on the same level as "our boys on the border." For many years to come, until one Sunday when the SABC cut me off mid-sermon, I trod the tightrope of trying to use this tainted medium to good purpose.

8

No Soft Landing

WHATEVER HOPES I HAD of a soft landing at Central Methodist Church in 1976 were to be dashed by June when Soweto erupted, but in the months before that I felt as if I were back in the fifties. Every Sunday, worship in the magnificent sanctuary began with the choir singing, "Drop Thy still dews of quietness, let all our striving cease," which was all very well, but it seemed out of touch with the energy of the city outside and the travails of a land edging toward upheaval.[1] Most of the worshippers—decent people mainly in late-middle age and above—commuted in from the white suburbs. Weekday organizations catered for their various fellowship needs, but none were addressing the central question of our time: What does it mean to follow Jesus in apartheid South Africa? In fact, very few CMC members would have felt that *was* the central question. Nor were programs engaging the city's needs. The old Methodist Central Hall had launched Johannesburg's first welfare organization—a team of deaconesses who visited the poor and needy—but that ministry had long been hollowed out and the Deaconess Society I inherited was just a fund.[2] My staff—an associate minister, an office secretary approaching eighty years of age, and four cleaners—was smaller than the team I had just left. CMC was like a giant ocean liner with no crew sailing serenely to nowhere in particular. Turning it around would require enormous effort, over the objections of most of the passengers. One evening during my first week, I slipped into the huge sanctuary illuminated only by the street lamps outside. The beautiful space with its nine hundred seats lent itself to awe. It was also deeply intimidating for one who was now expected to bring "a word from God" from its pulpit

---

1. John Greenleaf Whittier, "Dear Lord and Father of Mankind," *Methodist Hymn Book* (London: Methodist, 1933), no. 669.
2. Deaconesses—from the Greek *diakonia*, meaning "humble service"—were women ordained primarily to serve the poor.

each week. I knelt at the altar and asked for insight and courage. Insight so that what I preached would always have the ring of truth, and courage that I would never be afraid to declare it. A preacher's greatest foe is fear, and I sensed that a stern test was coming. Without a big dose of guts I would fail. But I also asked for love—something I wasn't very good at—because as I sought to move the congregation in a direction they would not like, I would need to love them without expecting to be loved back. I knew it would be hard. Then I had what some would call a vision: in the gloom I looked up at the gallery and imagined my dad sitting there as an eager twenty-four-year-old in the old Methodist Central Hall half a century before, listening to the great William Meara's preaching and being moved to offer his life to the ministry. I felt connection and a strong sense of continuity. The truth was that I was just part of a story God was writing. It had begun long before me and would continue long after I was gone. All God was asking from me was enough faithfulness to help write one chapter.

A painting of the Central Methodist Church, later to be named Central Methodist Mission (CMM), in downtown Johannesburg

Another early insight also helped. Rather than mess unduly with the weekly rhythms that were dear to the congregation, I would go around them. The old could continue while the new was built, and the test of relevance would ultimately decide what lasted and what would fade away. Thus liberated, I began to plan. I wanted to involve the four circuit congregations in a common strategy, pooling our meager resources and working as one.³ A number of training events to this end were held that year, and I was able to hire our first black staffers. In those days, most destitute people approaching CMC for help were white, and I enjoyed watching their faces when I referred them to "our social worker, Ms. Myeza." It was Hobson's choice—either submit to being interviewed by a black person or go with your prejudices and get nothing. Lindi Myeza started Zulu and black culture classes and began to endear herself to the congregation. It was tough to be the only black person at worship, but she brought real pizazz to the task and opened the way for others. Tentatively, a handful of black worshippers began to appear.

Not all the clergy colleagues I started with were as persuaded as I was of the way ahead; my successor at CCMC was unhappy about my plans, and he felt my leadership style to be high-handed compared to more laid-back superintendents in the MCSA. I'm sure he was right, but I was in a hurry: if we were to have any impact on a rapidly changing Johannesburg, we needed to move fast and move together. I understood when he chose to leave. Ultimately, the Johannesburg Central Methodist Mission (CMM), as we renamed the circuit in 1986, would have an inclusive team of five ministers and twenty-four lay pastors and staff, excluding janitorial staff.

All the while, clouds were gathering over Soweto.⁴ The apartheid regime's intransigence in forcing black school children not only to learn Afrikaans but also to accept the language of the oppressor as a medium of instruction made confrontation inevitable.⁵ We also had our own intelligence: Helen and Lindi were preparing to launch two preschool centers in Soweto. In the early months of 1976, future staff were coming to CCMC for training, and each time the news they brought was more disturbing.

With Helen and Lindi, I had re-started the My Brother and Me courses pioneered in District Six, and around March 1976, Lindi invited some forty youths from Soweto to join a similar number of whites for a six-week course. It followed a pattern similar to the earlier ones, but this time the atmosphere was especially tense. The Soweto youths were uneasy, bringing

---

3. The Johannesburg Central Circuit, as it was then named, consisted of Central Methodist Church, Civic Centre Methodist Church (my previous congregation), and two other small inner city congregations.

4. Soweto, standing for "South Western Townships," was the massed black housing area attached to Johannesburg where more than a million people lived in largely sub-economic city-owned housing.

5. Black school children spoke various indigenous languages at home, but English was the *lingua franca* traditionally used in schools. The Afrikaans-speaking apartheid rulers resented this and tried to make their language the medium of instruction for some subjects. It was this decision, on top of many other grievances, that precipitated the Soweto uprising.

an edge to their encounters with the generally older whites. We sometimes had to wait for them because of "difficulties" leaving the township. Around the fourth week—when in the normal course of events we expected things to be at their most tense—one of them approached me with tears of angry frustration on his cheeks. "I'm going home," he said, "I won't tolerate that white guy's arrogance anymore." It took a while to settle him. I knew whom he was talking about—a particularly loud and insensitive white minister had objected to what we taught about white privilege and prejudice. In small group discussion, this youngster had stood up to him and been steamrollered into silence. I tried to counsel him, affirming his courage: "You've got under his skin," I said, "he's hearing stuff about himself he knows is true, and he's never been confronted by a black person before. His real bullying self is coming out." I told him that most of the whites were profoundly impacted; he and his friends were doing an amazing job. He finally stayed, and at the end of the course his evaluation included the words, "When I came I wondered if I was a person. Now I know I am a person." His name was Tsietsi Mashinini. A few weeks later he was to lead the uprising that changed the political landscape of South Africa.

On Sunday, June 13, things were going to change drastically for my new congregation at CMC, too. I had received a plea from John Rees at the SACC whose staff were convinced that something horrible was about to unfold. "Would you hold a prayer service for us?" he asked, and that Sunday evening my congregation was shaken by the presence of black and white SACC staffers filling the front rows of the sanctuary. To add to their anxiety, Mrs. Winnie Mandela had arrived, too.

I welcomed the SACC as "Christ's peacemakers" who had been drawn by God into the struggle for South Africa's soul. In my sermon that night, I spoke about their need to stay centered: that in times of confusion and conflict "it is only when we're open to the eternal that we know what to do in the here and now." For real peace, South Africans needed first to face the ugly truth and then live the alternative. Racism was rooted in the "fear that casts out love," and people needed to see in us examples of the difference—people who genuinely sought to live and work together. Then SACC workers could be sure of the promise God gave to Jeremiah, to fortify them "*to stand fast against the whole land*" (Jer 1:18–19). It didn't matter if they never saw the results of their witness. It was enough that peacemakers were called God's sons and daughters—and were therefore the brothers and sisters of Jesus.[6]

Later John Rees wrote on behalf of the SACC staff saying they were strengthened: "All have mentioned in one way or another that it was as

---

6. Derived from Matt 5:9.

though we were being prepared for the week ahead."[7] If Rees was appreciative, others were not: letters and calls from white members reminded me that CMC was a "traditionally white congregation" and that a "convicted terrorist's" wife should not have been welcomed. Because I had warned of a possible violent uprising sparked by "the violence that is breaking [people] now," I was accused of "encouraging it."

The morning of Wednesday, June 16, began like any other. I had a full schedule of appointments and a funeral at 2:30 PM. During the morning, rumors began to spread of a massive school strike in Soweto. Looking down from my third floor office, I saw people gathering in small, earnest, very segregated groups. The funeral was barely over when John Rees called: *Could I come to SACC headquarters right away? Children were being shot in Soweto.* When I got there, SACC President John Thorne and a couple of other executive members were huddling with a field worker who had just come from Soweto. He described the stand-off between hundreds of students and a large police detachment, of flying stones, and a volley of shots. Now, he said, schoolkids were scattering and police chasing them down. Soweto had become a war zone.

Two things happened in Rees's office while I was there: the first was a speaker-phone call to Prime Minister John Vorster. John Thorne asked him if he knew what was happening, and he said he did. Thorne begged him to intervene by ordering a stop to police shooting. Vorster refused. "This was organized to sabotage my meeting with Dr. Kissinger," he growled, and we looked at each other helplessly, wondering at the overweening hubris of politicians.[8] What would kids in Soweto care about that? "This is on your heads," he said. "You people started this, so you can stop it." He was callous and the call pointless.

Then we heard that rail authorities had canceled commuter trains between Jo'burg and Soweto, presumably fearing that restive youths might bring their uprising into the city. Rees, who had superintended sections of Soweto for many years before the SACC job, saw it very differently. He began calling every authority he could, warning that if worried black parents working in the city were stopped from getting back to Soweto to see if their kids were safe, then indeed, the city *would* go up in flames. His wisdom prevailed, and the trains began to run again. Nobody knows how many lives John saved that afternoon.

---

7. Letter from John C. Rees, June 23, 1976.

8. Vorster had worked hard for an opportunity to persuade US Secretary of State Kissinger that apartheid was not as inhumane as it was painted to be and had at last secured a meeting with him for June 23.

Later, Desmond Tutu, recently appointed the first black Dean of St. Mary's Cathedral, arrived. He had driven out to Soweto but seen nothing. "I hear that police are driving up and down the streets just shooting at youths," he said and broke down in tears. "How can they do this? How can they just shoot kids?"

The days following were a blur of crisis meetings, emergency parents' committees, and the setting up of the Asingeni Relief Fund for victims.[9] It was not a week conducive to quiet reflection over what was happening. When Sunday came, I mounted the CMC pulpit to look out on a half-empty church. Angered by last Sunday's service and frightened by the events of Wednesday and following, many members boycotted the service. I read Jeremiah's words, "Would that my head were all water, my eyes a fountain of tears, that I might weep day and night for my people's dead!" (Jer 9:1). I continued:

> Last week I said that we had a choice between creating a real peace based on facing the truth—or having people rise up against the violence that is breaking them. Some of you protested that those words were too dramatic, but now we see, God help us, that they were not strong enough. In the horrors of just three days later, the choice was made.

I spoke of our guests from the SACC, who now were "haggard, drawn, and broken-hearted risking their lives to stand between their people and the police, pleading for an end to the violence of both. Nobody cared enough until blood was shed and death came to visit." Whites believed apartheid's propaganda that the line of racial separation helped "avoid friction," but instead it had become a battle line. "In war opposing armies wear different uniforms; apartheid has made our uniform the color of our skin," I said. Yet there was still time to be "courageous with love." I told the story of the black Soweto minister's wife who had ignored skin color, giving sanctuary to a terrified Afrikaans social worker who had run to the church for protection. "She incarnated our conviction that in Christ the dividing wall cannot stand. While the ruins still smoulder we must reach out our hands and ask and receive forgiveness. Because of Christ *the blood has already been shed*; we need not, we should not, we dare not shed each other's blood."

---

9. "Asingeni" means "We will not go in," referring to the school boycott. This emergency fund, entrusted to the discretion of the SACC general secretary and supported by churches all over the world, was set up to help families of those killed or swept up in police raids and detained without trial. It was also used later in more varied ways including funding the defense costs of those accused of "political offenses."

Things could never be the same at CMC after that. A war of attrition began between a section of the congregation and their new minister. It took various forms, none of them pleasant: there were the meetings with good, decent people who informed me regretfully that they could no longer remain at CMC because of "politics from the pulpit." Anonymous letters were less polite and other members simply slipped away to join suburban congregations. However, the only open rebellion was redeemed by farce: a rather tubby choir member (I can't resist mentioning that his day job was rat-catching) organized his male colleagues to stage a walkout the next time I mentioned apartheid. They didn't have to wait long. The large choir sat in steeply tiered seats immediately behind the pulpit, and as I moved into my sermon, I must have mentioned the forbidden word because the congregation seemed suddenly to be interested in what was happening behind me. Ignoring it, I ploughed on, but then some of the people in front of me burst out laughing, and I had to look round. The walkout had apparently begun well: the rat-catcher and his fellow gowned choristers had trooped down the steep stairs on one side of the choir gallery. At the bottom there was a sharp turn to exit into the choir vestry, and this is where rat-catcher came unstuck—or actually the opposite. As he swung round dramatically toward the exit, his gown caught on the balustrade. He was pulled up short, cannoning backwards into the person following, who did the same. By the time I looked, we had a Keystone Cops tangle of arms and legs and a highly amused congregation. The protesters finally sorted themselves out and left, and I made a lame comment about protests needing as much rehearsal as choir singing, but the event had made another wound that would need attention.

CMC's response to the Soweto crisis was multi-faceted. The church building became a refuge for kids wanting to study, and we offered extra classes there. Elizabeth and I opened our home to some traumatized Soweto youths, giving them a respite from the townships. On one occasion, we had Tsietsi's many siblings enjoying the pool in the manse garden until Alan had to dive in to rescue one kid whose excitement outstripped his swimming abilities. By far the most critical work, however, was done by a youth group that Lindi Myeza assembled to assist families who had lost young victims to police shooting or detention. They bravely visited some three hundred affected families and searched mortuaries looking for the bodies of missing school kids. Two of the group were ultimately detained without trial for more than three months. Lindi tells how they would come to her home after a heavy day for supper, debriefing, and prayers. One member of the group is today South Africa's president, Cyril Ramaphosa, whom she said was the theological conservative among them, then not too keen on political discussion!

With Lindi Myseza, our social worker and one of the heroes following the June 16 uprising

Late in 1976, Lindi herself was arrested and detained without trial. I was outraged and demanded to see Security Police General Johan Coetzee. I told him about Lindi's work and berated him for detaining an innocent person. Unmoved, Coetzee lectured me for some time on the "wiles of the communists," then, using his index finger, began to draw concentric circles on his desk. "We are going to stop this thing," he declared. "We arrested everyone in this circle, and it didn't stop. Then the next circle, then the next, and we'll go on until it stops." Then he looked at me with dead eyes. "And let me warn you, Reverend, that you're in one of my circles." I at least got to locate Lindi in the cells at a Soweto police station and saw her briefly. In short order three SACC staff were also detained without trial. Fortunately, although they were held in solitary confinement, none of them suffered torture.

Elizabeth was working overtime with Soweto victims, too. She had become John Rees's personal assistant in 1975 and was now interviewing bereaved families to aid them with burial money. Day after day, she heard ghastly descriptions of desperate searches through police mortuaries and the heart-wrenching moment of discovering a loved child's bullet-riddled corpse, often lying under a pile of others. It was traumatic work. Before the end of the year, the police had killed more than 660 schoolchildren.

Security police were meanwhile combing the townships for the leaders of the uprising, especially Tsietsi. He sought help from the Soweto Methodist Youth Center, where a courageous minister hid him. An informer told the police, and they came looking for him, only to be met at the door of the manse by a demure teenage girl dressed in a white shirt and black tunic—the standard female school uniform of the day. She opened up for them and watched while they searched every inch of the center and the manse. Thus disguised, Tsietsi lived there for some time before going into exile in August 1976.

Unbelievably, Helen, Lindi, and others were able to open their first preschool in Soweto in August. How they did it in the midst of the mayhem throughout those months remains a God-mystery to me. Both centers were staffed by Careways-trained preschool teachers. In a place of rampant violence, there was something crazily defiant about successfully birthing a preschool center whose aim was "to help children feel a sense of worth, become excited about life and the world around them, and come to know God as a loving Father."[10] The second Soweto center was opened in September 1977. Early evidence showed that kids who attended did "exceptionally well" in their first year at school.[11]

The reshaping of our work at Central had been interrupted, but the reaction to my June preaching made it even more imperative to proceed. My next step was to plan a weekly Academy for Christian Living that would be central to transformation. To act differently, people need first to think differently. Churches without a strong formational tool soon have a "balance of payments" deficit, becoming importers of how society thinks, instead of exporting transformative thought and action outward. People need a forum where they can drill down into the bedrock of Christian faith and practice and be helped to think and act like Jesus. The academy took education seriously. People registered and paid per course. A mandatory plenary at 6 PM was followed by supper, then participants could choose one of four electives:

---

10. Helen Muller, "Thlokomelong," document describing Aims, December 1980.

11. The Superintendent's Report for the year January to December 1977 was distributed at our annual meeting and then submitted to the Central District Office.

the first focused on biblical studies, a second taught theology, another addressed public issues, and the fourth offered skills. Semesters lasted six weeks on average. The academy drew on all ministers in the circuit as well as guest lecturers. Desmond Tutu, who is by discipline an Old Testament scholar, was one of our early presenters.

In the years following, between 60 and 120 people came each week to learn and grow. Some had been at CMC for decades and welcomed this new opportunity to deepen their lives. Others had been turned off traditional church but relished serious Christian education. They may have represented a modest percentage of the total membership, but it was the academy graduates—old and new—who became the leaders to help transform CMC.

It was while on a Life Line trip to Taiwan and Australia in 1977 that the temptation came. I had joyful reunions with Life Line friends from my Sydney days and preached in Alan Walker's pulpit. On the day I was to fly home, Sydney's CMM treasurers popped the question: Would I follow Alan Walker as superintendent minister when he moved on? The flight from Sydney to Johannesburg is a very long one, and little else occupied my mind. It should have been a no-brainer—Sydney's CMM was regarded as the most effective and exciting city church in the world. The offer represented the kind of challenge I had often dreamed of. When I shared the news with Elizabeth, she too was excited. Our days in Australia had been deeply happy, and she longed for our boys to be free of the shadow of compulsory service in the apartheid military. Yet, we decided not to rush it but to let the matter filter through our prayers for a while. Alan Walker's retirement was imminent, but no date had been set. In the end, we decided that it came down to a simple conviction: unless we sensed a clear and positive *call* we would be going for reasons of security rather than vocation. If we did that, then the pastor who touched down in Sydney would not be the same person they had invited. On the flight, I would have lost something irreplaceable, and they would be receiving a minister who had compromised his soul. I wrote the treasurers in those terms, declining the honor. Almost simultaneously, I learned that on their parish council were people who felt strongly that Alan's successor should be an Australian, and in the end an Australian preacher was appointed.

Other international invitations were to come from the United States and New Zealand, but while there was regret, there was no more temptation. We had worked it through together and were at peace.

9

Broken Open Church

IN THE YEARS FOLLOWING 1976, CMM was drawn ever more deeply into the maelstrom of South Africa's struggle. For me, that was inevitable for any congregation seeking to follow Jesus, but at the time many accused us of being political activists rather than faithful Christians. The distinction is important. My dad used to say that all discipleship "begins in theology and ends in politics"; in other words, our political principles need to rise out of the kind of God we believe in and the kind of world Jesus envisioned, and then be acted out where people live, love, hurt, and suffer. That is why I believed—and still do believe—that for Christians, opposing the ideology and implementation of apartheid was obligatory. There are plenty of political policies upon which Christians may legitimately differ without betraying their faith, but apartheid was not one of them. Like Nazism, its *herrenvolk* like racial idolatry and the ruthless oppression of its victims were simply evil. Nevertheless, the notion that political activism was all we were about would be a distortion. We were first and foremost a community where people came to discover their identity as children of God and to find purpose for their lives. The trouble was, of course, that we lived in a land where not everyone was respected as a child of God—and that required a response.

For me, the moment of preaching lay at the heart of what ministry was about, and far from thundering Sunday by Sunday about political issues, my passion was to offer people what Jesus called "life in all its fullness." I wanted everyone to know what a difference this Galilean carpenter could make to their lives, leaving them with a fresh vision of what he called the "Kingdom of God"—healed people in a healed world of right relationships—a world of joy, justice, and peace.

In Central's pulpit: the "moment of preaching"

Nothing was more fulfilling than journeying with my people through the forty days of Lent each year and into Holy Week. The drama of the Passion never failed to transfix and transform us. On Holy Thursday, the Service of the Tenebrae would unfold publicly under a great wooden cross in our foyer, doors wide open to the busy pedestrian mall. Afterward in the darkness, some of us would carry that cross upstairs into the sanctuary, where it towered over the crowded worshippers on Good Friday morning. Then the fallible preacher would dare the impossible: attempt to capture the mystery of God's great act of redemption in limited human speech. And each year, as if independent of my poor efforts, the impossible happened: the message burst through its confines and touched individual hearers. Many of the most effective new members of our church family traced their conversion to a Good Friday Service of the Cross.

Yet, to preach a message aimed only at personal transformation would have offered an impoverished "half-gospel." Good Friday could not have happened without Palm Sunday, when Jesus rode unarmed and alone against a great city to denounce a collaborationist religious establishment and confront the crushing power of Rome. Equally, Easter could not have happened without Good Friday, when the cost of taking on the "powers" was there for all to see—in a corpse on a cross.[1] The crucifixion was engi-

---

1. Walter Wink argues that the "principalities and powers" referred to in Scripture are not "angelic or demonic beings fluttering around in the sky," nor are they simply people in high places: they include the systems, "institutions and structures that weave society into an intricate fabric of power and relationships" as well as the spirituality,

neered by powerful vested interests just as much as by deformed human character, therefore wholistic preaching had to engage both. The surprise of Easter morning is about God gloriously endorsing the "wrong" person: instead of mighty rulers and pious priests having the last word, it was the broken, bloodied carpenter and his radical selflessness who heard God's "YES!" and continues to cause earth-shaking implications for the high and mighty everywhere.

So, when accused of stepping into political territory, I would argue the very opposite—that I was defending *God's* territory against trespassing politicians. It was South Africa's racist regime and right-wing clergy, not this preacher, who were the interlopers. Two thousand years after Jesus they were playing the same deathly games as Pilate and the priests of Jerusalem, trampling on the dignity of God's "little people." It was important to tell them: "When you mess with people made in God's image, you mess with God," and to warn them that no matter what suffering might lie between, they would lose in the end. Thus, these words preached in 1986:

> Let me say to Mr. Botha, "Apartheid is doomed! It has been condemned in the councils of God, rejected by every nation on the planet, and is no longer believed in by the people who gave it birth. Apartheid is the god that has failed. Let not one more sacred life be offered on its blood-stained altar. Open the prison doors! Call the exiles home! Burn the population register with its pornographic classifications of God's children by the color of their skin! Do it now, for as sure as God lives and Jesus is Lord, you will have to do it in the end."[2]

Again, this was not a case of looking for something "political" to say; it was stating a *theological* truth. Botha was tramping on God's turf and needed to get off. Of course, not everybody saw it that way, and some exploited the resentment many white members felt. In the late seventies, Johannesburg's now-famous Rhema Bible Church was launched and set up shop for some time in a nearby cinema. Its charismatic pastor Ray McCauley was studiously silent on apartheid but didn't hesitate to disseminate advertisements inviting those "tired of politics in the pulpit" and of the World Council of Churches to join his church.[3] It was unprincipled huckstering, but it

---

whether benign or demonic, at their core. Fallen powers congeal together into a "Domination System" that always requires violence to sustain itself. Therefore, it is not just individuals who need to be redeemed, but the "powers," too. Walter Wink, *The Powers That Be: Theology for a New Millennium* (New York: Doubleday, 1998), 1–11.

2. By the time this sermon was preached, Prime Minister Vorster had been replaced as head of the regime by Mr. P. W. Botha.

3. Rhema Bible Church now claims forty thousand members. At the Rustenburg

worked. Ray loved to boast of miracles in his church, but I told him the most amazing miracle to me was how his Pentecostals could wave their hands in the air and hide their heads in the sand at one and the same time. His congregation grew and mine shrank, but I took strength from the number of our members who were bearing the heat and burden of those days and working for change. Professor Trefor Jenkins was one. He and a couple of colleagues were waging an unpopular battle to expose the doctors who had permitted the torture that ultimately murdered Steve Biko.[4] Trefor wrote, "At a time when so many South Africans were being intimidated by the oppressive apartheid system and were being ground into a submissive state of passivity, worshippers at Central were offered the Christian hope and were sustained by it."[5]

However, the best sermons are often preached without words. We searched for a way to ensure that whatever the theme of a worship service, we would always remember people in detention and those suffering torture or other forms of apartheid oppression, so the Candle of Peace, Hope, and Justice came to the CMC altar. It was a simple white candle surrounded by coils of barbed wire.[6] At every service we paused to recall some victims or situation, reminding ourselves that no matter how cruel the barbs, the light "shines on in the dark, and the darkness has never mastered it" (John 1:5). Then we would light the candle and sing the prayer for Africa:

> God bless Africa,
> Guard her children,
> Guide her leaders,
> And give her peace.[7]

Conference between the Dutch Reformed, SACC-linked, and Pentecostal churches in 1990, McCauley publicly confessed that Pentecostals had been silent through a revolution.

4. Steve Biko was the charismatic young leader of the Black Consciousness movement. While he was being tortured in detention in 1977, in spite of his dreadful injuries, state medical examiners turned a blind eye to his condition and he died, naked and alone, in a prison cell.

5. Trefor Jenkins, "A Few Thoughts on Peter's Ministry," *What a Family,* November 1991.

6. The candle surrounded by barbed wire is the official logo of Amnesty International. I must now confess that in introducing it to our altar I failed to ask the appropriate permission. Ours was made by staff member Wendy Young, and I trust that its rapid spread across South African churches provided Amnesty with sufficient free publicity to earn me their forgiveness.

7. This widely used prayer is attributed to Bishop Trevor Huddleston, Community of the Resurrection.

The idea soon spread until similar candles stood on hundreds of altars across South Africa. I was amazed at the power of this simple symbol. Telling its story at the World Methodist Conference in Nairobi in 1986, a beautiful thing happened: British friends said that when they got home they planned to light their own candle every week to remember Elizabeth, me, and the CMC community. Such acts of encouragement cannot be measured. They not only kept that promise for seven years, but every week we received a card sending solidarity and prayers, signed by everyone at their Sunday dinner table. One carried four simple lines by Indian liberation theologian Samuel Rayan—words that have lived as a mantra in my head ever since:

> *A candle-light is a protest at midnight,*
> *It is a non-conformist.*
> *It says to the darkness,*
> *"I beg to differ."*

Central's radio broadcasts had always held a special place in South African life, and an early dilemma for me was whether to continue using the unashamedly propagandist SABC. A message from Nelson Mandela via a prison chaplain clinched it: he thanked me for the encouragement my broadcasts brought them on Robben Island, and I resolved to continue unless there was direct interference. It came in 1988 and was ostensibly about the candle. We had already clashed over a June 16 sermon, called "God's Future for South Africa," in which I had claimed that we were "infected with the diseases of racism and ethnic pride, worshipping a primitive tribalism that will destroy us all." It was time "to tell the people who propagate this kind of thing that they are a disgrace to humanity." The little red light in the pulpit suddenly went out, and I was off the air. The SABC claimed it was a fault in their studio link, but I didn't believe them. Now we had an open row. They took exception to our naming detainees and referring to "apartheid oppression" during our candle-lighting. In a tense meeting, they demanded that we exclude the candle from future broadcast services. With a straight face, I informed them that it was part of the Methodist liturgy and could not be excised. A Methodist colleague nodded loyally in support. Then one of the SABC moguls gave us a glimpse of absurdity. "Well then, Reverend," he said, "can you simply light it without saying anything?" I couldn't suppress a chuckle. The notion of sixty or more seconds of total silence in a radio broadcast brought to mind listeners all over the land scrambling to adjust their sets. These were *broadcast* experts?

Our fate was sealed, however. The SABC overlords admitted that the order to suppress me had come from "above"—their "above," not mine—and I was off the air for good, it seemed. In January 1990, a couple of weeks before Nelson Mandela was released, they changed their minds and CMC was invited back to the airwaves. We agreed, provided that "any further attempts to interfere with Methodist worship, including that very important moment when we light our candle and pray for the situation in our country, would not be tolerated."[8] When we returned, the national situation didn't seem to me that much different, so in my comeback broadcast I preached the same sermon, beginning with: "As I was saying when I was so rudely interrupted . . ."

But that was in the future.

Integrating the congregation was not simply a matter of inviting black people to worship. In theory, all Methodist services had always been open, but fixed attitudes and long custom were powerful deterrents. It took enormous courage for the few early black worshippers to walk into our imposing sanctuary with its all-white choir and pews awash with white faces. We needed a strategy to earn black trust. Part of it lay, of course, in educating the whites, two hundred of whom ultimately decided to leave rather than change. I only learned much later that when the first full-time black minister to join me presided at his first CMC Communion Service, one white communicant deliberately threw the consecrated bread to the floor rather than eat what he had received from his hands. Such were the early indignities some black persons endured.

The crucial step to integration began, quite appropriately, "underground." Deep in the basement next to our five-hundred-seat assembly hall was a large empty lobby space flanked by a well-equipped kitchen. This seldom-used area had direct access to the foyer and street via elevators and a broad staircase. From early on, I was impressed by its potential. Some people can visualize new concepts, but most need concrete examples. All my talk about a different kind of church—hospitable, diverse, and engaged with the needs of the city—could not match one working model, and the People Centre was to be that model. To a skeptical staff, I sketched out my dream of a bright, welcoming space with comfy armchairs and a modern restaurant where the humblest street cleaner would be served with the same dignity as any lawyer from the Supreme Court next door. It would be staffed by people with warm smiles, serving light snacks and tasty home-cooked lunches. There was little initial support, but I knew that unless this idea went ahead, nothing else would change. CMC needed to be irreversibly "broken open" so the real world could come in, and this was the way to do it. I didn't try to fund such a radical idea from CMC sources; a friendly foundation

---

8. Peter Storey, "CMM Back on SABC," *What a Family*, February 1990, 2.

put up the capital needed, and this went a long way to oiling the wheels. Lindi Myeza helped by demonstrating that nowhere could black people sit down to a meal. She challenged local well-known eateries to seat her, always to be rejected, and came back to tell her story. Now that finance was no problem, the project was grudgingly approved. With a small team, we set about transforming the basement. I was thrilled when a gifted and beautiful soul named Joan Rudolph left a high positon in the Central News Agency to become the People Centre's director. Joan was loved and trusted in the congregation and known to have superb catering skills. Soon she had assembled an excellent kitchen team and persuaded a group of white-haired CMC women to become volunteer table waiters.

The People Centre opened in April 1978 and from the outset was a resounding success. Ten thousand people of all races passed through its doors in the first six months, and for fifteen years after that, it served an average of two hundred meals each day. It was exciting to see black and white people eating together for the first time, but even more astounding was the notion of elderly white women serving black customers. Joan Rudolph was able to evoke a beautiful feel in the place. Clearing a table one evening, she found a paper napkin with these words scribbled by a customer: "Then there's all this—a stillness—a quietness—a people's place—an oasis in a steel city."[9] The People Centre was about lonely people finding fellowship, and hungry people finding food. It was also about black and white people finding each other. Johannesburg journalist Denis Beckett described it as "not quite charity, not quite commercial . . . at one table a millionaire Silk recharging from the pressure of prowess, and at the next someone who you suspect would never see a square meal were he not seeing it here."[10] I made sure I ate there on Wednesdays when Joan's magnificent lemon meringue pie was on sale.

Of course, it was illegal. Apartheid's Separate Amenities legislation forbade mixed restaurants, and we soon attracted police attention. But we skated round registering as a restaurant by obtaining a certificate from the city health department permitting us to prepare food. That never ended the harassment, but when the cops came we assured them that all we were doing was providing for our congregation—some of whom were black. It wasn't a lie: John Wesley had called the whole world his parish, so why could we not claim Johannesburg—and everyone in it—as ours?

The People Centre opened a new future for CMC: the building at last had a "heart," a warm, human-scale place of hospitality. Black people

9. Helen Muller, "The First Milestone—Hospitality to Thousands," *What a Family,* June 1979, 9.

10. Denis Beckett, "The Closing of Johannesburg's People Centre," *Sunday Star,* March 1993.

began to feel at ease in the building, paving the way for deeper involvement in CMC, and although it took time, white members began to embrace the fact that this was what the future was going to look like. CMC was also gaining a unique reputation as the "Church of the People"—the place in the city where black and white South Africans could break bread together.[11] Beckett recalled that "The criterion for admission was simple ... you pitched up. This place was for anyone—not nominally for anyone, as is common—but really for anyone."[12]

Now that we were more confident of the hospitality we could offer, we moved outward. A talented new staffer trained and led a multi-racial team to visit in the flatland around us. Each year they knocked on more than one thousand doors, welcoming new arrivals, helping them settle into the city, and inviting them to the People Centre and CMC—and many came. We developed a charter describing who we were and the disciplines we were committed to. Unsurprisingly, it contained those four priorities that I had articulated ten years before when we left Sydney. Following John Wesley's example of "making it easy to come, but hard to stay," we welcomed all unconditionally, but those desiring to deepen their relationship with us had to journey together for eight weeks in a New Life Group, learning to embrace our charter disciplines while also exploring their own gifting.[13] New members committed to be faithful at worship, attend the Academy for Christian Living or the GIFT groups that met in people's homes, give sacrificially, and involve themselves in one or other of our ministries to the city.[14]

Other ministries followed with different degrees of success. Our efforts to love and serve the people of the city were wide-ranging and included addiction and housing services, ministry to janitorial workers, prisoner reentry assistance, hospital and nursing home care, and even an Afrikaans-language service. This latter initiative failed to win a following, but Workers' Worship every Wednesday lunch hour did take hold, offering prayer and a brief message to about sixty people from surrounding workplaces. A dramatic moment in its life was when a man walking past heard the singing in

---

11. Certain luxury "international" hotels received permission to host foreign business people of color in their restaurants, but ordinary South Africans were not permitted to take advantage of this.

12. Denis Beckett, "The Closing of Johannesburg's People Centre," *Sunday Star*, March 1993. The People Centre operated for fifteen years until it was closed two years after I had left CMM in March 1993 "due to the present economic climate."

13. Wesley preached in the open air, welcoming all who were "moved," but those who responded to the gospel were immediately placed into disciplined "classes" under a lay leader to enable their spiritual growth.

14. GIFT (Growing in Faith Together) groups met in people's homes around the city and suburbs.

our chapel and came in, standing uncomfortably at the back until everyone had left. He told me that he had been on his way to the hotel next door, intending to throw himself from its roof, but the hymn had been a boyhood favorite, and he felt impelled to come in. That moment began a way back from his despair.

At the beginning of the 1980s, rent control in the city ended with the passing of the Sectional Title Act. I attacked it in the media as a "Landlords' Act" gouging poorer tenants. After one radio interview, an irate landlord called me, saying I was naive and ignorant of the problems he had to deal with. When I disagreed, he suddenly said: "I'll tell you what, Reverend, you can have my block of flats! I'll sign it over to you right now. Let's see if you can make ends meet trying to run it." And he did. I was gobsmacked but was not going to duck the challenge, so we soon found ourselves legal owners of Villiers Court, a slightly shabby block of fifty-six apartments a couple of streets away from CMC. With it came its tenants, most of whom were elderly disability pensioners, and a tough Afrikaans-speaking caretaker. The vision we set for ourselves was to prove we could bring a block like this up to acceptable standards and create a sense of security, community, and mutual care among its residents—all for the low rental of forty-eight dollars a month. I knew this was a job for miracle-makers and asked John Rees to manage the property while I gave Joan Rudolph the job of "creating community." We had to raise $80,000 for renovations—an enormous sum in those days—and we did. Every flat was repainted, rewired, re-carpeted, and fitted with a new stove, and the presiding bishop officially named the building Cornerstone House in October 1981.

Not all was plain sailing with our tenants. One had been a famous boxing promoter and journalist with an easily aroused temper. He was known to walk the passageways brandishing a revolver. For a time, I was probably the only Methodist minister in the world keeping a brothel because one resident was definitely earning an interesting living. A lesbian couple occupied another flat, which was no problem for me, but our caretaker, of conservative views and limited English, sometimes got confused between the two flats and grumbled about the "lesbitutes" in the building.

Our tenants were initially suspicious of us. On Christmas Eve, just three months after taking over, a group of us gathered in the courtyard and began to sing carols. Looking up at the encircling six floors, we could see one or two heads leaning over the balcony but nothing else. We were clearly not welcome, and when a couple of unsavory missiles came dropping down, we departed. But the residents had not reckoned with Joan Rudolph's stubborn love: later that night, she and her team crept along every floor, pinning a bright Christmas stocking to each door. Inside were some useful gifts, and a card from the "new owners" wishing the occupants a merry Christmas. Things began to thaw after that, and when one tenant moved out, we turned that flat into a community space, furnishing it with comfy chairs, tea-making facilities, and a TV. Slowly, community began to happen. Cornerstone House operated for eight years until bad damage from the Khotso House bomb blast opposite and other factors forced its closure. When it did, I felt that a lot had been achieved. We had been the first to operate an ordinary block of flats on a non-profit basis, providing pastoral care for residents. I said that this "showed the way for other, better-funded organisations . . . [and] at least we know that we began something with Cornerstone that lives elsewhere in a number of similar projects."[15]

Financing the rapidly expanding work was a never-ending challenge, but in 1985 we clinched a unique property deal promising us a more stable future. The old hotel next door was demolished, and construction of the prestigious Johannesburg Sun hotel begun. The developers came to me with an intriguing proposition: Would we be willing to sell them our three floors of surplus bulk? "Bulk" was apparently the amount of volume a building with our footprint was permitted to occupy, and it seemed that because Central had built only four floors out of a possible seven, we had not used our full allowance. Selling our unused "bulk" to the Sun people would enable them to add another couple of floors to their hotel. This kind of negotiation had never happened in South Africa, but we were assured that it was common in New York, and we got down to business. In the end, they got their "bulk" in exchange for $130,000, eight permanent staff parking spots, and fifty free spots on Sundays for our congregation. In addition, we would remodel our facility, replacing our small parking garage with three shops, two of which would be rent-producing and the third given free to Operation Hunger. All of this for some fresh air! I dined out for a long time on that deal.

The one hundredth anniversary of both CMC and the city of Johannesburg were celebrated in 1986. This was also the year that the MCSA Conference recognized us as the first Central Methodist Mission (CMM) in the land.[16] The name change was significant because it acknowledged that we were unique both in our city location and our multi-racial character. Unlike suburban or township churches, a CMM was given freedom to seek financial and other forms of support from the nationwide church. For me the new name was also a badge of courage, a salute to those people of color who had risked so much to integrate CMM.

15. Wendy Young, "Cornerstone to Close," *What a Family*, August 1989, 3.
16. We had fought for this classification to be established in the MCSA to encourage city ministries across the land to become multi-racial and enable them to retain a viable witness in the face of much heavier costs than those in the suburbs and townships.

CMM in 1990: a non-racial congregation emerges, modeling "God's future for South Africa"

In the late 1980s, two new staffers joined us, each of whom had sacrificed significant salaries to work with CMM. Wendy Young expanded our children's work by adding two preschools to our after-school ministry, so that each day we were caring for more than 220 children. Judy Bassingthwaite began a ministry on the unforgiving streets, identifying many colonies of homeless people living in wretched conditions. Sis' Judy, as she came to be called, moved with extravagant compassion among these most vulnerable of human cast-offs, ensuring food and medical care and becoming their champion in the endless stand-offs with the city government.

In 1988, my Annual Superintendent's Report noted that "the non-racial character of CMM has reached 'critical mass,' no longer a white congregation with black participants but a community of firmly non-racial character not only in our worship but in every part of our life." It recorded that we were now the most integrated congregation in the MCSA, and "the prophetic decision made more than ten years ago by what was then an all-white congregation—and the price that had to be paid—have been justified." It had seemed too high a price at the time: there were days when I truly feared I would be remembered for shutting down the MCSA's flagship church. Yes, we had lost some two hundred members, but looking at the smaller but much more diverse community we had become, I knew that in spite of the pain, it had been cheap at the price.

Central Methodist Church had been broken wide open.

10

Ministry with a Whiff of Tear Gas

SOME YEARS LATER WHEN the post-apartheid Truth and Reconciliation Commission (TRC) began its work, one of the commissioners, Dr. Fazel Randera, visited me. He was responsible for setting up the TRC hearings in Johannesburg and came with a request.

"Bishop," he said, "we're hoping very much that you will permit us to hold the Jo'burg hearings at CMM."

I was taken aback. "We would be deeply honored," I replied, "but the hall only holds five hundred people, and it's below ground. If the air-con gives trouble, you'll have problems. I really don't think it would work."

"No," he interrupted, "I'm not sure you understand me. It's the *church* we want, not the hall."

"But Fazel," I said, "have you thought this through? You're a Muslim, and some of the victims telling their stories will be of other faiths. Surely they will be suffering enough pain without being in a place with 'alien' religious symbols like our sanctuary."

Once again Fazel hardly waited for me to finish. "Peter," he smiled, "there's nothing alien about your sanctuary. It belongs to the people. It's the place that gave us shelter, where we could speak out, protest, and mourn our dead. In the dark days we came there time and again. We can't think of a better place for truth and reconciliation to happen."

For someone who believed as fiercely as I did that the church exists, not for itself, but for the world, here was an amazing affirmation that CMM had become that kind of church. I readily gave my blessing, subject to the approval of my successor at Central, and I kept my composure until Dr. Randera had left. Then I sat down and thought about the import of his words and of all the times when CMM had been in the eye of the storm, and how many, many people had been sheltered and embraced, encouraged and affirmed there—and I was overcome with gratitude.

Much of our witness for justice rose out of simply trying to be faithful pastors and was interwoven with the daily joys and frustrations of ministry, but that was not enough: God and the circumstances required more. As Fazel's words explained, in the struggle years CMC was impelled—not for the first or last time—to demonstrate the ancient Judeo-Christian practice of *sanctuary*.[1] Believers in a God who is our "shelter and refuge" and a "safe retreat" and who follow a Christ who began life as a refugee, are called to offer sanctuary always (Pss 46:1; 31:3, 20; 91:2; Matt 2:13–15). One of my earliest decisions at CMC was to replace the tall, forbidding wooden entrance doors with plate glass ones: people needed to know that this place welcomed them. We began to house vulnerable civil rights groups like the brave people of the Conscription Advice Bureau and Actstop.[2] Our evening services provided a meeting point for Conscientious Objectors unwelcome in their home churches. The Detainees' Parents Support Committee, who cared for the families of people detained without trial, met in our premises and were tear-gassed there more than once.

Embattled trade unions gathered in the underground hall and sometimes overflowed into the People Centre, much to our customers' discomfort. Joan Rudolph and her successors showed enormous grace when this happened, but the subtext was easy to read: "Peter, how can we run a restaurant with war-like chants thumping through the walls?" I did my best to say sorry, but how could we refuse? Where else could these people vent their frustrations without having their heads beaten in?

The largest such gathering took place during the violence-wracked transport strike of 1987.[3] Denied a place to meet, 2,500 railwaymen—most of them migrant workers brandishing *knobkieries*—descended on us.[4] I had two problems: the first that they were armed, and the second, where to put them? All I could do was stand at our doors refusing entry unless they stacked their "traditional weapons" in the foyer. To my relief they complied. We packed about fifteen hundred into every inch of the nine hundred-seat sanctuary, then into the five hundred-seat hall, with the rest filling stairways

---

1. For the full story of CMM's unique history as a sanctuary and especially its recent care for refugees, read Christa Kuljian, *Sanctuary: How an Inner-City Church Spilled onto a Sidewalk* (South Africa: Jacana, 2013).

2. The Conscription Advice Bureau was a front for the banned End Conscription Campaign. ACTSTOP was the Action Committee to Stop Evictions.

3. The South African Railways and Harbour Workers' Union strike had led to seven workers being killed by police and sixteen thousand dismissed. Some workers themselves committed horrific acts. Their meetings were repeatedly broken up by police. Ultimately the strikers prevailed and the workers were reinstated.

4. *Knobkierie*: wooden stick with a knotty or carved club head at one end, claimed by some rural Africans as a "cultural weapon."

and lobbies. The protest songs began in the sanctuary, rumbled down the stairs, and ended a few beats behind in the hall. They were remarkably well-behaved, but I didn't want to be around when they got back to the foyer and tried to sort out whose *knobkierie* belonged to whom.

CMC was also the venue for crowded memorial services, the first being for Steve Biko when he died a tortured death in prison in September 1977. I do not recall another death in the bad days that so stunned South Africa's black population—until Chris Hani was gunned down in his driveway in 1993—yet most whites had no idea who Steve was.[5] His charismatic leadership had produced the Black Community Programs that turned around many a hopeless rural settlement and gave them self-respect. Who is to know what our country may have looked like had he lived?

Another of the dead slaughtered on apartheid's altar was thirty-one-year-old Jeanette Schoon, this time assassinated together with her six-year-old daughter Katryn in June 1984 by a letter bomb sent to her in exile in Angola. Her parents were amazingly brave. They buried their daughter and granddaughter in Angola but asked me to host a service for her at CMC. I'm not sure I've ever been more affected: the sheer calculated ruthlessness of this act of state terror touched an anger deep within me. Jeanette was a courageous student leader who had suffered sixty-eight days of detention without trial and then slipped across the border with her spouse Marius Schoon on the day of their wedding. When she became a mother, she withdrew from political work for the sake of her children. She had written to her parents assuring them that they would be safe—and then this. Marius was away and two-year-old son Fritz was playing outside the range of the detonation. They could not attend the service, of course. As I prepared to preach, a picture kept coming to mind of a police explosives technician coldly assembling the fatal piece of mail that would take the lives of a mother and child in another country. I was filled with a cold fury: "The Bible speaks of the fallenness of humanity," I said. "It speaks about people who 'love darkness because their deeds are evil.' Today we are reminded again of the depths of evil to which human beings can sink. We can only speculate on her murderer or murderers; but whoever they are, *I want them to know right now that they have damned their own souls.*"[6]

---

5. Hani was a charismatic younger leader of the ANC armed wing and widely seen as a possible successor to Nelson Mandela. After returning from exile, he was assassinated by a white right-winger.

6. We now know that the bomb was organized by notorious secret-police operative Craig Williamson, who confessed at the Truth and Reconciliation Commission (TRC). For his arrogance and lack of remorse, I have found him the most difficult to forgive. The bomb-maker was one Roger "Jerry" Raven. Both were amnestied by the TRC.

These occasions were not without enormous stress. Inside, I was not always popular with the crowds. No matter how passionate or painful the event, party banners or flags were banned from the sanctuary.[7] Sometimes over-exuberant activists would sneak a big banner in and try to hang it behind the pulpit just before proceedings began, but I would have none of it. We may have been the "People's Church," but in the sanctuary they were in God's space, not to be hijacked by any political movement. Outside, the police always surrounded our premises, and often they pursued some of those attending afterward. Sometimes the unmistakable sting of tear gas wafted about. Describing one such scene, a journalist used a sentence that gave me joy: "What struck this bystander," he wrote, "was that here, come to life, was that thing so often wished for, a 'relevant' urban church."[8]

A favorite police ruse was to call in a bomb threat, hoping to cause a disruption or cancellation. CMC was a large, complicated building with a hundred possible hiding places, and guiding the squad and their sniffer-dog through it all was tedious and time consuming. The dogs apparently thought so too, with one deciding to stop and defecate inside an almost inaccessible air-conditioning space. We had mixed feelings about these searches, suspecting that if there was a device, it could quite possibly have been placed by the police themselves. In the end we ignored the threats.

The CMM building also became a venue for exhibitions, some of them very uncomfortable. I walked through our front doors one morning to be met by a gruesome sight: hanging with nooses round their necks from a long crossbeam spanning the foyer were what appeared to be six life-sized hooded corpses in orange prison uniforms, with hands tied behind their backs. I had forgotten that a lawyer-activist had asked whether an anti-death penalty group could mount a five-day exhibit. I had happily consented but had no idea how realistic it would be. Using dummies, the exhibit replicated the horrifying group executions that happened every Friday morning at Pretoria Central Prison. Once over the shock, I was glad we could play our part in highlighting this barbaric practice, but the People Centre's business did suffer that week.

In 1980, our entire clergy staff got arrested. We had joined some fifty others in a protest march to Security Police headquarters to demand the release of Congregationalist leader Rev. John Thorne, who had been taken a

---

7. We also banned the national flag, but not only because it had come to represent the hated apartheid regime. The post-1994 South African flag is also not permitted in Methodist churches, not out of disrespect, but simply because Caesar's banner has no place in the house of God.

8. Beckett, "The Closing of Johannesburg's People Centre," *Sunday Star*, March 1993.

couple of days earlier. The Security Police, led by notorious torturer Colonel "Rooi Rus" Swanepoel, swooped on us—somewhat unwisely—right outside the *Star* newspaper building and shoved us into waiting vans, getting us to our destination earlier than planned.[9] Then we were dumped into some very unhygienic prison cells. The eight of us in our cell were dressed not very practically in our clerical collars and cassocks. The whole purpose of prison is to intimidate: the noise, shouting, rattling keys, and clanging iron doors, the guards in their boots and leather belts and guns and the rest, are all about power. So, with a slam and a rattle an officious young guard shoved his enormous key into the door of our cell and—oops—the key wouldn't turn. We watched for a while as he wrestled the key, but the door just wouldn't lock. I thought this a good moment to remind him in Afrikaans of the Bible story of Paul and Silas in prison—and the way an angel of the Lord had freed them (Acts 16:16–34). The young white Dutch Reformed lad in his big uniform began to look less sure of himself. Finally, in words that could have been written for a comedy, he gave up and said, "Look, you're priests. Please promise me you won't come out of here!" In that comic moment, the power equation was inverted, testifying to God's sense of humor. The open door allowed us to check on other prisoners during the night, but the next morning we were all back in place and able to offer our guard our own version of "do yourself no harm, we are all here!" (Acts 16:28).

Facing the magistrate the next morning was a noisy business. Clergy from all over had come to support us and were singing and chanting in the corridor and outside the windows. Some of us—including Beyers Naudé and Desmond Tutu—had decided to refuse bail, only to find that an "anonymous person" had already posted bail for us. Clearly the authorities didn't want further publicity and wished us gone. It was the first of five arrests for me, and I determined to always carry a toothbrush in the future.

Each annual remembrance of the 1976 Soweto student uprisings brought nationwide clashes with security forces—always followed by more deaths. As the tenth anniversary approached, we searched for a creative way to commemorate June 16 that would demonstrate to the people of Soweto that their pain was felt by ordinary South Africans—the "silent majority" who were perhaps too cautious for public protests. Elizabeth's brother and a friend came up with the astounding idea of "A Garland of Flowers for Soweto." Why not invite people everywhere to send flowers with messages to their compatriots in Soweto? The idea immediately caught on. We raised

9. "Red Russian" Swanepoel was notorious for having ordered the police to shoot protesting schoolchildren on June 16, 1976, in Soweto. He headed up a task force in the following days that was responsible for killing many more. He was also the much-feared chief interrogator of the Security Branch, overseeing the torture of many detainees.

consciousness by placing newspaper ads with a daisy to cut out, color yellow, and display on the rear windows of cars. Then on June 15, 1986, real flowers with their notes attached were to be sent to a suburban church, from which they would be taken the next day into Soweto.

On the morning of June 16, arriving at the designated church, I found a squad of riot police outside, obviously hoping to intimidate donors, but not quite sure how to bully families, including small children, delivering bunches of flowers. Once inside, I found myself wading into a foot-deep sea of flowers filling the church. There were flowers from every corner of the land and further afield: deliveries from celebrities like Sting, Sidney Poitier, and Harry Belafonte were lying alongside tiny posies with touching messages:

> We come to Soweto to wish you "shalom" and pray these flowers will keep the hope of freedom alive in your hearts.

> In anguished memory of the thousands who have died violently and tragically in Soweto and other tormented townships since 16th June, 1976. We mourn with you and pray for a just peace in our beloved land. May God be with you.

> My family is praying very hard that our country may have peace and justice. We grieve with you for the deaths of your children and the suffering and fear with which you are now so familiar.

> These flowers are a token of our sympathy and our longing to reach across apartheid barriers to our fellow citizens.

The police squad watched while we loaded cars and pick-up trucks and set off for the various entrances to Soweto, but armored vehicles had preceded us, blocking all entrances. The police there dumped and trashed some loads and turned others away. The van I was in slipped through by following close behind an ambulance racing to Soweto's main hospital, but we got no further. Surrounded by police, we laid out our flowers against the hospital wall, while across the road residents of the black township applauded. The police ordered us to leave, but we insisted that one of our number, Rabbi Adi Asabi, should pray. In the magnificent tradition of the Hebrew psalmists, Asabi offered a lengthy lament, calling down the Lord's judgment on a long list of apartheid's sins. Later, we heard that as soon as we had left, the police trashed everything.

However, unknown to us, Elizabeth's brother had a plan B. He had hired a light aircraft, loaded it with flowers and messages, and flown over Soweto, throwing them out of the plane's door. No police force could stop him up there, but as luck would have it, one flower got stuck in an air intake, and it took all the pilot's skill to land safely.

That day, motorists with yellow daisies in their rear windows were being stopped by traffic cops, and some were arrested. Flowers that survived were delivered to the "non-white" hospital in Jo'burg, and the day ended with a packed service at CMM, dominated by a yellow flower wreath in memory of the 1976 victims. We could take comfort in the fact that their memory had been honored—and while thousands of flowers failed to reach their target, there was a warm response from Soweto residents and, more importantly, to our knowledge, no more youths had died in confrontation with police.

Two years later on the eve of another remembrance of the Soweto uprising, our Sunday school children had decorated CMM's foyer with moving prayers for peace. That night, CMM's exterior walls received a different decoration: leftist political graffiti was splashed all over them, implying that some of the human rights organizations which we sheltered had desecrated our church. But one of our janitorial staff had seen the perpetrators at work, and the next day he identified one of the culprits among the Security Police when they arrived to monitor our June 16 remembrances. When I preached later, I reminded the congregation that Jesus had anticipated people acting against the Church "because they do not know either the Father or me" (John 16:3). The people who did this were "heathens who had defiled God's temple" (Ps 79:1), and as such, worshipped another god: "Oh, they may have some god," I said, "most people do. My guess is that theirs is the tribal god of the white race. They bow to the idols that so many worship in this land, but they do not know the God and Father of our Lord Jesus Christ." "That's why, if we identify them," I said, "we will prosecute them, and when they are found guilty, I shall ask the magistrate to sentence them to worship here every Sunday for six months, to sing with us, to pray with us, to pass the peace of Christ with us, to hear the liberating Good News of God's grace with us, to break bread with us . . . so they may find God!"[10] When I went to press charges, it became clear that it would make our only witness—a young black cleaner—far too vulnerable, so I left it.

At about 1 AM on August 31, 1988, the apartheid state committed its most outrageous act of terrorism against the Christian Church. Using between sixty and eighty kilograms of explosives, a hit-squad led by their most feared assassin, Eugene de Kock—nicknamed "Prime Evil"—blew up Khotso House, headquarters of the SACC and a number of other activist

---

10. Peter Storey, "Sentence Them to Church!," in *With God in the Crucible: Preaching Costly Discipleship* (Nashville: Abingdon, 2002), 118.

organizations. The blast was enormous: the explosives had been placed near the elevator shaft in the basement parking garage—blowing the elevator out the roof and devastating each floor of the six-floor building. I was woken soon after by a call from John Rees; I dressed quickly and raced into the city to be met by a scene out of Dante's *Inferno*. Fires were still burning in the street, now littered with rubble, glass, and twisted metal. The windows of Khotso House gaped emptily, with ripped curtains and blinds hanging out of them. Part of the face of the building had been blown off, revealing the foyer, where a large tapestry depicting Christ as the "Prince of Peace" was strangely undamaged and now exposed to the world. In the unpredictable way of explosions, the floor of the foyer had been sucked down onto the demolished cars in the basement, injuring the security guard who was now sitting in pain on the curb. He later testified in court that I had taken him to hospital—something I don't remember. Cornerstone House, CMM's apartment block for disability pensioners, was directly opposite, and shrapnel from the explosion had ripped into its frontage and destroyed all its windows. Fortunately, most of the residents had their beds under the windowsills of the sturdy building. Shrapnel had blasted through above their beds, embedding itself in the interior walls of their bedrooms. I found some of them wandering around in their nightclothes covered in dust and blood from lacerations on their faces and forearms. The total number of injured was twenty-three.

The *Citizen* newspaper later published a photo of a police explosives expert escorting us away from the entrance of Khotso House after refusing us entry early that morning.[11] Some years later, he asked the Truth and Reconciliation Commission for amnesty for having been one of the squad who planted the bomb. SACC staffers began to arrive with the morning crowds, and it was gut-wrenching to see the shock and horror on their faces as they came around the corner to find their workplace destroyed. We moved among them, telling them quietly to remain calm and make their way to CMM, just two blocks away. There, at the usual time for SACC morning prayers, we gathered in CMM's chapel and began worship. It was a deeply shocked group who tried to sing Psalm 23 together, but they were also a sign that the witness of the SACC against the powers would not be deterred.

---

11. Peter Delmar and SAPA, "SACC slams blast," *Citizen*, September 1, 1988, 2.

Residents cleaning up Cornerstone House after the bomb;
John Rees can be seen on the right

Soon, every nook and cranny of the CMM building was cleared and turned into office space for the SACC. Other city churches followed suit, but of course the destruction of computers, files, and other records set the work back enormously. It would take some years before we knew that this devastating act of violence was done on the express instructions of President P. W. Botha.[12]

12. P. W. Botha, former Minister of Defence, had succeeded B. J. Vorster as head

Early in November 1988, a man with a heavy Afrikaans accent phoned in a chilling threat to my secretary: "Tell your boss Peter Storey 'I'm watching you; your time has come. Some of your black servants are already suffering.'" He claimed to belong to the "Wit Wolwe."[13] Days later, twenty-one-year-old right-wing Afrikaner Barend Strydom went on a shooting spree in Pretoria. He cold-bloodedly murdered eight black persons, wounding sixteen more. On being arrested, Strydom said he was the Wit Wolve leader. The police decided that there was no movement—that he was the only wolf. If they were right, then the call to my office came from Strydom himself, and it is still an uncomfortable thought that I was on his list.

The phrase "Prayer and Protest" came to describe gatherings where CMC's pulpit was a platform for prophetic resistance. The biblical prophets—including Jesus—disturbed the sleep of the powerful with God's voice for justice, and CMC made space for the prophets in our broken land to be heard. For a while, we could offer better protection than more exposed venues, but as confrontations escalated, the powers showed scant respect for church spaces. In 1977, for instance, the Security Police raided Khotso House and held the staff—including Elizabeth—hostage for many hours as they searched different offices. Riot police tear-gassed political funerals and trashed the Methodist Youth Center in Jabavu, leaving it in a shambles. Churches of other denominations suffered a similar fate.

Our turn to be violated came later. On December 6, 1988, a meeting nearby protesting the Delmas Treason Trial was banned at the last minute.[14] Word went round to disperse and reassemble at CMC, and soon the church was packed. The protest was resumed, this time as a "prayer" gathering. I was sitting behind the pulpit while church leader Dr. Allan Boesak addressed the crowd when I got word that a "whole lot" of police were outside. I went to investigate and sure enough, a platoon of men in full riot gear carrying sub-machine guns was stationed in front of our doors. Seeking out the officer in charge, I asked him why they were here—we were holding a perfectly orderly meeting. He replied that the meeting was banned, and his men were there to disperse it.

"You must be mistaken," I said. "The banned meeting was at Wits University. This is Central Methodist Church."

---

of government. The position of prime minister had been supplanted by an executive presidency.

13. White Wolves.

14. The Delmas Treason Trial involved the prosecution of twenty-two activists and lasted from 1985 to 1988. Eleven were found guilty, but this verdict was later overturned by the appellate division of the Supreme Court.

"Don't be funny with me, Reverend," he said. "We know who's in there, and we're coming in."

"Listen, Captain," I remonstrated, "this meeting isn't in the hall. It's in the church sanctuary. You guys have never invaded a church. If you do that, you cross a line. There will be hell to pay if you dare to invade a Christian church."

In doubt for a moment, he turned and spoke into his radio: *"We have a problem,"* he said. *"The priest says they're in the church itself."*

Then came the reply, and on hearing the word *"Move!"* crackling through his radio, I turned and ran up the stairs and down the aisle into the pulpit, stopping Boesak in full cry. I told the congregation that we were about to be occupied by riot police and to stay absolutely still in their places. There were only two major staircases down to the ground floor, and I was desperately concerned about what would happen if a crowd approaching one thousand people stampeded. Before I got the sentence out, the police were streaming into the church. The sight of some sixty men in full riot gear, positioned around our communion rail pointing their weapons at the congregation was frightening, but to their credit everyone stayed calm and seated.

The officer, pistol on hip, joined us in the pulpit and barked at me in Afrikaans: "Tell them they've got four minutes to disperse."

Again I remonstrated: "That's impossible! It takes much longer to empty this church. I know this. Let me calm them and dismiss them."

While we were arguing in the pulpit, an older, more conservative member of my congregation did an amazing thing. With dignified anger at the riot squad's lack of decorum, he got up and approached them. "Take off those helmets," he instructed. "Don't you know you're in a church? Show some respect!" It seems that some of the young Afrikaners in the squad were from God-fearing homes, because a few of them sheepishly removed their visored riot helmets, trying to tuck them under their armpits. In spite of the anxiety of the moment, I couldn't suppress a small smile. The police captain realized I was right about the dismissal and grudgingly agreed to my request, whereupon I announced that the service had been declared illegal and that we would have to leave—after a closing prayer. With that, I lifted my hands and began to pray. It was a long prayer. I wanted to at least challenge the power equation: Why should a bunch of policemen have all the authority? So, while the officer repeatedly growled, *"Finish off, priest, finish off!"* I managed what I hope was a dignified ending and pronounced the benediction. With that the people left quietly, and there were no arrests.

Police invade CMM in 1988: with Rev. Frank Chikane and Dr. Allan Boesak while an armed police captain tries to halt my prayer

Ministry in such a massively stressful context was never easy and could not have happened without remarkable people—not only on the CMM staff, but among my lay leaders. At some time, I asked the six senior leaders if they would meet with me and my associate ministers weekly at 6:30 AM. It meant that we could deal with urgent issues, yes, but more importantly, that we could pray together and hold each other accountable. Some of them lived in distant suburbs, others nearby, but with deep faithfulness they came into the heart of the city before daylight each Wednesday for years. I see their faces now and give thanks for them. They kept me strong.

By 1991, I had been twenty years in the circuit—sixteen of them at Central Church. Much of what I had hoped to achieve had come about. Central had been broken wide open in a number of important ways. We had turned to face the gritty needs of the city and committed to numerous ministries of healing and service. While a significant group of white congregants had rejected transformation and left us, our church family of around six hundred had found a "painful togetherness" and begun to look more like God's future for South Africa. People of color now topped 50 percent, and one of my proudest possessions remains a 1990 photo of the congregation, showing a beautiful rainbow community. Our voice had been heard nationally and could not be ignored, and CMM had become known worldwide for its effectiveness as a city church.

We had also waded right into the thick of the political struggle—not as a tool of any political formation—but retaining our integrity as *church*. I never forgot that the Dutch Reformed Church's early identification with suffering Afrikaners had later turned into theological capture by a nationalist apartheid ideology. I also knew that in the present struggle even the "good guys" would not be above using us, and I was determined not to get sucked in that way because no matter how noble the cause, there would come moments when those same "good guys" would need to be held accountable, too.

Quite early during these years I had also been thrust into national leadership positions, first as president of the SACC and then as presiding bishop of the MCSA, followed by the ongoing task of bishop of the district.[15] Crazy as it sounds, these additional responsibilities had been carried out while still leading CMM, but by 1991 my synod judged that the burden had become too great and voted to separate me from circuit ministry at the end of that year. I would now be like Anglican and Catholic bishops, without a congregation. I understood the need, but looking back I know that I lost something life-giving and precious. For a minister, there is nothing more fulfilling than to walk with your people through their various life challenges, offering them each Sunday the "bread of life" and seeing them grow in faith and character. More than we admit, we pastors live by our congregation's faith as much as our own, and my heart broke at the thought of leaving CMM's people and pulpit. For me, the sixteen years there—with four before that up the road at CCMC—would always be the apex of my life as a preacher, pastor, and sometimes maybe a prophet.

---

15. See chapters 13–16.

11

Public Square Encounters

THE WORK OF A minister is more varied than many people know, and the special circumstances of South Africa's years of travail made it even more so. During the CMM years and beyond, as I became involved in wider leadership, there were many fascinating, robust, and sometimes life-threatening encounters with people on all sides of the conflict as well as in the international arena.

In 1980, I returned from speaking at the World Methodist Youth Conference just in time for the meeting of church leaders with P. W. Botha. It was our first, and P. W. was somewhat taken aback when Bishop Tutu asked to pray before we started. He clearly wasn't happy with the prayer because he warned that the next time we met he would make sure that his principal military chaplain was there to pray instead. We waded in with the calls that would become a mantra in the years ahead: commitment to common citizenship for all, abolition of the pass laws and forced removals, a uniform education system, and a "national convention" that would include the jailed and exiled leaders of the people. My contribution was to remind him that the churches had "branches" in hundreds of places where his party had never been and that our take on the situation was far closer to the grassroots than his. Botha responded to the different inputs in a more conciliatory tone than expected and proposed a second, all-day meeting. We left with mixed feelings. On the one hand, I told the media that there was a "very wide gulf" between us, but that more genuine conversation had taken place that day than "in any other talks in thirty years." I said I believed it was possible "to speak to people without surrendering principles."[1] I was wrong this time: despite our efforts, the promised all-day follow-up never happened. The project died after we discovered that at the very time we

---

1. John Allen, "Church-State gulf exists but talks will be resumed," *Star*, August 8, 1980.

were meeting the prime minister, his government was secretly funding the right-wing Christian League of Southern Africa, which was dedicated to smearing the WCC and the SACC. Desmond had also made a long trip to Europe and America, infuriating P. W. by lobbying church and political leaders for tougher action against the regime. P. W. immediately removed Desmond's passport, preventing any further international travel. Our next meeting with him would be a long time coming.

"Bye-bye. We must meet again sometime."

The Gulf: hanging on to Desmond Tutu as he farewells P. W. Botha after our 1980 meeting

The most remarkable assembly in the history of the MCSA was called "Obedience '81" and took place in the winter of that year. For seven days, eight hundred Methodists met to stake out our convictions about what obedience to Jesus would mean in the 1980s. Apartheid's alienating power was driving deeper fissures into the already tenuous unity of the MCSA, and black Methodists were despairing of whether their "multi-racial church" could be trusted to stand by them in their struggle. Most white Methodists, persuaded by government propaganda, were shockingly ignorant of their fellow Methodists' suffering.

The gathering was unique in a number of ways. Clergy and laity, young and old, women and men, and black and white were selected on a proportional basis, ensuring that Obedience '81 was completely representative. Delegates signed a covenant promising full participation and committing to stay to the end, regardless of how frustrated they became. The "bottom-up" decision-making process was also unique: every delegate was required to journal each evening, recording all insights during the day. Early in the morning, each met for prayer with one other person—a "faithful friend" chosen for them from a different background—to share their journaling. These pairs fed their insights into a larger group of about twenty that met immediately afterward. There were forty such groups deciding what concerns and convictions they would convey to a "listening committee" that was also uniquely inclusive. Nominations for it were held open until all eight hundred participants were satisfied that their concerns were represented on it. I was tasked with chairing this committee, and when we first met, I wondered how this disparate crowd of some forty people could ever reach a consensus. We met each day and brought drafts of the emerging message to no fewer than three plenary assemblies for discussion, revision, and more work.

It became clear that two great concerns were paramount. The first was the need to rediscover and contextualize the missional and evangelistic passion of our heritage. There were powerful calls for a new commitment to spreading the gospel in the Wesleyan spirit in Southern Africa. Moved by these calls, more than fifty participants offered themselves for full-time ministry. The second was whether black and white Methodists would stand in solidarity with one another in confronting the powers as the apartheid state entered its most oppressive decade. Midway through the gathering, a black minister brought things to a head with a brutally honest challenge to white Methodists: either they were with the struggle for justice or against it. They had to choose. For many whites, this was the first time they had been upbraided by a black person, certainly in such terms, and his address became the tipping point. Some broke down and others threatened to go home, but many more knew that it was time to change. Remarkably the covenant held and of the eight hundred participants, only one broke ranks and left the gathering. The moment when Obedience '81 came closest to exploding gave opportunity for God's truth to break in.

A seasoned political journalist wrote that he knew of

> no other meeting of this size and lasting so long, where blacks and whites were in a situation of continuous and intensive confrontation and debate, telling each other with brutal frankness

and honesty how they saw and experienced their fellow Christians on the other side of the apartheid fence.[2]

The next days were marked by a quiet determination to move the MCSA into a more radical obedience. Resistance to change began to melt away, clear convictions emerged, and the work of the many-opinioned listening committee became easier. After consulting the plenary for a third time, they asked a small multi-racial team to work on a final text. I took four clergy and a layman to my office, and we labored through the night. One by one, sleep overtook our partners until only two of us were left. We put the finishing touches to "The Message of Obedience '81" at 4 AM, and later it was unanimously adopted by a standing vote.

Obedience '81 was called "probably the most important assembly yet held by any church in South Africa."[3] In the years that followed—the bloodiest years of the struggle for freedom—its "Message" was used to hold Methodists accountable. Its power lay not only in its words, but also in the way it had come about. Methodists may have failed it in many ways, but none could deny the commitment they had made in a week of painful togetherness. The "Obedience Charter," as it came to be known, pledged the MCSA to "henceforth live and work to bring into reality the concept of an undivided Church and a free and just Southern Africa."

Another powerful experience for me in 1981 was to attend the WCC Central Committee meeting in Dresden, East Germany—the first to ever meet behind the Iron Curtain. Our links with the WCC were precious to us, and this great ecumenical body was unwavering in its support for our anti-apartheid struggle.

Dresden had been almost obliterated during World War II when Allied bombers ignited a firestorm that killed twenty-five thousand people, and it had suffered under Communist rule since 1945. The city center was still dotted with gutted ruins, and as we moved into our accommodations, I wondered how we would relate to the people of this grey police state.

I had no idea how their faith would move and humble me.

In the dusk of the first evening, our convoy of buses moved down to the venue. We could see people in the gloom outside, but they were being held back by the dreaded *Volkspolizei*. We disembarked into an eerie silence, thick with suspicion and fear. Then we moved into the great *Kreuzkirche*—the Church of the Cross—which had been rebuilt only that year. Elliptical in shape, it had two balconies, one above the other, both empty. We took

---

2. J. H. P. Serfontein, "Shock Therapy Opens Eyes at Assembly," *Sunday Times*, July 19, 1981.

3. Serfontein, "Shock Therapy Opens Eyes at Assembly."

our seats in the nave, feeling uneasy and insecure. Then we heard a shuffling sound: the people of Dresden had been permitted to come and watch this service and were moving into the balconies.

The service began. The organ thundered out with Luther's "A Mighty Fortress Is Our God," and as we stood to sing, something happened: we felt what seemed like raindrops falling on us. We looked up, and there were hundreds of faces looking down on us, hands reaching over the balconies, each waving a white handkerchief. The people were smiling and weeping, both at the same time, and their tears were falling on some of us. That is how our "enemies" welcomed us, and in spite of all their Communist rulers' attempts to stop them, they continued to do so in the days that followed. The Christians of East Germany had endured thirty-five years of persecution, intimidation, and harassment and simply proved that when life gets most intense, God becomes most real. In the days following, wherever we went, people would come up to us in the street, smiling and saying, "I too am a Christian."

Like the East Germans, those who took a public stand against the South African apartheid regime had to reckon with our own secret police, the "Security Branch." Sometimes their activities were less secret than others. Our youngest son Alan—waiting for letters from his girlfriend—couldn't understand why mail seemed to arrive only once a week. When he asked the friendly mailman, he was told, "Sorry, man, but we have to wait for the Branch to come on Wednesdays to read it before we can deliver." On another occasion, I was having a long telephone conversation with my presiding bishop when a voice suddenly interrupted: "Oh, you two are speaking shit!" Apparently we had tried our phone-tapper's patience once too often. More serious were the anonymous calls and occasional death threats. Our sons developed different ways of responding, our youngest's being a pithy "Fuck off!"[4] Mysterious objects were left at our front door, one a parcel emitting an ominous ticking sound, which I gingerly carried to the back garden and dumped into the swimming pool. It turned out to be harmless.

If one was black, however, Security Branch attention could be much more scary. On June 20, 1986, I was phoned in the early hours of the morning by the wife of Rev. Ike Moloabi to tell me that he had just been picked up by the Security Police and taken away in his pajamas. Ike was a fine minister stationed at a black township eighty miles away. I immediately departed, and by 8 AM another minister and I were making the rounds of the police stations looking for Ike. As was usual in these detentions, there were denials of any knowledge of him, but when we got to the town prison,

---

4. Bold for a ten-year-old and definitely learned outside our home.

someone let slip that he was indeed there. As his bishop, I demanded to see him, and it worked. We were put in a room with some rough benches, and an Afrikaans prison officer brought Ike in. He was still in his pajamas, shivering in the cold, and clearly frightened.

We were not allowed to say much to each other, but I had brought in my pockets some bread, a small chalice, and communion wine, so I asked the guard if we could give Ike Holy Communion. He agreed. Spreading a handkerchief on the bench between us with the bread and cup upon it, I told the guard that Methodist Communion was open to all and invited him to join us. After some hesitation, he accepted. Having broken the bread and shared it between the four of us, I passed the chalice first to Ike and he drank. Then, because we had a "stranger in our midst," it seemed right to pass the cup to the officer. Now, this white Afrikaner had a dilemma: if he wanted to receive the means of God's grace, he would have to place his lips for the first time in his life on a cup from which a black man had just drunk. For what seemed an eternity he held the small chalice in his beefy hands, just looking at it. Then he lifted it and drank—and at last I saw the hint of a smile on Ike's face. Finally, I confess to introducing a variation in the liturgy. "We Methodists always hold hands when we say the Grace," I said and asked the Lord to help me keep a straight face as prison officer and prisoner held hands while I recited the ancient words of benediction. There was no miraculous release after this. Ike was kept some time longer, but while he remained there, he and this guard were strangely bound to each other, and the power equation between them was not the same. We should never underestimate the power of the holy. Rituals we have grown accustomed—and maybe inured—to in the sheltered walls of our sanctuaries can have a dramatic impact when performed "out of context," such as this one was. It is why, when confronting the armed might of the state on the streets, we clergy made a point of wearing our cassocks and stoles. We wanted Caesar to know he was making war on the church of God.

Of course, this didn't necessarily protect us. In 1988, a number of church leaders went on the shortest protest march ever. Five days after the banning by the government of seventeen anti-apartheid organizations and a number of their leaders, a protest service was held in St. George's Cathedral in Cape Town on February 29. I spoke the "sending forth" prayer: "Go now in the spirit of Christ into a land of hatred, take his spirit of love into this city of division, take his spirit of unity into these streets of violence, take his spirit of peace and go now with God." Well, we didn't really go anywhere. We set out to march on Parliament only to be confronted by a large group of police right outside the cathedral. They ordered us to disperse, so we knelt on the sidewalk instead. Our pavement prayer was short: those of us in the lead of the procession were physically lifted off our knees, and my feet never touched the ground until I was pushed into the back seat of a police car and driven to the police station. Why the police took all this trouble I don't know, because we were not even booked before being warned and released. The rank and file of the protest were not so fortunate. They were attacked with a high-powered water-cannon, and 150 clergy were arrested—something of a world record, I would think. While they were being processed, we returned to the cathedral and held a press conference.

A scarier encounter was with militant youths in 1990. A courageous Catholic priest in Soweto embarked on a hunger strike protesting the escalating violence, and I wanted to go and pray with him. Our son Alan joined me. Parts of Soweto were in flames, and a heavy pall of smoke hung over the area. The priest was lying on his bed with a group of people around him, and we shared together and prayed. Afterwards, we found our return littered with felled trees, making driving very difficult. As we picked our way slowly through these barriers, sometimes driving on the sidewalk, something tapped my side window. It was a 9-millimeter automatic in the hands of a youth of about sixteen. He was very agitated and shouted at me to roll down my window. As I obeyed, the gun barrel was pushed into my ear, and I was told to get out. A group of youths, all very menacing, surrounded our car, opening Alan's door and pulling him out, too. I didn't know whether they were an ANC self-defense unit[5] or drugged kids taking advantage of the general anarchy to hijack us. The youth with the gun seemed to be the only one armed, and his weapon was now pointed at my chest while he continued shouting. It was a very tense stand-off and there was not much I could think of to say. Gambling that the law of averages would favor me, I said, "Some of you are Methodists. Do you want to shoot your bishop?" There was a pause in the shouting, and the group went into a huddle, and I tried to keep calm while they consulted, presumably about our lives. At that moment, somebody approached from across the road. Alan remembers that he seemed to be telling them who I was. The huddle suddenly broke, and the leader came back to me, stuffing the pistol into his trouser waistband. "Sorry, Bishop," he said, and we shook hands. Then they let us go. As we drove away grateful that our church's witness still had some influence even over these wild youths, our relief was tempered by the realization that, in spite of some of them likely being linked with the MCSA, they too had become infected with the false trust in violence.

---

5. Armed ANC-supporting youths called "self-defense units" were set up to protect their neighborhoods, but the line between defense and thuggery was crossed regularly.

In September of 1986, Desmond Tutu was enthroned as the first black Archbishop of Cape Town, leader of the roughly two million Anglicans in Southern Africa. After the pomp of the service in the cathedral, Elizabeth and I went on to a stadium to join the ten thousand people who greeted the new Archbishop. There we separated, because I had to be on the podium to welcome Desmond on behalf of the wider ecumenical church family. Bareheaded and in my black cassock, I looked a little out of place among all the be-mitred Anglican bishops of the province resplendent in their white and gold. I guess this is what it means to be a non-conformist, I thought. When it was my turn to speak, I reminded Desmond that we had shared the same small town as children, "I in privilege, you in poverty."[6] South Africa had separated us, I said, but the church of Jesus brought us together. We had prayed together, gone to prison together, been deported together, "and today we can thank God together that this vast gathering is a sign of a new South Africa." There was thunderous applause. "Today we salute your service to the ecumenical movement but even more we salute you as a symbol of hope for the hopeless, as a voice for the voiceless, and as a servant of the cross," I said. "Today is a word to those in power that apartheid is doomed."

By the late eighties, some unexpected and influential people were beginning to use their positions to push for change. One Sunday evening, a distinguished-looking man in his early sixties slipped into the back pew of our chapel at CMM. He attended a couple more services before introducing himself as Ian McCrae, the CEO of Eskom, South Africa's subcontinent-wide energy utility. He slipped his card into my hand and asked if I would have lunch with him. Some days later, we met in his office in Eskom's headquarters, and as we ate he drew my attention to a large oil painting. It depicted one of Eskom's mighty generating stations with power lines running off toward a distant city. But the painting held a surprise: under the power lines was a tree and a small rude dwelling with a black family living there. "I keep that in my office to remind me why I'm really here," he said. "We have more power than we need in this country, yet families like that live by kerosene lamps." He went on to speak of his dilemma. Because he kept the lights on in South Africa, P. W. Botha's Security Council and the military knew that he could also switch them off. He was being drawn into their web with a view to weaponizing electric power as part of the "Total Strategy," but he wanted to use the massive utility to free people, not hold them to ransom.[7] Could I

---

6. Ermelo, in what was then called the Transvaal, where Tutu's father was a teacher for some time and mine the local Methodist minister.

7. The "Total Strategy" was P. W. Botha's response to what he called the "Total Onslaught" against South Africa by "communist-inspired terrorism." While communist ambitions for Southern Africa were real, the regime used the situation to militarize

put him in touch with the "real black leaders" so he could hear from them how best to do this? I was impressed with him and undertook to make the contacts secretly. He could not be seen publicly to be consulting any but the regime's "tame" black surrogates. I met McCrae late one night in the underground parking garage of the Sun Hotel where we swapped cars, and I drove him into Soweto to meet with a small group of leaders. He listened intently as they described life in Soweto, the vagaries of the electricity supply, and problems of payment for the poor. As if by arrangement, there was a power outage while they spoke, and the meeting continued by candlelight. McCrae agreed to process what he had heard and report back. My role ended by hosting the feedback meeting at CMM in December attended by Soweto heavyweights. I do not know what flowed from any further meetings but got the feeling that he had run into a wall at the Security Council end. I took some solace in knowing that one of the people who literally wielded power in our land had been moved to try to act for the greater good.

In November 1990, the SACC linked up once more with African Enterprise to bring churches together for a conference at Rustenburg. It was the first time in many years that SACC member church leaders were meeting their Dutch Reformed counterparts as well as engaging the Pentecostal family of churches. The rationale behind the conference was simple: if South Africa's divisions were to be healed, it was time for the churches to heal theirs. I confess to having had little appetite to engage with church leaders who—either by support or silence—had nourished and extended the life of apartheid. But after a tense beginning where we eyed each other suspiciously, a prominent Dutch Reformed theologian came to the podium.[8] His words would transform the spirit of the gathering:

> I confess before you and the Lord not only my own sin and guilt and my own personal responsibility for the political, social, economic, and structural wrongs that have been done to you, the results of which you and our own country are still suffering from, but vicariously I dare to do that in the name of the Dutch Reformed Church of which I am a member.

For a while there was a stunned silence: you could have heard a pin drop. And then Archbishop Desmond Tutu bounded up to the platform and looked at us all and said, "Well, my theology tells me when someone confesses, I have no choice. I must forgive." That was a moment of breakthrough, and from then on a spirit of confession moved amongst

---

white South Africa and ruthlessly suppress blacks and anyone who questioned their policies.

8. Professor Willie Jonker of Stellenbosch Dutch Reformed Church Seminary.

us all. Ray MacCauley stood up on behalf of the Pentecostals and said, "We sinned. We preached individual salvation without social transformation. We were neutral and therefore we collaborated with apartheid." That left us. We may have been the "good guys" who had led the struggle, but we also had failures to confess: "Some of us were bold in denouncing apartheid but timid in resisting it. We failed to give support to courageous individuals at the forefront of protest. We spoke for justice, but our own church structures continued to oppress."[9]

The Rustenburg conference was costly for the Dutch Reformed Church, especially when their moderator stated "unambiguously" that his denomination fully identified with the theologian's statement. As a result of that confession, some thirty thousand members of the denomination walked out in anger and started a new whites-only church, the Afrikaans Protestant Church. Dutch Reformed Moderator Prof. Johan Heyns, with whom I worked late into the night helping to write the Rustenburg Declaration, was later assassinated by an unknown gunman. It is thought that his turning against apartheid was seen as an act of treason against his *volk*.

Rustenburg had many positive results: one being that it enabled a capacity for peacemaking that was going to become very necessary between 1990 and 1994. If the churches had not found that moment of healing, if we had not bowed our heads and confessed our own failures, we could not have played the crucial role required of us in two important bodies that saved South Africa: the National Peace Accord and the Truth and Reconciliation Commission. Both of these uniquely South African initiatives required a new spirit of working with former enemies, and I doubt that either would have been possible unless estranged churches had found each other first.

---

9. The Rustenburg Declaration, November 1991.

12

Shadows of War

THE CLAMOR WAS ALMOST unbearable. Every rivet in the big Super Frelon helicopter seemed to be crying out as we winged across the bush. The ground was so close that I felt I could lean out of the open door and touch our shadow as it leapfrogged the trees. I'd been told that we had to fly this way to avoid ground fire from the SWAPO "terrorists," and I could see it made sense.[1] My escorts, an army colonel and two South African Defense Force (SADF) chaplains, were hooked up to the intercom system. I'd been given earmuffs to dampen the noise and couldn't hear their conversation. However, the colonel hadn't bothered to hide his dislike; I knew I was an unwelcome guest and my presence strongly resented. It was easier to stare out the door at the blurring scrub than to try and engage them. Looking about me, I wondered again what I was doing in an SADF chopper in the middle of a war my country was waging in the thick bush of the South West Africa/Angola border.[2]

It was 1985, and I was now the head of the Methodist Church of Southern Africa. As early as 1970, church and state in South Africa had engaged in an increasingly tense exchange over issues of military chaplaincy, conscription, and the "Border War." Behind these loomed the overarching debate about violence itself. Under the influence of Gandhi and King, and mentor Alan Walker, I had come to a personal position of Christian

---

1. SWAPO—the South West Africa People's Organisation—fought a twenty-three-year guerrilla war to liberate what is now known as Namibia from South African control. It ended in 1990 with Namibian independence.

2. The "Border War" loosely describes all the conflicts fought by the SADF not only against SWAPO in what was then South West Africa, but against Angolan, Cuban, and some Russian fighters deep in Angola. It also includes the role of the SADF in covert warfare in Zambia, Rhodesia/Zimbabwe, and Mozambique. Apart from SWAPO forces and Angolan soldiers, over the years of war a total of some 600,000 white South African conscripts and 400,000 Cuban conscripts were rotated through the war zone.

pacifism, hoping that I would find the courage to live it out. As a cocky seminarian, I had argued confidently for the "Just War" position, but no longer. Try as I might, there was no way that I could imagine Jesus in a military uniform. I had become convinced that nonviolence was his way and that the church's compromise with war since the time of Constantine was its longest and most tragic act of disobedience. With war there were no winners, only blood and more blood.

However, I never lost empathy for the people in uniform. Not only had I been one of them for a while, but the sacrifices of World War II had been stamped too deeply into my early consciousness to join the peace movement's sometimes glib condemnations of the military. I still appreciated the Just War position even though I could no longer defend it and felt for those who made the dreadful death and life decisions of command— who had to just "do these things and say our prayers at the end."[3] I shared Gandhi's view that practitioners of nonviolence should not scorn military bravery, but exceed it by being willing to die but not to kill. For me, the real problem lay not with the soldiers, but with the politicians who sent immature eighteen-year-olds to fight their wars and die for their ambitions. As a father of four sons, I cared particularly about young conscripts sucked into the SADF, and as a minister I cared about colleagues tasked with giving them spiritual care as chaplains. This may appear to have been a conflicted position, and of course it was, yet perhaps no more conflicted than that of Jesus the nonviolent liberator giving time and compassion to an officer of the occupying Roman army.

P. W. Botha asserted that "the honor and duty to defend one's country should not be made subservient to one's religious convictions."[4] A statement like that asked for confrontation, and that is what he got at the 1974 SACC National Conference. One participant proposed that because the SADF was defending an unjust and discriminatory society young conscripts should be encouraged to refuse service and the churches should reconsider seconding ministers as military chaplains. I supported the main thrust of the resolution but decided to engage him about the withdrawal of chaplaincy. The vast majority of SADF personnel were young conscripts who would be abandoned to the care of Dutch Reformed chaplains, most of whom were part of the apartheid brainwashing machine. I was determined that they should not be left without some spiritual succor. After a tough debate, my amendment was carried, leaving our chaplains in place

3. Nicholas Monsarrat, *The Cruel Sea* (London: Cassell, 1952), 200.

4. Gary Thatcher, "South Africa's conscientious objectors," *Christian Science Monitor*, September 4, 1980. Botha was minister of defense prior to becoming prime minister and later president of South Africa.

but calling for "reconsideration of the basis on which they were appointed." It also sought to investigate ministry to the pastoral needs of those who had left the country and joined the liberation movements.

The "Conscientious Objection" resolution broke on the nation like a thunderclap. Botha immediately introduced the Defense Further Amendment Bill with a $12,500 or ten-year prison sentence for anyone who encouraged another to refuse military service. This was later watered down to six years, but still made counselling potential objectors a high-risk business. Meanwhile, choosing to be a CO carried an automatic six-year prison sentence. When I became minister of CMM in 1976, we offered an office to the Conscientious Objectors' Advice Bureau, and I was in awe of several elderly ladies who trod a legal tightrope, risking their own freedom as they helped troubled conscripts make decisions that could involve six years behind bars. Theirs was a role truly subversive of the "powers," played with sweetly innocent smiles and cups of tea in their office one floor above mine.

On Sundays, CMM used to hold a small evening service in our ground floor chapel, and because we were known to be sympathetic to COs, numbers of them attended. Their own congregations had coldly rejected them; here there was warmth and welcome. The presence of these young men always challenged me. Some of them were already on trial for their convictions, others had yet to face arrest. No cheap religiosity would do for them; the gospel that had inspired them to sacrifice needed now to strengthen them for suffering.

Then, in one of God's amazing ironies, the dynamics of our evening worship became even more unique. Following the Soweto uprising, the black townships had been occupied by the military. Young white conscripts who had been told they would be facing an enemy on the northern borders of the country were now patrolling the streets of Soweto. One Sunday evening, just as worship began, there was a screech of brakes outside the chapel, some barked orders, and the clumping of boots in the foyer. I continued with the service, but it was hard to concentrate, and the COs inside the chapel were white-faced and anxious. World War II veteran Ken Roberts went to investigate and found an entire platoon of uniformed SADF medics in the foyer. They came from barracks on the edge of Soweto and were in the charge of a young corporal—also a conscript—who was a Methodist and had decided they should go to church. CMM was the only Methodist Church he knew of in Jo'burg, and he asked if they could enter. There was one problem, however. Ken pointed to the pistol on his belt and said, "You can't bring that into our chapel." The corporal was apologetic; they were not allowed to drive anywhere without one of them being armed. I know nothing of the negotiation that followed, save that the weapon was handed to Ken, who spirited it away to a safe place for the duration of the service, and the soldiers joined our conscientious objectors for worship. This arrangement went on for some months, and it was fascinating to see the engagement between them over coffee after each service. Here was a group of young white South African males similar in all respects save one decision: to accept conscription or resist it. After some stiffness and suspicion, it seemed to me that an unexpected sympathy grew between them. Our COs knew how difficult their own choice had been and cast no blame on those who had found it easier to "go with the flow" when the call-up came, while at least some of those in uniform expressed a sneaking respect for contemporaries who were facing six years in prison for their principles. Standing in the foyer after worship and watching a soldier and a CO talking animatedly, I marveled at the miracle. Where else, I wondered, could two groups of youths who had chosen such radically divergent futures be able to pray together, share together, and perhaps find respect and understanding? Where else but in the welcoming embrace of Christ's church? Maybe they were discovering together that whether in uniform or facing prison for refusing to wear one, all were victims of the same evil system and all shared the need for grace and courage to face whatever lay before them. Some years later, I met that young corporal once more: this time he was a candidate for the Methodist ministry. He spoke of how those CMM chapel services had played a part in his call to ministry. Even though we opposed the presence of troops in Soweto, he had found welcome, not judgment.

Army occupation of the townships was initially seen as an improvement on the trigger-happy police patrols they replaced, but as soldiers got involved in house-to-house searches, reports of some atrocities emerged. A "Troops out the Townships" campaign gained traction and resistance grew. Youths were digging trenches to trap the ugly armored "Caspirs" used by the police and stringing wire across streets to try and decapitate soldiers riding in high, open troop carriers. In February 1986, a concerted attempt was made by the churches to get the government to withdraw the troops. After a fruitless trip to Parliament to plead for withdrawal, Desmond Tutu and I went to the stadium in the teeming Alexandra township, near Johannesburg, to report back. The arena was packed with forty-five thousand angry residents. We squeezed our way through those tightly jammed on the field itself and climbed on the back of a flatbed truck. As Desmond began to use the PA system on the truck, his voice broke. "I have nothing to bring you," he said. "We have failed." The anger in the crowd was tangible, and he spoke again, in Xhosa and Sotho, but any attempt to offer hope was drowned out. There was nothing for it but to leave. We jumped down from the truck and some men formed a wedge to get us to our car. Once there, a group of youths surrounded us. "Why should we let you go?" they shouted. "You come here with nothing and leave us to these soldiers who are killing us!" It was a very scary moment, but they finally let us leave. As we drove away, Desmond wept. "They are right," he said. "We brought them nothing."

As a bishop, one of the portfolios assigned to me was that of military chaplaincy, responsible for implementing our church's policy and caring for the welfare of our chaplains. I found very quickly that they divided between those who were clergy wearing the uniform in order to do their job and those who did the job *for* the uniform. There were ministers of integrity and courage who were willing to embrace this deeply ambivalent role for the sake of getting alongside the young and often frightened conscripts who were the cannon fodder of the apartheid wars. Other chaplains enjoyed the military too much and had not only absorbed its culture but also big doses of the "Total Strategy" ideology. These were the people we needed to weed out. Among the truly dedicated chaplains, some paid a heavy price for their loyalty to the MCSA and its position on the South African struggle. The chaplain-general to whom they answered was a pastor of the apartheid-supporting Dutch Reformed Church. During the notorious political indoctrination classes run by Military Intelligence, he had warned against "Tutu and Storey and other dangerous subversives," implying that we were both communists. One of our chaplains immediately protested, demanding that the general meet with the chair of the MCSA Chaplaincy Committee—myself. An embarrassed chaplain-general ended up apologizing to me, asking me to convey his regrets to Bishop Tutu, as well. These moments of small triumph were of course meaningless in the larger scheme of things, but I admired the courage and loyalty of a young chaplain being willing to call out his general in that way and suffering the attendant consequences.

I had experienced something similar myself when Bishop Tutu and I traveled to Namibia in 1982 to investigate allegations of SADF atrocities in the conflict against SWAPO. We listened to horror stories of how a brutal police counterinsurgency battalion, co-founded by multiple murderer Colonel Eugene de Kock, used to rampage through villages in their Caspirs, dragging the bodies of killed "terrorists" in the dust and often leaving flattened dwellings behind them. Several tribal leaders had been killed for alleged sympathy with SWAPO and captured land mines had been planted by SADF operatives near their villages, with deaths of innocent villagers blamed on the "terrorists." It was a dirty war.

On our return to Namibia's capital, Windhoek, we called a press conference to expose some of what we had seen and demanded an immediate withdrawal by both sides to end the suffering. "South Africa is in an unwinnable war," I said. "Every military victory of the South Africans is a political victory for SWAPO."[5] Unknown to us, the hotel we used was partially occupied by the SADF, and the press were highly amused at attending an anti-SADF "presser" a couple of floors below a military headquarters. Less amusing for me, however, was the knowledge that my two eldest sons, John and Christopher, were current naval conscripts. There was no way they would escape some of the fallout of their dad now being a whistle-blower, and I felt for them. The press conference struck a nerve. Government-supporting media and the military were quick to counterattack: an Afrikaans newspaper carried a cartoon showing Desmond and me welcoming a thuggish, heavily armed "terrorist" with Tutu saying, "I greet you—not as Communists or Marxists, but as beloved Anglicans and Lutherans."[6]

"I greet you—not as Communists or Marxists, but as beloved Anglicans and Lutherans."

The SADF said it was "obvious that the Rev. Peter Storey and the SWA churchmen with whom he had discussions, have either been misled by the stream of twisted propaganda emanating from that sinister tool of Russian expansionism SWAPO, or are in cahoots with that organization."[7] The day

5. Alan Dunn, "Withdraw and end the suffering—SACC," *Star*, February 19, 1982.
6. By cartoonist Gregory Boonzaaier, published in *Beeld*, February 20, 1982.
7. "Denial on 'Atrocities,'" *Cape Argus*, February 25, 1982.

after the press conference, we sat in the Windhoek airport lounge waiting for our flight home surrounded by fellow passengers, all of them white and many in uniform. They subjected us to the most poisonous glares I can remember, and I expected someone to get up at any moment and assault us. It was around the time of Evensong, however, and Desmond Tutu opened his Missal and began to quietly say his evening prayers. Nothing would divert him from his spiritual disciplines.

The real heroes of our conflict with the SADF were the COs. They were not many, but one after another they made their compelling witness and suffered for it. As the years passed, their numbers grew. The state grudgingly introduced a "Religious Objector" category, but the government remained unmoved by any "selective objection" based on the immorality of the Border War.

In 1985, as head of the MCSA, an invitation arrived for me to accompany other church leaders on an SADF-sponsored trip to the "Operational Area" in northern Namibia. I knew of these tours, where VIPs were wined and dined and given the propaganda line from morning to night, and I refused the invitation. At the same time, I felt a pastoral responsibility toward Methodist youngsters caught in the SADF web. So I waited for a decent interval and then made an official request to visit Methodist conscripts in the Operational Area. The SADF people were enraged, but I knew that in terms of a longstanding church-state concordat, they were obliged to give someone in my position the access I requested. In May, I met up with the unhappy colonel and the two SADF chaplains on the Angolan border. We boarded the Super Frelon chopper and headed off into the bush. I had specifically asked to meet with conscripts in more exposed situations, and the low-altitude rush across the bush brought us to them.

We would come upon a fire-base in the middle of nowhere, where the bush had been cleared for a couple of hundred meters in all directions and high berms bulldozed out of the sand to form a perimeter. A watchtower or two overlooked the bush. Behind the safety of the berms was a small canvas village surrounding a headquarters tent and a mess-tent. To one side were makeshift showers and latrines and the helipad, on which we descended with an enormous racket, whipping up a stinging cloud of sand. This was as close as any civilian would get to the sharp end of the Border War. We never stayed longer than an hour before flying on to the next fire-base, and at each one I was met by anyone not on patrol who wanted to join me. The largest group consisted of about twenty-five young conscripts. I was honest with them, saying that while the Methodist Church could not support this war, I knew that they hadn't asked to be here, that they were maybe scared, and that we cared about them very much. They were remarkably open with me: like soldiers everywhere, they hated the boredom and, yes, when on patrol they were often afraid. One of them was bold enough to talk about the corrosive effect of hate. "We're taught to hate here," he said, "and I fear what that is doing to me." Others nodded as he spoke. I had already seen the evidence while drinking some coffee in a HQ tent: ghastly photos of mangled corpses looking down on us—trophies denoting the fire-base's "kills"—and I had wondered what long-term damage these crude "motivators" wrought and what price would one day have to be paid for such violations of human decency. It was not easy to respond to him. We talked about the God who I believed never left us, even when we walked into places God didn't want us to go. I asked them for telephone numbers of parents and girlfriends, promising that I would call them all when I got home. Before parting, we said prayers together, and then I shook their hands and got back into the chopper.

The next day, I finally flew back home in a military transport. Once there, I began to place telephone calls: late into the night, I called parents and girlfriends to tell them that I had seen their soldier son or lover a dozen or so hours previously and that he was "okay." When I first identified myself, the reaction was usually one of suspicion or outright hostility. Why would someone with my political reputation be wanting them—and at that time of night? Then, when the purpose of the call was communicated and messages shared, the chill slowly melted, replaced by thanks and appreciation. "We stand against this war," I said, "but we care about those caught up in it." It was a good night's work, and I went to sleep alongside Elizabeth in the small hours thinking about young men on two sides of a dirty war, sleeping fitfully that night in exposed places, each seeking courage for this needless conflict.

At the 1987 Methodist Conference, some of us called for the MCSA to make a radical break with its past and become the first mainline denomination to declare itself a "Peace Church." In so doing, we would join the small group of Christian bodies like the Mennonites and Quakers who renounced violence, refusing to let their members take part in war. After a vigorous debate, it was surprisingly agreed to refer the issue to all circuits across the country for discussion. My episcopal area as bishop covered Johannesburg, Soweto, and the mining towns to the southwest, passing through several archconservative areas. In the middle of a war, Methodists got down to arguing whether their denomination should commit itself to pacifism, but many local superintendent ministers ducked the issue rather than face uproar. I was invited to some angry meetings and was fascinated to see how this issue united whites and blacks in opposition. Whites were outraged that their church was asking them to "stand by and let the communists take over the country," while blacks could not believe we wanted their liberation movements to lie down while the army and police "just mowed them down." I tried to interpret to each the dilemma of the "other" with little success and came away more convinced than ever of how different things might have been if the MCSA had been more integrated at grassroots. Instead, Methodists were shouting past each other—and in some places, no doubt shooting at each other. While driving to one of those meetings out in the country, I came across the sobering sight of a long convoy of SADF tank carriers bearing heavily damaged tanks and other armored vehicles. The picture of those twisted wrecks stayed to haunt me. Men had died inside of them. The murderous waste of war was there before my eyes.

The next Methodist Conference received reports from the circuits and districts and came somewhat regretfully to the conclusion that the Methodist people were not ready to embrace the Peace Church notion. Pacifists would remain a small minority, and the church would have no new prophetic word for a nation torn in two.

Throughout these years, the shadow of the inevitable call-up of our four sons had hung over us. We were concerned for their physical safety, of course, but there was the deeper matter of integrity. The concept of "moral injury" is relatively new: it refers to the character damage soldiers experience, not so much from what they have suffered, but because of what they may have *perpetrated*. We hated to imagine any of our boys actually killing another person, never mind a fellow South African. Because of this, I had hoped very much that my naval background would count in getting them into the navy, where chances of this happening were much smaller. In spite of their putting up a good case, when John's and Christopher's papers arrived, they were both headed for the army. We were still trying to come to terms with this when sheer coincidence opened a door. Passing the SA Navy recruiting office in Pretoria one day, I heard someone shouting my name. Looking in, I was surprised to see a person whom I knew from my naval training. Now he was a naval captain and apparently in charge of recruiting. He surprised me with the warmth of his welcome, as if unaware of the wide gulf that alienated me from the SADF and its actions. After chatting for a while, he asked me about my family, and I took my chance: "Can you believe," I said, "that my two eldest boys have both been called up for the army? Two sons of a naval officer made to wear khaki!" My captain friend's reply made my heart leap: "Ag, we can't have that, Peter," he said. "Give me their details, and I'll look into it." It was as simple as that. New papers soon arrived, and instead of the army, John and Christopher both left for naval training. I know that I compromised my principles that day in Pretoria, for interests that were very personal, but I think I can live with that guilt—and I remain ever grateful for that chance meeting and the captain's generosity.

In late 1989, 771 young white men from all over South Africa announced that none of them would fight in the "Apartheid Forces." I was grateful that our four sons were among them. John and Chris had decided to refuse any further call-ups. David was a law student receiving legal deferments but decided to refuse when the call came. Alan took a more direct course to CO status.

Needing space to think through his call-up, Alan had followed seminary graduation by spending 1988 working in Australia and returned with his mind made up: he would be a CO. He had a profound commitment to nonviolence, and although his objection was solidly faith-based, he decided to reject "religious objector" status because it discriminated against secular moral and political objectors. So he began to prepare himself for six years in jail. He felt called to seek ordination as a minister, and while in Australia he had preached his first sermon in a Sydney church. It was titled "The Only Thing God Cannot Do," the theme being that God was unable to stop loving us. It happened to be on my fiftieth birthday, and news of it was a special gift.

With sons David, Alan, Christopher, and John

In April 1989, with Alan back home, a small group of Methodists, ordained and lay, met in a retreat to launch the Methodist Order of Peacemakers (MOP). After much agonizing and praying, those who felt ready to do so gathered in a circle to make our commitments. On the table in the center of the circle, handwritten and fresh from our struggles, lay the pledge of the new order. It read simply:

> I desire to model my life on the nonviolent way of Jesus;
>
> I therefore renounce violence and pledge myself to engage actively in the work of peacemaking.
>
> I will seek to live by the rule of life of the Methodist Order of Peacemakers.
>
> I accept that this commitment may be costly to me, but make it trusting in Christ who strengthens me.

Alan went first to the table, signing his name, followed by Elizabeth and myself and seventeen others. It was a holy moment, made solemn by the tremendous price that Alan and some of the others were ready to pay for that simple promise. South Africa now had the harshest penalties in the world for conscientious objectors.

While waiting for the axe to fall, Alan pursued ordination. In 1991, he was appointed to a conservative church, whose supervising minister was a gung-ho part-time SADF chaplain with no sympathy for Alan's stand, and the congregation chose to simply ignore his agony. The day he was required to report for military training, he reported to the military base as required, declared his refusal, was arrested, and ordered to appear in court on April 15, 1991. The End Conscription Campaign (ECC) came to his support: "We need men of peace like Alan Storey working among South Africans and building the spirit of the new nation, not wasting time in prison," they declared.

Through all of this, my bizarre relationship with the SADF continued. On April 6, Elizabeth, a number of MOP members, and I were arrested by an army officer for demonstrating outside an SADF recruiting exhibit at the Rand Show. Having confiscated our anti-SADF placards, he marched ahead of us, ramrod stiff, not knowing that he was displaying the top poster to good effect to the watching crowd. We followed happily.

Eight days later, on the evening before Alan's court appearance, we held a prayer service in our "COs' Chapel." It was crowded with friends and activists. Some had plastered the city with posters of Alan with the words: "Rev. Alan Storey—On Trial for Non-violence." I struggled through a short homily, rather choked up with the thought that by the end of the next day our fourth son might vanish for six years into the maw of South Africa's prison system. I wanted people to grasp why he was doing this: "Many say that the stand he is taking is unrealistic," I said, "that because we live in a fallen world realism requires us to use blunt instruments like violence." Alan, however, had a different sense of what was real: his starting point was the cross of Jesus—God's way of confronting evil with radical love. "That is the reality that Alan lives by," I said, "and that is why he cannot support the unrealistic and outworn way of violence." Our son was going further than simply refusing to use violence to defend apartheid: "He is saying that he could not use violence even to destroy it." This service, though painful, was also a deep celebration. I said that Al had made the biggest discovery of all: *being real was to be loved, to love and to refuse not to love*—even though, as the Skin Horse once told the Velveteen Rabbit, "it might hurt sometimes."[8]

The poster plastered all over downtown
Johannesburg before Alan's trial

8. Margaret Williams, *The Velveteen Rabbit; or How Toys Become Real* (Boston: David R. Godine, 1983), 4–6.

And so we went to court. Our son was calm but pale. The courtroom slowly filled, and we waited for argument to begin. In the end, it was a strange anticlimax: the magistrate informed the crowded room that at the request of the attorney general, he was adjourning the trial. Something was afoot. We didn't know it at the time, but we were witnessing the beginning of the end of the conscription system. Alan appeared again in May with a similar outcome. Then in June, at his third appearance, the SADF withdrew all charges against him. He was a free person, which of course he had always been—a truly free person. The entire conscription edifice had begun to unravel. After honoring all the past COs who had been imprisoned, he talked of his own pain: "I think back on the many days I broke down and wept, agonizing over my decision." Then he declared joyfully, "I testify to the truth that God's power is made perfect in weakness. When I am weak then I am strong."

My last duty toward SADF personnel was in May 1997, when I made a public plea to ex-conscripts to apply to the Truth and Reconciliation Commission while there was still opportunity. I attacked the military for "sitting tight, arrogantly hiding behind a dubious code of unit loyalty and oaths of secrecy" and called for ex-conscripts to come forward and expose the human rights violations of the war. The militarized apartheid ideology had conscripted not only their bodies but also their consciences: "By coming to the TRC you can reclaim your consciences and expose the truth." A last word was for those who had refused conscription: "Those who paid the full price, not only of imprisonment, but the sneers of a misguided white public . . . I salute those young men today. They were the conscience of South Africa's white youth and the most obvious victims of conscription."

Over the quarter century that conscription was in place, some 600,000 white youth were called up, to become in the words of Theresa Edlmann, "both victims of a system and perpetrators in its name."[9] The SADF was never defeated in the field, but too many of its members were internally damaged because of what South Africa's dirty wars demanded of them. Moral injury manifests itself still in men in their fifties, sixties, seventies, and eighties. Our culpability has yet to be exorcised.

---

9. Theresa Edlmann, "The Scars of Conscription," *Natal Mercury*, September 3, 2015.

13

Perfect Storm

I HAD SERVED IN the leadership of the South African Council of Churches (SACC) since 1975 and was elected its president soon after Bishop Desmond Tutu was appointed as general secretary in 1978. His task was to give day-to-day leadership to the council and its large staff while implementing the policies laid down by the Executive over which I presided. The SACC was the leading church organization opposing the apartheid state, and while technically Desmond's boss, I saw my role as giving maximum support to him as he became the primary spokesperson of that resistance. We were virtually standing in for the black leaders who had been thrust into prison or exile, and our actions attracted the glare of media attention as well as uncomfortable government and Security Police scrutiny. My time in leadership also brought a personal crisis that was to test my friendships and push my sense of integrity to a breaking point.

It was late on Friday, April 10, 1981, when the blow came. Desmond Tutu and I had spent the day engaging with church leaders from all over the country about the fallout from Desmond's latest overseas trip. He had enraged the regime once again with his calls for economic pressure on South Africa, and they needed to hear firsthand what he had said, and why. Now they were gone, and we were joined by our chief administrator and our lawyer, who brought news that would shake the SACC to its foundations over the next three years. It seemed that while the police were investigating misappropriation of SACC funds by a staffer, they had stumbled on *prima facie* evidence that John Rees, the previous general secretary, had stolen money from the council. At that moment, they were waiting outside wanting us to sign an affidavit laying a complaint against him.

For a while, we sat in stunned silence. It was too much to take in. My first thought was that this was the work of the Security Police and that if there was evidence, it must have been planted. Knowing John as I did, there could be no other possibility.

I had first met John Rees in 1967 when we both served on the MCSA's Commission for the Renewal of the Church. I took an immediate liking to this dynamic young layman's quick wit, sharp mind, and seemingly boundless energy. At the time he was in the very senior echelons of the Johannesburg city administration, having started as a humble clerk. He had been converted through the Methodist youth camp movement and had been an ardent youth leader. A later turning point in John's life was his selection to attend the Fourth Assembly of the World Council of Churches. To this thirty-year-old who until then had experienced little beyond local Methodism, the discovery of the church's worldwide ecumenical family was mind-blowing—and its agenda even more so, as this was the first of the more radically engaged assemblies of the WCC. Its message spoke of listening to "the cry of those who long for peace; of the hungry and exploited who demand bread and justice; of the victims of discrimination who claim human dignity; and of the increasing millions who seek for the meaning of life." Acknowledging that human beings had not yet learned how to live together, the assembly vowed to "seek to overcome racism wherever it appears."[1] John heard a personal call to live a more ecumenically inclusive, socially engaged Christianity. When the position of general secretary of the SACC was advertised, he decided to apply. The position in this modest, underfunded organization had always been held by a senior clergyman, and John was not the only one surprised when he was appointed.

By the time our family moved to Johannesburg in 1972, John had transformed the SACC into a formidable organization. New divisions had been established, staff hired, and much wider contacts established with churches in Europe, the United States, and the rest of Africa. My relationship with John grew at three levels: a personal friendship that would last until the night he died, a stimulating and business-like engagement in the SACC, and an exciting and virtually indispensable collaboration in the development of the Central Methodist Mission.

Elizabeth became involved in the SACC before me. Soon after we arrived in Johannesburg, John's lone secretary used to bring Elizabeth her overflows of work, and this developed ultimately into a position as John's PA. Elizabeth was to serve three general secretaries in that position: John Rees, John Thorne, and Desmond Tutu. For my part, I began attending the Executive in 1975 and was elected a vice president in July 1977. John was

---

1. *Message of the 4th Assembly of the World Council of Churches*, Uppsala, Sweden, 1968.

punctilious in avoiding SACC shop-talk away from those meetings and never attempted to use our friendship to influence any position I might take as an officer of the council. In any case, we thought we would overlap for only a brief period because John had decided to move on.

It was his involvement with CMM that had us working most closely together. I have never met anybody more disciplined and indefatigable. John rose very early and after spending time in prayer and gathering his thoughts for the day, donated at least two hours to his church commitments before arriving punctually at his office at the SACC, and later the SA Institute of Race Relations. His role at CMM expanded over the years: teaching a teenage class each Sunday morning, organizing fundraisers, and being a circuit steward of the mission.[2] His biggest commitment was to manage Cornerstone House, our block of flats for disability pensioners. In the multitude of tasks involved—fundraising, preparation of leases, dealing with difficult tenants, the total renovation of the building inside and out—John was key, and he accounted for any finances to the last cent. We also worked together more widely. He ran the African Old Age Pensioners Scheme and built the first home for the aged in Soweto. He established Meals on Wheels in three black townships and managed Methodist Relief, a massive feeding project. Together, we worked at a national level on the MCSA Renewal Commission and Obedience '81. While never quite acknowledging it to each other, we both told others that we were best friends.

This, then, was the man who I was now asked to believe was a thief. Because I would not, my fate was to be inextricably bound to John's in some of the most painful years of my life.

After seven years heading the SACC, John had resigned. He had grown the council exponentially from a handful of staffers to a complement of over forty persons overseeing thirteen different areas of mission including home and family life, justice and reconciliation, theological education, bursary funds, inter-church aid, and mission and evangelism. He had also seen to it that the ratio of black divisional directors to white had changed significantly: seven of the twelve were now black persons. We replaced him with Rev. John Thorne, a distinguished previous president whose tenure was very brief. John Rees was called back to hold the fort while we searched for another GS, this time the Anglican bishop of Lesotho, Desmond Tutu. I was privileged to nominate Desmond for the job, and he was appointed in 1978.

As senior vice president, I often found myself leading Executive meetings and even national conferences, often on short notice. Thus I chaired

2. Circuit stewards were the lay leaders of a circuit, responsible with the superintendent minister for its proper administration and for the care, housing, etc., of all the ministers in the circuit.

Desmond's very first meeting where it was agreed that John Rees would stay on for a couple of months as the new GS settled in. During an extended overseas trip by Desmond in 1979, I found myself navigating problematic issues involving staff suspected of dishonesty.

Investigations showed that some $35,000 dollars was missing. The evidence pointed to the chief accountant, Mr. Elphas Mbatha. Desmond Tutu laid charges against him, and he later stood trial for fraud. He was discharged for lack of evidence, but it was during the police investigation into this case that they claimed to have uncovered evidence against John Rees.

That fateful meeting in Desmond's office would be the first of many agonizing debates as people wrestled with their loyalties toward John on the one hand and the apparently damning evidence on the other. That first night, a pattern emerged that would typify most of what followed. I was adamant that on the basis of my knowledge of John's character, he was innocent of a crime; whatever the evidence, there would be an explanation. Desmond took a more measured view: while we might have full confidence in John's integrity, we could not rule out the theoretical possibility that a felony had been committed. Moreover, he was concerned about the racial sensitivities involved. We had signed the necessary affidavit to charge a senior black staffer, and now we were being reluctant to do so in the case of Rees, a white man.

The police then joined us in the person of Warrant Officer Allan Mills of the Commercial Branch. Mills was an unprepossessing, mousey man whose complexion matched his grey suit, but he was on a mission. He produced evidence that sums of money had been placed by John into at least twenty-one different personal bank accounts and immediately applied pressure. Rees, now director of the prestigious SA Institute of Race Relations, was about to go overseas on a fundraising trip. "We believe that he is a flight risk," Mills said, "because this case will ruin him." Meanwhile, our administrator had been scrutinizing the evidence and said he needed more to persuade him that the funds in those accounts were SACC monies. Mills became agitated and used the race card. "Mr. Rees is a thief. You acted quickly in Mr. Mbatha's case, and now you are reluctant." We responded that this was completely different: in John's case he had absolute discretion over massive funds to disburse as he saw fit and could not be thought to have behaved improperly "at the first whiff of suspicion." While assuring the police that we would not stand in the way of any bona fide investigation, we declined to sign the affidavit.

When Mills had left, we instructed our attorney to contact John and seek explanations around the disputed funds. I had listened with care and watched the interchange. Mill's smugness galled me. I had a strong feeling that something beyond the normal was happening here—something malevolent—but I couldn't put my finger on it. So I expressed the only certainty I had at that moment: "I continue to have full confidence in John's integrity and would be unable to sign that affidavit. If the Council comes to a point of doing so I will almost certainly have to resign." So, from the beginning of what became known as the "Rees Affair," lines began to be drawn.[3]

Three days later, our attorney reported on his discussions with John. He had ascertained that John oversaw two discretionary funds. The first we knew about: the SACC Asingeni Relief Fund had been set up after the 1976 Soweto uprising. It evolved into support for a wide range of victims of the regime and was always at the complete discretion of the general secretary. Unknown to us was an unrelated secret fund involving some $300,000 over the last four years. John was bound to total confidentiality about its operations and the principal's terms, whom he refused to identify. He said that this fund had made advances to the Asingeni fund on occasions when Asingeni was in deficit, and the checks the police had produced of apparently SACC funds going into John's personal accounts were "repayments from Asingeni." Our attorney confirmed to us that such a fund existed and was satisfied from John's disclosures and the "somewhat scanty documentary evidence" that John had not committed a felony, even though placing the monies into his private accounts "may not have been wise."

Feeling the need for wider counsel, we decided to invite all local SACC Executive members to meet at CMM the next day. At that meeting of thirteen highly trusted people, I outlined the "very grave situation" and asked for their help. Some wanted me to recuse myself because of my pastoral relationship with John, and others felt I should remain in the chair, but I felt it best to leave the meeting, which decided that another senior attorney should look into the matters and report back.

I had meanwhile turned to Philip Russell—at that time Anglican bishop of Natal and an honorary vice president of SACC—for counsel. Philip was one of the wisest people I knew, and his carefully reasoned reply confirmed me in my stand. Both the donors and the SACC Executive had entrusted John with a very large fund and placed it completely in his discretion. Given the times we were living in, it was no surprise that both donors and recipients might well demand absolute confidentiality. John had to make subjective decisions alone about large disbursements, and having put him in that position, it was up to us either to remove him if we were not prepared for the risks involved, or to trust him. "When one moves in the area of trust, one is guided not simply by 'hunches,' but by experience,"

---

3. Minutes of Presidium meeting, Office of the General Secretary, April 10, 1981.

Philip wrote and went on to state "categorically" that nothing John had ever done during his time at SACC had given him any reason not to trust him completely. He did raise one flag, putting into words something all of us who knew John were aware of: "I refer to his love of the dramatic. I do not regard this in any sense whatsoever as a character blemish, but it could have resulted in his overreacting to a situation, over-moving in the direction of super-confidentiality."

Then John broke his silence. In a strong letter to us, he detailed his extensive service to the organization and explained the various discretionary funds he was authorized to oversee while general secretary, including the Asingeni fund in which 60 percent of the disbursement was confidential based on the SACC's guidelines. He told us about the separate super-confidential fund, known as ACTIPAX, that was unrelated to the SACC. In order to ensure confidentiality, he told us he created new accounts to handle transactions for both these funds, and in some cases, transactions passed through his own personal banking account. John then listed some of the ugly ways in which the Security Branch had sought to discredit him and lamented the prospect of us being manipulated by the government to punish him.

Despite this compelling letter, not everyone on the SACC Executive was convinced, and I wondered whether they still trusted my judgment. Yet, by a strange irony, on the very day that John wrote his letter, Desmond Tutu asked that I permit my name to go forward to the National Conference for election as president of the SACC.[4] Desmond wrote, "If you believe that the Holy Spirit has a hand in things such as elections then you should not want to frustrate him so early." Amidst the high drama, life had to go on.

The evening before the vote at the May national conference, I had supper with Desmond and thanked him for the painful but rich privilege of working with him. "It's been quite a ride," I said, "but tomorrow it ends." I was quite sure I wouldn't be elected; not only was I one of only two white candidates out of six nominees in an overwhelmingly black conference, but the shadow of the Rees issue hung over us all. Elizabeth was already picking up rumblings in the corridors of Khotso House about my protecting John "because he was white." I was proved wrong, however: to my utter surprise, I was elected with three times the votes of the runner-up. Desmond wrote again, thanking me for my "wonderful, costly, and prayerful support." It *had* been all of those things. I was utterly committed to ensuring that Desmond should never be without my support both in prayer and action. I believed in him, believed that God had called him to this task, and regarded my role as being

---

4. Until this date, I had held the position of senior vice president but had filled the president's role for many months because the elected president was a habitual absentee and had been prevailed upon to resign.

his loyal shield. We had developed a friendship based on mutual respect and appreciation of one another's gifts. I admired his Christ-centered spirituality, natural warmth, prophetic insight, and sheer guts; he liked my preaching, my "way with words," as he put it, my clarity of thought, and the way I guided difficult meetings. He would come back to his office and tell Elizabeth how much he had felt supported by his president. Yet neither of us was afraid to challenge the other. That was the way it should be. We made a good team, but we were about to be painfully tested. As the weeks rolled on, Warrant Officer Mills seemed to relish dropping regular tidbits of added information by way of our administrator, who said he was now satisfied that "SACC funds were being held in accounts beyond the council's control." While some of my colleagues believed that nothing had changed in principle, I had the growing impression that Desmond was having doubts.

At a full Executive in April, I tried to sum up the situation. We had invited the police's attention by charging Elphas Mbatha. They had a *prima facie* case against John, evidence which, in the absence of a reasonable explanation, indicated that a crime had been committed. If there was political pressure behind Mills, they would probably go ahead whether or not we laid a complaint; therefore, our decision came down to what we believed about John. He had vowed to go to jail rather than reveal details, so we had to rely primarily on our experience of him and the testimony of our attorney. It was all about John's character and the fact that we had trusted him with the SACC for seven years, as well as giving him total discretion over large sums of money. We also had assurances regarding the existence of ACTIPAX. "If all these together amount to a 'reasonable explanation,'" I said, "then we should refuse to lay a complaint."[5] If not . . . I didn't want to contemplate that.

The Executive decided not to lay a complaint.

In October, Elphas Mbatha was found not guilty for lack of evidence. The case was widely reported for two other reasons: First Warrant Officer Mills used his time in the witness box to allege that John Rees had placed SACC funds in fifty-one different bank accounts and that the SACC had refused to lay a complaint; and then the magistrate had lambasted Desmond Tutu, accusing him of making Mbatha a scapegoat for SACC's "chaotic" finances. It was time to go public.

Desmond Tutu and I held a press conference, and I covered every step we had taken since April when Mills first approached us, saying that the National Executive had consistently concluded that Mr. Rees had acted with complete integrity. Desmond followed up with a fiery response to the

---

5. Notes on SACC Executive meeting, Khotso House, April 22, 1981.

magistrate: "I will not be deterred by all the vilifications and denigrations and personal attacks ranging from prime ministers to magistrates," he vowed, and then outlined the steps taken to correct the SACC's financial problems. I also issued a statement defending Desmond and criticizing the magistrate for "emotive rather than judicial expressions of opinion."[6]

The hue and cry escalated, however, with newspapers joining less friendly media in calling for full disclosure. *The Cape Times* recommended a "full and public inquiry with all due speed."[7] *The Sunday Times* front page yelled: "Churches in New Cash Row."

Facts unknown to me were also emerging. One of my SACC colleagues had received $9,500 to start a shop in Soweto, and Desmond himself $16,000 toward his Soweto house. It didn't seem to matter that my colleague had suffered in solitary confinement for fifty-six days and certainly qualified under the Asingeni rubrics, and that John had identified a completely separate anonymous donor for Desmond's gift. Events were outpacing us. When the full Executive met in October, I reported on the confluence of different problems, each of which was bad enough, but together had led us to a point of crisis. The matter was now one of public interest, and we needed to satisfy the public about our bona fides. The upshot was that the Executive decided it had no option but to set up an "urgent commission of inquiry" headed by a senior advocate to look into our financial affairs from 1975 onward.

But it was all too late. We had exposed ourselves, and the regime moved swiftly to outflank us. Early in November, Prime Minister P. W. Botha announced a judicial commission of inquiry into the SACC headed by Justice C. F. Eloff. It had wide terms of reference, and we soon received a letter demanding that we hand over an endless list of documents.[8] Every nook and cranny in the SACC and of our lives would be under scrutiny for years ahead. Our intention to set up a church-driven commission stumbled on for months but became irrelevant. All attention would now be on the tribunal under Justice Eloff and on the almost inevitable trial of John Rees.

In spite of growing tensions, I still felt able to straddle the demands of my loyalties to Desmond and the SACC and to my friend John. In November, I chaired a particularly intricate meeting with church leaders to decide how to respond to the Eloff Commission, and Desmond Tutu wrote me a gracious letter: "Thank you for who you are," he said, "and for chairing a tricky

---

6. "SACC President Hits at Remark from Bench," *Star*, October 10, 1981.

7. "Editorial," *Cape Times*, October 15, 1981; "Editorial," *Rand Daily Mail*, October 28, 1981.

8. Letter from Mr. M. L. Marais, Secretary to the Commission of Inquiry into the SACC, December 3, 1981.

session so competently." He felt that we had emerged from that encounter much closer to one another than before the meeting.

During the June national conference, I did not dodge our crisis in my presidential address. "The years of crying God's words of warning and calling for God's compassion and justice could be coming to a climax for us. The long shadow of state action stretches across this council and therefore over the church." There would be those hoping that this would be an excuse to strike at the heart of Christian opposition to injustice and to silence our voice. But we would not be silenced. Apartheid was "the most radical dismemberment of any nation since the partition of India." The sons of black and white South Africans were being poured into the bottomless pit of war, and churchmen were being beaten in churchyards, their arms broken by police whips.

Yet, in all of this, there was good news: Jesus had said, *"When all this begins to happen, stand upright and hold your heads high, because your liberation is near"* (Luke 21:18). The stones of South Africa's temples were already tottering, and the false god of apartheid was failing. Yes, the Council was not perfect and the powers were trying to discredit us, but that did not matter in any ultimate sense. I reminded them that just as the media were trumpeting our troubles and our "crisis," 123 ministers of the Dutch Reformed Church had come out saying they couldn't worship at the temple of apartheid any longer. "When you see these things happening, know that the heart of the battle is already won." Whatever happened to us, we needed to be confident of that. Our task was to live in "God's future" now: in that future compassion and caring would rule—so we should live that way now. While the world lived by the love of power—we should live by the power of love now, and by truth, and by justice, and by nonviolence. This was the Christian hope, not some sentimental optimism, but "the insight which enables us even in the darkest hour to know that Christ is Lord."[9]

I would need a strong dose of my own medicine in the days following.

In a week of what the media called "high drama," Desmond Tutu announced that he was returning the money he had received from John Rees. Then, while I was deep into chairing the national conference, someone came in and whispered to me that the police had arrested John. They timed it as dramatically as possible to coincide with our conference, marching into the boardroom of a company where John was accepting a donation for SAIRR and taking him away. I delegated the chair and raced into Johannesburg. We reached the magistrates' court just in time to join John's deathly pale wife,

---

9. Peter Storey, "Stand Upright—Your Liberation Is Near!," Presidential Address SACC National Conference, June 1982.

Dulcie, in one of the grimy courtrooms as John was brought in to be charged with fraud, and failing that, theft. He was released on bail, and we spoke briefly before I returned to the conference, where I convened an emergency Executive during a recess. I was sick in my stomach as I reported the morning's events. Then I offered my resignation, but the Executive wouldn't hear of it and instructed me to continue in leadership. The conference later passed a resolution assuring John of their "love, concern, and prayers."

That same day, I was told that as a potential prosecution witness, I was forbidden any contact with John. That was deeply painful: he was not only my friend, but I was his pastor. The ban remained in place until the end of his trial. The people of CMM were also stunned and confused, but after being apprised of the story in its entirety, the Leaders' Meeting took a brave vote: John was told that they continued to believe in him and whatever other positions he might lose through all this, his role at CMM would continue as before.

Tensions rose in the months leading up to his trial. An example was a meeting where we struggled for hours over the complex question of privilege and of whether the SACC had an obligation to help John finance his defense. Some felt the SACC did not have an obligation—Desmond reminding the meeting that no such help had been given to Mbatha. But others differed. SACC had always helped accused people get a fair trial. Desmond drew a line: if we decided to finance John's defense, he said, he "would need to reconsider his position." Trying to prevent a complete fracture, I informed the meeting that Methodists were rallying around John and raising the necessary funds; he would not need SACC help. At the same meeting, we were warned that the Eloff Commission had been hard at work turning over every stone in our affairs and was ready for hearings.

It was a perfect storm.

14

Bearing Witness

WE COULD EITHER LET the Eloff hearings intimidate us or we could use them as a platform to tell the world what the church of God was really about. We believed that at the heart of the encounter lay the question of our theological identity: these turbulent priests who dared to speak truth to power and to defy the state—who were they really representing?

It was decided that Desmond and I would offer the SACC's main evidence. He would lead off, establishing the SACC's mandate from Scripture, the church, and from God. Then other witnesses would deal with nitty-gritty questions of detail, and I would "book-end" the SACC's case with a closing statement.

Desmond's evidence was a tour de force. Naming it "The Divine Intention," he began:

> My purpose is to demonstrate from the Scriptures and from hallowed Christian tradition and teaching that what we are as the South African Council of Churches, what we say and do, that all of these are determined not by politics or any other ideology. We are what we are in obedience to God . . . we owe ultimate loyalty not to any human authority however prestigious or powerful, but to God and to his Son our Lord Jesus Christ alone, from whom we obtain our mandate. We must obey the divine imperative . . . whatever the cost.
>
> I want to underline that it is not the finances or any other activity of the SACC that are being investigated. It is our Christian faith, it is the Christian churches who are members of the SACC on trial. . . . We are on trial for being Christian. . . . It may be that we are being told that it is an offence to be a Christian in South Africa. That is what you are asked to determine. And that is a theological task through and through.

Then, much to the obvious bemusement of Judge Eloff and his tribunal and to the enthrallment of the public gallery, Desmond waded into a sweeping journey through the Scriptures from Genesis to Revelation, spanning the doctrines of creation and the fall, of incarnation and salvation:

> I will show that the central work of Jesus was to effect reconciliation between God and us and also between men and men. Consequently... I will demonstrate that apartheid... is evil, totally evil and without remainder, that it is un-Christian and un-Biblical... I will show that the SACC and its member churches are not some tuppeny-halfpenny fly-by-night organisation. We belong to the church of God... universally spread through the whole inhabited universe.... It is the body of Jesus Christ... and it is a supernatural, a divine fellowship brought into being by God himself through his Holy Spirit.

Then an early ultimatum:

> With due respect I want to submit that no secular authority nor its appointed Commissions has any competence whatsoever to determine how a church is church nor what is the nature of the Gospel of Jesus Christ. With respect we do not recognise the right of this Commission to enquire into our theological existence and therefore into any aspect of our life as a Council. Only our member churches can call us to task. If we have contravened the laws of the country then you don't need a Commission to determine that. There is an array of draconian laws at the disposal of the government.

This bishop of the church was not going to be intimidated:

> I want the government to know I do not fear them. They are trying to defend the utterly indefensible. Apartheid is as evil as Nazism and Communism and the government will fail completely for it is ranging itself on the side of evil, injustice and oppression. The government are not God. They are just ordinary human beings who very soon like other tyrants before them will bite the dust. When they are taking on the SACC they must know that they are taking on the church of God... Christ has assured us that his church is founded upon a rock and not even the gates of Hell can prevail against it.

Some five hours later, he completed his statement. It stands as one of the great documents of Christian witness.[1]

---

1. Evidence-in-Chief of Bishop Desmond Tutu, General Secretary of the SACC,

Then the examination began, led by Advocate Klaus von Lieres und Wilkau, whose Prussian name suited his demeanor. He set out to show that the SACC, far from being a primarily religious organization, was a tool of the ANC and its communist allies, busy fomenting revolution. He grilled Desmond for some twenty hours, but there was something pathetic and clumsy about the bullying von Lieres trying every which way to shake a theologian of Tutu's stature. The bishop remained firm.

In the next weeks, others came forward either to vilify or defend us. My old nemesis, secret police General Johan Coetzee, was one of them, alleging that we were giving money to the terrorists and demanding that the SACC's overseas funding be cut off. The right-wing Christian League of South Africa, a body secretly paid by the government to smear the SACC and WCC, also weighed in against us. On the other side, we smiled as the head of our Justice and Reconciliation Division, when attacked for being the "brains" behind our alleged left-wing machinations, insisted on giving long, dry, theological, and biblical responses to von Lieres, clearly frustrating our prosecutor.

Then it was my turn. Early on March 9, 1983, I drove to Pretoria, praying that the knots in my stomach would ease. It was a Wednesday, and I had spent the weekend dictating my eighty-four-page statement. There was no time for revision on the Monday or Tuesday because, ironically, I was leading a retreat for Methodist military chaplains wrestling with how to represent the gospel in the deeply compromised context of the SADF.

The commission met in a modest hall in the optimistically named Veritas building just off Church Square. Supreme Court Justice Eloff and the other four commissioners—all white males—were seated at the far end. There was a small press and public gallery, and to the left were the tables for counsel. In the middle of the room was a single chair with a small table. This was where I was to spend a total of twenty-six hours, and it suddenly felt a very lonely place. I muttered to myself Jesus' words about not worrying what to say when brought before "rulers and authorities" (Luke 12:11–12) and settled in for the ordeal.

The judge welcomed me courteously and asked if I had an opening statement. I answered, "Yes, quite a lengthy one," and he bade me begin. I identified myself first and foremost as a minister of the gospel of Jesus Christ. Whatever my status, nothing was more binding on me than my vows of ordination. All other loyalties, whether to nation, family, people, or party, were subservient to this. None could live up to the high calling

---

presented to the Eloff Commission of Inquiry on September 1, 1982, published as Desmond Tutu, *The Divine Intention* (Braamfontein: SACC, 1982).

of Christ, but the "supreme improbability" of the Good News was that when we failed, God met us with his grace and forgiveness. As the SACC, we were not perfect, but without disrespecting the commission, we were answerable to an authority way beyond them and would not accept having our motives and intentions decided by them. Any anger in my responses to the "hard and cruel things said about us" would not be because of personal grievance but because "truth had been violated, the church misrepresented, and our Lord grieved."[2]

I said that it had been strange listening to the evidence thus far. Witnesses had painted a picture of the SACC as serving dark intentions and designed to bring chaos in our land. "The SACC I know is a different one: it is an attempt against the heavy odds of prejudice, the captivity of the past, and the oppression of the present, to be a light on a hill and a transforming leaven in a land of division, hopelessness, and fear." Our detractors seemed to have read history with one eye closed. We were accused of being allies or willing dupes of international communism and its surrogates, but I had waited in vain "to hear one word about the other makers of history in our time: the inventors of apartheid. To examine our role without taking cognizance of that context was like trying to understand Abraham Lincoln without mentioning slavery or Dietrich Bonhoeffer without mentioning Nazism." Our role in SA arose out of two great realities: the first being our understanding of Scripture, a point made powerfully by Bishop Tutu, and the second being the great corporate sin of apartheid. Quoting my dad twenty-four years earlier, I said, "Apartheid is a sin against the Father who wills that all should be his sons and daughters; and against the Son who died to reconcile all people to God and to each other; and against the Holy Spirit who makes all of us one in the bonds of peace."[3] Further, if you once accepted that apartheid could be right anywhere, then you were saying that Christ's act of reconciliation on the cross had failed everywhere.

My task was to show that our concern with socio-political, economic, educational, and human rights issues was as much part of the evangelical gospel as winning disciples, and I used John Wesley and the Wesleyan movement as my model. I reminded the commission that the eighteenth-century evangelical revival was the most widespread since biblical days, yet Wesley insisted that it was never only about individual conversion. I listed the practical programs he set in place to educate and uplift the poor

---

2. Evidence-in-Chief of Rev. Peter John Storey, President of the SACC, presented to the Eloff Commission of Inquiry on March 9, 10, and 11, 1983, published as Peter Storey, *Here We Stand* (Johannesburg: SACC, 1983).

3. Clifford K. Storey, President's Address to the Annual Conference of the Methodist Church of Southern Africa, East London, October 1957.

and ridiculed the charge that the SACC's support for the new black trade-union movement was subversive. "It was in fact the Evangelical Revival that gave birth to Trade Unionism." The breeding ground for the SACC's concern for human rights, justice, and reconciliation was not Marxist. "These very same concerns were the hallmarks of powerfully spiritual men who lived a hundred years before Marx was heard of." I said that I resented "hearing my Christian heritage being cheapened by naive inferences reminiscent of McCarthyism."

Referring to those we chose to aid, our decision to help political prisoners and support their families was because they were the most despised ones of South Africa—the equivalent of the "least of Jesus' brothers and sisters" in the Gospels (Matt 25:31-46). We were under Jesus' instruction to go to them.

To the accusation that we were in cahoots with the ANC, I countered that an alliance with any political organization would cause us to surrender our "prophetic distance," a vital element of our integrity. Further, the strength of the SACC's witness was the very fact that it neither held nor sought temporal power. "The only man to be trusted is the one who seeks nothing for himself—so also in organizations." I quoted my own words to the prime minister: "We have no dreams of power, we pose no political threat. In secular terms this Council is quite powerless. You can close us down tomorrow. Can you not believe then that the cry we raise comes not from some political strategy but from the heart... that [we]... are in touch with more grassroots people than your racially excusive party can ever be? Why would we bother if it were not for the fact that people are suffering?"

To the accusation of being fellow-travelers with the communists, I said: "If I walked out yesterday and found that it was snowing, and if the person walking next to me was a communist and said, 'It's snowing,' I don't believe I would have a moral obligation to say it was *not*." Some political formations might well take stances similar to those of the SACC, but there was a radical divergence around the issue of violence. While we could understand those whose frustration led them to abandon peaceful methods of achieving their ends, I said that "I could not belong to a body advocating violence as a means of change, and I am confident that neither would any of our member churches." Nor could we countenance acts of terrorism, whether by liberation movements or the SADF.

Speaking of Desmond Tutu's role as both servant of the churches and prophet in their midst, I defended his right to go out ahead of us. I quoted our member churches' declaration after a controversial speech: "We will not allow any single member of the Body of Christ to be isolated for attack where we are sure that his primary commitment reflects—as does Bishop

Tutu's—those values for which each of our member churches firmly stand." Then I closed by reminding the commission that something similar to this hearing had happened a very long time ago:

> In the Book of Acts, there is the record of the early Apostles on trial before the Sanhedrin. The reason why the work of the Church didn't come to an end that day was because of two actions: the first was the fearless witness of Peter the Apostle, standing for the truth even when threatened, and obeying God rather than men. The second actor was one of his hearers who was open to the truth, the Pharisee Gamaliel, who though he didn't have any reason to like the Christians, discerned the ring of truth in their words. He said "Keep clear of these men . . . for if this idea of theirs is of human origin it will collapse, but if it is from God, you will never be able to put them down, and you risk finding yourselves at war with God." The result of that encounter long ago, was there for all to see.

The presentation took four hours, and I was questioned for two days after that, generating 250-odd pages of question and answer.[4] I remember the judge showing a special interest in the social impact of the Wesleyan revival. He wanted a book about Wesley to read over the weekend. By one of those inexplicable coincidences, I was broadcasting from CMM that weekend, and on the Monday he told me he had listened. He grilled me himself on my definitions of apartheid and of what I meant by corporate sin—and about violence. He struggled to accept my argument that a young black man living under the humiliating constraints of apartheid might come to believe that "unless he did something, he would die with his dompas still in his hand . . . still condemned and branded by the accident of a black skin."[5] I had said that any reasonable person would understand such a young man, saying, "Let me rather die with a gun in my hand than come to old age that way," but Eloff couldn't get his head around that idea and rejected it.

Elizabeth was able to attend some of my testimony and felt that "it was like an exam taken on all your learning, studying, reading, and living, your whole life." At some point she found herself descending in the elevator alone with a Security Policeman who had attended most of the hearings. Out of the blue he made some complimentary remarks to her about my "integrity." Taken aback, she tried to engage him further, but he said nothing more and stepped out very quickly when they reached the ground floor.

---

4. *Record of the Commission of Inquiry into the SACC*, vols. 41–45 (Pretoria: Lubbe Recordings, 1983).

5. *Dompas* (literally "stupid passbook").

For Prime Minister Botha, the Eloff affair brought forth a mouse. I had come to sense that the judge was at heart a decent, fairly non-ideological person, and his 450-page report reinforced that impression. Of course, there was predictable criticism of the SACC's engagement in social, political, and economic matters and especially the council's financial affairs but otherwise the commission gave Botha very little. It suggested framing legislation that could ensure tighter controls on the finances of bodies like the SACC but significantly failed to recommend declaring the SACC an "affected organization,"[6] saying that such an action would have "been seen as restricting religious freedom." It said that even though the money spent on helping the needy and deserving "can only be described as meagre compared to that used for political purposes, innocent people would suffer if the organisation were to be rendered largely ineffective."

There is no doubt that the government was both angry and disappointed, but Desmond Tutu was not going to let the commission off without a scolding. He could find only one point of agreement with them—that they had little understanding of theology, so how could a fair judgment be expected? "It really was like asking (speaking respectfully) a group of blind men to judge the Chelsea Flower Show."[7]

For me the most significant moment of the Eloff Commission hearings was in mid-March when there was a stir and a shuffling in the public gallery and a group of churchmen from all over the world entered the hall and demanded to speak on behalf of the council. They came from Germany, Britain, Scandinavia, and the United States, representing great bodies like the World Lutheran Federation, the EKD (Evangelical Churches of Germany), the Anglican communion, and the National Council of Churches in the USA. They spoke with force and conviction, leaving no one in doubt that an attack on the SACC was an attack on the world church. I remember my eyes filling in wonder at being part of this amazing entity—body—movement—and thinking at that moment of those in power in South Africa: "You guys can't win; you're up against the church of God."

I also breathed a prayer of thanksgiving that we had been able to get through the Eloff hearings united and together.

Meanwhile, thirty miles away in Johannesburg in the Supreme Court, right opposite CMM, another drama was moving inexorably toward its climax. There John Rees cut a lonely figure as the state piled up the evidence

---

6. Such a declaration would have crippled the SACC by preventing it from receiving any monies from outside of South Africa. At the time 96 percent of the council's $4,428,000 budget was sourced internationally.

7. Shirley Du Boulay, *Tutu: Voice of the Voiceless* (London: Hodder & Stoughton, 1988), 178.

against him. The judge was Richard Goldstone, who would go on to stellar heights as one of post-apartheid South Africa's first Constitutional Court justices—and then the International Court of Justice in the Hague. He was one of those jurists who had managed to remain relatively untainted in a distorted judicial system, and I had no doubts about his fairness. Bishop Tutu's evidence in the trial became controversial: first, he declined to comment on the state of the administration when taking over from John, but when pushed indicated that he was "very unhappy" from the start. There were sharp differences with John's advocate over whether he had known and consented to the withdrawals John had made following Desmond's arrival. This was, as I recall, a major dissonance between the two narratives.

John's attorney led him through what was almost a lone defense. Elizabeth was one of the witnesses called to testify to his lifestyle. "He was so punctilious that if he sent a personal letter from the SACC office, he wanted to know right away what the postage cost was so as to reimburse it." She spoke of their modest home, always in mint condition but offering no signs of extravagance.[8] It also emerged that some of the "fifty-one bank accounts" that Mills had made so much of had never contained more than a few rands. But in the face of John's silence, there could only be one outcome. His main defense was no different than what our attorney had come back with almost exactly two years previously. Now, as then, his only hope of proving it was to offer up names of people he had helped who could verify his story, something he had vowed never to do, even at the price of going to prison.

Like so many others, the judge seemed to be looking for a hidden key to the puzzle. A *New York Times* journalist wrote that Goldstone "leaned over backwards to avoid any suggestion that he was joining the Government's vendetta against the Council."[9] On the face of things, Goldstone appeared to have no option but to convict him. He found John guilty of twenty-nine of the forty-three counts of fraud and alternately theft involving $220,000 of SACC money. All that remained was for pleas in mitigation of sentence and John's likely imprisonment.

Late that night I ignored my ban and visited a very broken man. What passed between us remains in the sacred space of pastoral confidentiality, but it was a conversation of searing honesty, and I came away affirmed in the one certainty that had held me throughout the long saga: John may have made stupid mistakes, but he had not enriched himself by one penny. I didn't hesitate to join others in witnessing to John's virtues

---

8. Anton Harber, "Rees led a modest life, fraud trial told," *Rand Daily Mail*, April 21, 1983.

9. Joseph Lelyveld, "Fraud Case Splits South Africa Church Group," *New York Times*, June 21, 1983.

and long list of accomplishments on behalf of the poor and marginalized. Elizabeth had created a scrapbook with a similar record and messages from around the world that we handed in, too. The judge quizzed me at length about what he called the "riddle" of John's character. I spoke about John's love for the dramatic and of the psychological danger that lurked for people who could daily dispense large sums to others—that with the good they were doing sometimes came a sense of omnipotence. But I also underlined the reality of the risks involved in helping political fugitives and the effect that had on him.

Leaving the court with Elizabeth after we testified in the Rees trial

In the end, John was sentenced to ten years imprisonment, suspended conditionally for five years, and fined $22,000. I rejoiced that he would at least go free but being familiar with his deep pride in his name and integrity, I knew he had suffered a blow from which he would never recover.

It remained for me now to consider my position with the SACC. Unlike some others of John's friends, I had no difficulty in understanding Desmond Tutu's anger at John, and therefore to some degree at me. Here he was—the first black SACC general secretary—just three years into his tenure and under sustained attack from the regime, plunged into a crisis threatening the very life of the council, all because of the actions of one man. Whether John acted rightly or not, his case doubtless emboldened Botha to trigger the Eloff Commission, which in turn virtually immobilized the council for two years. If I were in Desmond's shoes, I would have found it impossible to hide my frustration, but he held it in through the multitude of meetings around this issue and, whatever he felt, he went along with our decisions not to lay a complaint. After the trial, however, his anger exploded in ways that were unhelpful.

Though desperately torn at times, until Goldstone's verdict I felt that I had honorably managed to balance my loyalties to both my general secretary and to a key member of my congregation, and to each as friends. The Friday night after John was sentenced, the SACC Executive met to discuss the implications of the trial. On the Sunday I woke to a story in the *Sunday Express* reporting on the meeting, quoting Desmond saying that I "had accepted the guilt and betrayal of trust" by John, and speculating about my probable resignation.[10] Desmond and I had a pact that we would always offer the media a united front, and a journalist had managed to fracture it. I was furious. I called him, berating him for speaking about me. Desmond didn't hold back either, letting some of his frustrations fly, too. It was short, sharp, and painful—and the only time we ever had heated words. Within hours I apologized. However this disastrous situation affected us, we should not be divided. We had prayed together, marched together, gone to jail together, and looked death in the face together. Surely—whatever happened—our friendship should not be allowed to founder under the weight of this crisis. He replied with a gracious apology himself.

However, the national conference was fast approaching, and the next Executive would be discussing whether or not to sue John for the money he was supposed to have stolen. I couldn't be part of that. The time had come to end the agony, and in May I resigned.

"The presidency of the council is a symbol of unity in the SACC, which is itself committed to the unity of the church," I said. "By God's grace we have been enabled to demonstrate that unity throughout the Eloff Commission and the Rees trial." Both had now come to an end, and "I have been given to understand that the position I have taken could prejudice that unity and thus be a disservice to the council. To imperil that unity would be out of character with the love and respect I have for the SACC."

I reminded my colleagues that circumstances had dictated that I had chaired the Executive for five of the nine years I had served with them, and we had become a non-racial ecumenical team "tested by fire and made stronger by adversity." I fully understood the hurts that had come recently to each member of the team and the anger that some felt. I added that I continued to hold Bishop Tutu in the highest esteem together with all those with whom I had walked.

---

10. Wilmar Utting, "Churchmen meet to decide on action over Rees," *Sunday Express*, May 22, 1983.

"I pray for you today," I said, "in the hope that now that the law has been the law, the church will be the church."

It was a deeply sad moment for me, made even sadder by Elizabeth's resignation as Desmond's PA later that day. She loved Desmond deeply but had been asked to type one too many personally painful documents and felt she had to end their five-year working relationship. From one of the most significant secretarial jobs in the country, she became unemployed looking for temporary work.

John took a position as head of a home for mentally challenged children and poured his prodigious energy into ensuring their well-being. To visit him there was a beautiful thing. Children with these needs have few boundaries, and I loved seeing them mob and lovingly maul him every time he emerged from his office. This warm yet private friend who had left the courtroom not long ago with his reputation in tatters seemed to be finding some healing in their embrace.

My strains with Desmond took very little time to heal. As a pastor, I think he understood how standing by one of my parishioners could be a priority. However, according to Shirley du Boulay, what he *did* question was my refusal to admit John's guilt. She wrote, "His final wistful comment on the matter was 'I only wish I had a friend like that.'"[11] He sent me a letter following the June national conference telling me of the standing ovation they gave me *in absentia* and of their invitation to become a life vice president. I asked for time but later accepted the honor.

Meanwhile, after some unusual bleeding, John was diagnosed with the most virulent strain of leukemia, and I was privileged to walk with him through the months of suffering and the work of dying. He lived just long enough to see the birth of a new democratic South Africa. A unique mark of respect had come from the judge who had sentenced him: he asked John to chair the Goldstone Commission's Committee on Children and Violence—a monumental report which he just managed to complete.

More than one thousand people of all races packed the CMM sanctuary for John's memorial service. Offering the eulogy, I said:

> Many opponents of apartheid suffered, but John's crucifixion was of a uniquely excruciating kind. It was not his vision, nor his convictions that were put on trial, but that place within himself that he prized most dearly, his integrity. Given the evidence before him, the judge had little option, but the real truth, which will one day be revealed, lay in what wasn't before that court.

---

11. Du Boulay, *Tutu*, 180.

I pray that one day, those who John saved and hid and fed and enabled to escape the Security Police with the money he is supposed to have stolen, will find the courage to stand up and testify. But even if they never do, from the times we talked together, prayed, and wept together, I testify today that John's conscience was clear. His family knows that and so do many others.

But who was this man?

I was reading the beatitudes of Jesus this morning. They tell of the kind of people who Jesus needs to build the kingdom of God. Those beatitudes are appropriate for John: he knew his need for God, he knew sorrow, he was of a gentle spirit, he hungered and thirsted to see right prevail in this land, he showed mercy and he was pure in heart. He was a peacemaker and he suffered every kind of calumny for the Lord's sake.

And he was my friend.

15

National Leadership

BEING ELECTED PRESIDING BISHOP is the highest honor the MCSA can bestow on any of its ministers—and the toughest job. In my day, the expectations were almost absurd. Known then by its more humble Wesleyan title, the "President of the Conference" carried all the responsibilities of leading the largest multi-racial denomination in South Africa while still serving a local church and running its district. The saving grace was that the term of office in those days was just one year before handing over to a successor.[1]

Time-honored usage required that voting for the top position be without nomination. This was designed to discourage individuals from politicking as "candidates." As a young minister back in 1969, I had enthusiastically lobbied for another to be elected to this position, but the experience had left me uncomfortable, and I decided "never again." So when delegations came to me in 1982 and 1983 asking me to "stand" for the office, I shooed them out: "Nobody 'stands' when an election is without nomination," I said, and I truly meant it. Nevertheless, I found myself runner-up in the voting in 1982 and was voted president-elect a year later. I would take office in October 1984, presiding over the ten-day Annual Conference in Pretoria before leading the denomination until October 1985.

The conference made a big moment out of such elections. Elizabeth joined me as I responded later to the vote, bringing to mind the people and influences that had shaped my life. I was somewhat overwhelmed, recalling that my dad had been similarly honored twenty-eight years before, something unique in MCSA history. What I didn't say was that the vote offered some healing after my anguished decision to resign the SACC presidency six months earlier. I knew I had done right to stand by John Rees, but it had left

---

1. The position of presiding bishop of the MCSA is now a full-time appointment, carrying no other responsibilities. The incumbent is elected for a five-year term, renewable once.

me in a very empty place, feeling bereft and alienated from the ecumenical community that Desmond Tutu and I had led. Now, here was my "mother"—the Methodist Church—seemingly affirming the path I had walked and inviting me back into national leadership.

The election, while presaged by the close vote in 1982, was still a punch to the solar plexus. Was I ready for this? I was forty-four; only one other had been younger than me when elected. Given that I was not wildly popular among white colleagues and was elected on the first ballot, it had obviously happened with overwhelming black support. While I was grateful for that, South Africa was hurtling toward the abyss, and my year of office—1985—would be the most fraught and violent yet. Only a brash fool would not have quaked at the prospect.

Then came an unexpected challenge. I was asked to co-lead an ecumenical delegation to the United States and Europe in the spring of 1984. Our tasks were to alert the world to the way forced removals were destroying black community life and to seek additional pressure on the regime. My co-leader was Roman Catholic Archbishop George Daniel, and our delegation was a mix of seven clergy with on-the-ground experience in the barren resettlement areas where victims of the policy were dumped. We were armed with a powerful exposé of the government's "Relocation" policy, and the group appointed me as spokesperson.[2] The first engagement was at the United Nations in New York addressing the ambassadors of the Africa Bloc. We then went on to meet with UN Secretary-General Dr. Pérez de Cuéllar. He listened intently to the case as I put it. Already three-and-a-half-million black people had been robbed of their citizenship, uprooted—some more than once—and sent to so-called bantustans. The regime was planning the same fate for at least two million more black people, and the only thing that could stop them was massive international pressure led by the UN. Pérez de Cuéllar needed no convincing; he assured us of maximum support, and we went from his office to a press conference.

---

2. South African Council of Churches, *Relocations: The Churches' Report on Forced Removals* (London: Catholic Institute for International Relations, 1984).

Addressing UN Secretary-General Perez de Cuellar (far left) while leading anti-forced removals delegation to the US and Europe; Co-Leader Archbishop George Daniel is on my right hand

In New York, we also met with President Reagan's Under Secretary of State for Africa, Dr. Chester Crocker. He was pleasant enough but clearly committed to Reagan's policy of "constructive engagement," which he felt would eventually win. We could not agree. He had the cold detachment of a distant analyst but was unconvincing to those among us who had recently come from the suffering of South Africa's dumping grounds. As we left, we found the South African Ambassador to the US, Mr. Brand Fourie, waiting in the anteroom. He doubtless felt the need to follow up on our visit with Crocker in case we had been too persuasive. As we passed him, he spat out the word, "*Skande!*"[3]

In Washington, DC, we covered the same ground with both Democratic and Republican members of Congress. The courtesy with which we were met from both sides of the aisle was very different from the coarseness of present-day US political discourse, and the anti-apartheid cause gained endorsement from significant Republicans like Mark Hatfield and Richard Lugar as well as the more predictably supportive Democrats.

We then visited the United Kingdom and the foreign ministers of a number of European countries. There was a not-so-funny-for-me comic moment in London, where we arrived on a Saturday afternoon. Our delegation was to supply the preacher the next day at Westminster Abbey, and we had delegated the task to Archbishop Daniel. While we checked into our

---

3. "Scandalous!" (Afrikaans).

hotel, George went to his accommodations at a Catholic convent. At supper, a waiter informed us that British Summer Time began at 1:00 AM Sunday morning and that clocks needed to be advanced by one hour. Next morning, we reached the Abbey in good time, but as the minutes ticked away there was no sign of the Archbishop. We were already formed up to process into the Abbey when someone said, "Looks like you're the preacher," and my stomach heaved. There was no way I could pluck a decent sermon out of the sky. At that moment, by the grace of God, Archbishop George appeared with his usual beatific smile, thinking he was just over an hour early. Nobody at the convent had told him of the time change, and his smile vanished when he saw us lined up and beginning to move. "Did they change the time of the service?" he asked, hastily donning his cassock. "No, George," someone said. "God changed the time all over Britain. Now get in line!"

Our itinerary had been designed to preempt a trip P. W. Botha was planning for June. He had secured his first meetings with some European heads of state, including UK Prime Minister Margaret Thatcher and Chancellor Helmut Kohl of West Germany. We wanted to make sure that wherever he went he would be dogged by questions about forced removals. Soon, however, it was I who found myself at the center of controversy, and sadly, on the wrong side of a spat with one of my heroes, Alan Paton.[4] Calling the forced removals policy "apartheid's own version of a 'final solution,'" I listed some of the similarities between the ways in which unwanted people were treated by Nazi Germany and the way they were being treated by the South African government—the stripping of citizenship rights making people aliens in the land of their birth, shipping them off into a limbo where their continued existence was totally ordered by the whim of their rulers—all because of their race and the determination to be rid of unwanted people. I added: "If the six million people treated this way by the Nazis had been dumped in those places without being killed, there would have been very little difference between the two policies." The statement was not strictly untrue, but it received an outraged response. We had been followed everywhere by South African newspaper reporters, and they pounced with headlines like: "Storey—SA policies like Nazi Germany—Only Gas Chambers and Mass Murders Missing."[5] Then lion-hearted author and liberal prophet Paton ripped into me in the *Sunday Times*.[6] He scolded me for

---

4. Nobel Laureate Alan Paton authored *Cry, the Beloved Country*, the first book to arouse international indignation at South Africa's racism. He later became the leader of the multi-racial Liberal Party until it was banned by the regime.

5. See Peter Storey, "SA Policies like those in Nazi Germany," *Star*, April 3, 1984.

6. Alan Paton, "Letter to the Editor: Violation of Truth and of the Language," *Sunday Times*, April 22, 1984.

violating truth and the English language. "How the two situations are 'fully comparable' when the two most terrible happenings in all history are missing, I just cannot comprehend," he wrote, warning me that I would never win over "backward white Christians" with such "unhelpful hyperbole." I defended the accuracy of my comparison as I had originally stated it but tried to learn something from this most trenchant of apartheid's critics: if comparisons are too emotive, they become the focus instead of the wrongs they are intended to highlight.

When P. W. Botha arrived in June, the media did tackle him wherever he went about his forced removals policy, and when he met leaders like Thatcher and Kohl, the *New York Times* wrote of a "staged frostiness." In fact, Helmut Kohl, who typically sat on a large upholstered sofa for photo opportunities with foreign guests, actually had the sofa moved out of his office for Botha's visit.[7] Hopefully, the work of our delegation contributed some of the frost. Botha seems to have gotten the message anyway because forced removals tailed off, and the additional two million people marked for "resettlement" stayed put.

In June 1984, I received a letter from Nelson Mandela, now a prisoner in Pollsmoor Maximum Prison. He wanted to congratulate me on my election to lead the MCSA and mentioned my broadcasts from CMM. Knowing that his letter-writing privileges were still limited, I was deeply touched by this kindness. He ended by saying, "I look forward to the day when I will meet you and your wife in the flesh and shake your hands very warmly."[8]

Approaching the church's national conference in 1984, I decided that the theme would be "hope." We were entering a make-or-break period in the South African struggle, and I wanted to point the nation toward the high road of peacemaking and justice rather than the violent abyss yawning before us. I began my addresses by offering a theological foundation: for Christians the *wellspring of all hope* lay in the Jesus event. That was the center of all history for us, and because it was the night of my induction, it seemed right to speak very personally about my own faith:

> My testimony is simple: Jesus told a story once that leaped across 2,000 years and flashed into my life, of a son and a father, a far country and a family home. That story explored the geography of my soul ... it told me I was a long way from home. But it also told me something else: that there was someone back

---

7. James M. Markham, "Europeans Give Botha a Frosty Visit," *New York Times*, June 10, 1984.

8. Handwritten letter from Nelson Mandela dated June 11, 1984. It was twenty-one years since, as a fresh-faced young minister, I had visited him and his comrades on Robben Island.

there scanning the road each day.... Since then I have come to discover something about myself: there is the self I know and despair of—the self-truth if you like. But this is not all: there is another truth about me in the heart of God. The self-truth says, "Make me a servant, I have sinned." The God-truth says, "*This my son was lost and is found again, was dead and is alive.*" Tonight, I celebrate Jesus for showing me the God-truth about myself. That is the truth I must trust for him to make me the person he sees in me.⁹

I invited all our ministers to be "Messengers of Hope," challenging two forms of theological despair, "obscurantist spirituality that led to pietist escapism—and ideological captivity that led to ultimate disillusionment." Each was a heretical "half-gospel," and only the whole gospel of Christ would suffice. Turning to Methodism's founder as an example of holistic faith, I reminded them that "John Wesley's theology was beaten out on the anvil of his daily battle with personal and social evil in a brutalized society very much like our own." Real hope was born in the inward life of the soul because "hope's final fortress is the heart," but it needed to be realized in concrete action. Rather than being part of the nation's disease, the church had to be the place where "the love of God leaps across the parallel lines drawn by history." I pleaded for a much more rapid implementation of racial integration within the denomination. Undeterred by claims that many blacks were also uneasy about full integration, I said "all that proves is that the Bible is right—none of us has a monopoly on sin. There are times when God's Spirit requires of us something none of us wants, but which all of us need."¹⁰

The beginnings of the nationwide unrest and security crackdowns that were to bring 1984-85 to a boiling point were already upon us, and the conference was anything but placid. Early on, news came of six thousand police and soldiers invading Sebokeng, a black township sixty minutes from Pretoria. I sent a task team to investigate and after hearing their report-back, brought the conference out in a two-hour vigil of protest, calling on army conscripts to "refuse to be part of such actions." The conference went on to encourage opposition MPs to resign their seats to demonstrate that Parliament had lost any legitimacy.

I welcomed Bishop Desmond Tutu to receive our congratulations following the announcement of his Nobel Peace Prize, which, I said, was the world's emphatic rebuke to the findings of the Eloff Commission. "Now

---

9. Peter Storey, "The Wellsprings of our Hope," President's Induction Address, MCSA Conference, Pretoria, October 1984.

10. Peter Storey, "Ministers as Messengers of Hope," President's Address to the Ministerial Session, MCSA Conference, Pretoria, October 1984.

you belong to the world," I said to him, "but we are so proud that you first belonged to us." A session that evoked animated discussion was about the meaning and significance of Black Consciousness, a subject the church had tiptoed around for too long.

"Now you belong to the world!" Welcoming Nobel Laureate Desmond Tutu to the MCSA Annual Conference

My main address, "Finding Hope for South Africa," began with its own comical mini drama. Earlier I had dubbed the SABC "the prostitute of the airwaves" for becoming a slavish government propagandist, and the public broadcaster had withdrawn their TV crew in a huff; but now, because of a leak that I would be calling for an end to the ANC armed struggle, they wanted to come back. They made the mistake of arriving noisily to set up their cameras in the church aisle after my address had begun. I ordered them out.

I had recently been given secret intelligence showing that both the SADF and the ANC were estimating that the full-blown civil war we were heading for on our streets and in the countryside would take around three million lives—most of them black—before it was exhausted. Listening to some of the self-proclaimed "radicals" around me, I was convinced that few of them had any idea what a real war involved. The current clashes in the townships were horrible, but they were minimal compared with the devastation and bloodletting that could lie ahead. I began by saying that the intensifying violence across the nation had exposed a widespread despair. The regime was at the peak of its military power but had actually run out of road: "the granite wall of apartheid is riddled with cracks," I declared. "It is ready to fall on its builders, and they don't know how to dismantle it. They are haunted by the knowledge that no government can defend itself indefinitely against its own people." On the other hand, the dispossessed in our land were lashing out with "the rage of a despairing people," and the liberation movements were equally bound by narrowing options. There were now thousands of exiles who saw their choices in starkly simple terms: "they have only two ways of returning to this country—on their knees or with a gun in their hands, thus their commitment to the armed struggle." South Africa was like Gulliver, a great giant bound and made helpless by a web of consequences, and the desperate danger was that we would adjust to them so that they became inevitabilities.

There was need for a "strategy of hope." The church had to live a *prophetic evangelism* that offered the cross "not as a formula whereby to escape our dilemma, but that place where we nail ourselves to God's passion—and where God nails us to our neighbor." Turning to the convictions that had for so long sustained my own faith, I said that the first need was for *fearless witness to the truth*. Then we needed to *bind up the broken* because compassionate caring was not a diversion from the main struggle for freedom; it was a sign of hope: "It is by the costly caring for the broken that we earn the right to speak at all." A third priority was for the church to *live the alternative* in what I called the "pain of togetherness": "I say to black and white today, South Africa waits to see a working model—a visual aid—of things we believe to be the will of God." Calling for ways *to bring actual change* that were "consistent with the mind of Christ," I wanted to confront the war-drums now beating so loudly on both sides of the struggle:

> In war violence is glamorized, people are dehumanized, truth becomes propaganda, morality is destroyed, and reconciliation is impossible . . . war is always the *ultimate despair*. . . . To those who believe that military might can repress the aspirations of a subject people, I say: "in the long-term your hope is vain and your war unwinnable." To those who believe only war will bring the change they want, I say: "the instrument you are using will bring more suffering on this land than it has ever known and you will inherit ashes."

Therefore, a failure to urgently explore every avenue for negotiation now was "criminal." There were certain steps that *could* lead to a just peace. "Statesmanship," I said, was when "leaders are willing to risk greatly for the sake of averting even greater catastrophe" and, for South Africa itself, two great acts of statesmanship could break the impasse:

- The liberation movements should renounce the armed struggle.
- President Botha should withdraw troops from the townships, unban the liberation movements, and invite them home to "talk instead of fight."

"Then," I said, "let there commence the long process of seeking together with other authentic leaders . . . a truly new dispensation for South Africa to which each party can say 'yes.'"[11]

My proposals now sound tame, but at the time they were almost unthinkable and sparked widespread debate in the media. *The Sunday Star* saw my "dramatic call" as "an attempt to break the impasse between the Government and . . . movements like the ANC,"[12] while *The Rand Daily Mail* asked, "Who can deny the relevance and force of that message . . . ? The deadlock has to be broken, and as Storey notes, it requires a two-fold commitment: the exiled movements must abandon their armed struggle, and at the same time the Government must unban the movements and invite them home to talk."[13] Desmond Tutu, who was present at my address, supported my call but wanted an assurance that it included authentic leaders in prison and exile, which in my mind, of course, it did. Dr. Allan Boesak rejected it, indicating that only the government could end the cycle of violence because "it started the violence in the first place."[14] I wondered whether the dead in the coming holocaust would care much who started it; the question was how to end the cycle of death in a way that opened new possibilities of life. I knew that my call needed much refining, but I also had no doubt that the path of negotiation was the only alternative to bloodshed on a massive scale unimagined by some of the more shrill voices on the stage.

My final address at the Conference Communion Service was a simple evangelical sermon accompanied by an altar call. God still has surprises: among the many who came forward to kneel there were one of the SABC crew and a probationer minister about to be ordained that same day. Now, having successfully navigated the conference, the real work of leadership would begin.

---

11. Peter Storey, "Finding Hope for South Africa," President's Address to the Representative Session, MCSA Conference, Pretoria, October 1984.
12. "Editorial," *Sunday Star*, October 21, 1984.
13. "Editorial, *Rand Daily Mail*, October 24, 1984.
14. Peter Sullivan, "Tutu backs peace call," *Sunday Star*, October 21, 1984.

16

Among God's People

THE PRESIDENT TRADITIONALLY SPENT much of the year visiting the eleven districts, and I had asked to hold "teaching retreats" for clergy and laity on my travels. These went well, and I enjoyed the teaching role, but the real work of leadership was dictated by the escalating crisis in the land. In January 1985, I found myself in a light plane rushing to preach in the burnt-out ruins of a historic church, destroyed by fire two days after hosting the funeral of a riot victim. "God's tears flow with yours," I said. "This place of peace is now one of the symbols of South Africa's pain and division. Violence will lead us all to hell, but we cannot preach against violence unless we can show people a better way. We have to plant the tree of justice in our land, then we'll see that one of its fruits will be peace."

I traveled throughout the country visiting church members in rural areas living amidst deep poverty. I came away touched by the faithfulness and sheer strength to survive among the poorest of our people. During these travels, I was able to meet with Winnie Mandela, who was living under banishment.

In March, police shot dead twenty-four funeral mourners right in front of the Methodist Church in an Eastern Cape township. With many townships ablaze and increasingly under siege, I felt it crucial to expose white Methodists to what was happening to their black counterparts. "It is wrong that many of our members continue to worship serenely while innocent people are being killed on the doorsteps of our township churches," I declared.[1]

---

1. Peter Storey, Statement by the President of the Methodist Church of Southern Africa on the Langa Shootings and other Violence in SA, March 25, 1985.

"Violence will lead us all to hell": preaching in
a burnt-out church in Grahamstown

I directed that all districts should convene one-day "Crisis Synods" and locate them right in the conflict-ridden townships, where they could see the devastation and listen firsthand to the experiences of the suffering people, and more than 1,500 clergy and laity did so.[2] Whites who had the courage to leave their privileged "bubbles" to attend these synods in the burning townships were deeply shocked by what they saw and heard. In a message to be read in all pulpits in the land, they said: "We are living in a time of tragically fulfilled prophecy. Our pleas and warnings all went unheeded

---

2. The MCSA was divided into eleven districts at that time. In each district, the annual Synod of clergy and lay leaders, presided over by the bishop, usually assembled in June. The call for additional one-day "crisis" synods in April 1985 was unprecedented.

and we must now minister in the chaos and suffering which has resulted." There followed a list of actions taken or planned in regard to confronting government, calls for withdrawal of soldiers from the townships and that conscripts be allowed to refuse such duty, reaffirmation of our unequivocal opposition to violence as a means to either prevent or achieve change, and a repeat of our call for a national convention involving all authentic leaders. It was time to "end this agony."[3]

As president, I felt called to visit the MCSA's ministry to Angolan refugees in Rundu on the northern border of Namibia. Whole families had risked the crocodiles of the Kunene river to escape war-torn Angola, and we had an effective ministry among them, with a school, chapel, and clinic. Pastor Ludwig Hausiko ministered to them and wanted to show us a new clinic in the bush. Together with his bishop we got into his jeep-like vehicle and set off on the rutted road parallel with the river border. The pastor had only one speed—flat out—and it seemed soon that our wheels were more off the ground than not. When I suggested he slow down before he killed us, he looked round, teeth bared in a wild smile, and shouted above the noise: "Land-mines!" I never said another word.

The clinic was a tiny prefab on the banks of the river and was sadly lacking in supplies. I wondered what good it could be. Then Ludwig took us on a hike along a narrow defile cut through the tall thick grass until we came to a small clearing. There, on the carefully swept sand, logs had been laid out like pews and a forked stake with a flattened paraffin tin nailed on it had been driven into the ground, forming a lectern. Under the scant shade of a thorn tree, in the silence and the heat, we waited. Then we heard singing. Into the clearing came some twenty women, all very thin. Their clothes consisted mostly of sacks—either of rough hessian or the lighter muslin used for flour bags—with holes for head and arms. These women were victims of the war, their menfolk dead or fled, who were trying to survive in the bush. Yet here they were, carrying millet-fronds and waving them as they sang. Ludwig turned to me: "They are saying that they are glad to meet their President and they want to say thank you for the clinic." Their faith and devotion was mind blowing. We had church together for an hour and then, as we left that little clearing in the middle of the bush, Elizabeth whispered, "We've just been in a cathedral."

In July we travelled to war-torn Mozambique. The Marxist government was locked in a grim war with South African-backed RENAMO[4]

---

3. "A Message to the Methodist People," signed by Rev. Peter Storey, President of the Conference, Rev. Stanley Mogoba, Secretary of the Conference, and ten District Bishops, May 7, 1985.

4. *Resistência Nacional Moçambicana*, a guerrilla army trained and supplied by

forces. Elizabeth had decided "for the boys' sake" that it would be too dangerous to have both their parents in the war zone, and I agreed, but she later changed her mind. "I just had a strong feeling that I must go," she said. "I felt God saying, 'You can walk with the people in their pain—just be obedient.'" We were met by our local bishop who packed us into his pickup truck. The capital Maputo was derelict. Electricity supply was sporadic at best, with people in high-rise buildings cooking their food on open fires at ground level then climbing maybe eight stories to their apartments. There being no spare parts, cars that broke down stood abandoned in the streets, their wheels removed. An air of fear and decay pervaded the tree-lined avenues as we drove to the only major hospital. There we visited Rev. Chikona Matussi, one of our clergy who had lost a leg in a RENAMO ambush. It was a battle to get to him because of the many beds crowded into the ward. There were no serious medicines, and he was in anguish, surviving his amputation without painkillers. Later I met with the government director of Justice to talk about Methodist Relief and how best to deliver aid to the impoverished country.[5] He was frank about the need. "Mozambique is like a baby," he said, "born in pain and naked, needing food, clothes, shelter and education." Then he made a rueful confession: "I'm a Marxist, Reverend," he said, "but I'll tell you now that the only people I can trust to get food to those who need it most are the churches." He thanked the MCSA for what it was doing in this regard.

The country was effectively cut in two by RENAMO, and we couldn't reach Methodists in the north, but we took the ferry across the estuary and deep into the bush on the southern side to visit Rev. Matussi's former congregation. There we were welcomed with a heartbreaking song:

> *Only a true friend comes when there is trouble,*
> *You have come when it is not safe to come.*

These people could live relatively normal lives between sunrise and sunset, but when darkness came they took their children and faded into hiding places in the bush while RENAMO roamed. The little corrugated iron church was full of people, many of them youngsters. It had bullet holes in its walls, letting in pencils of light while I preached. Elizabeth spoke with great power about the woman whose backbone was straightened by Jesus: "With his healing touch this stooping woman was freed to stand up straight and look into eyes filled with grace and love and could now look other people in the face

---

Rhodesian and South African special forces in an attempt to terrorize and destablilize Mozambique, which was offering shelter to the ANC in exile.

5. Methodist Relief was at that time a sophisticated aid operation run by the MCSA.

too, with dignity and full personhood" (Luke 3:11–22). My wife spoke of her fears about coming to Mozambique. "Violence makes us fearful," she said, "but God straightened my back and said, 'Go and do not be fearful.'" Wherever we went, her message touched the women, who were clearly suffering most in this war. Nobody ate before noon, but amazingly, people in abject need shared out of their poverty. A bowl of water was brought for us to wash our hands, then another bowl containing rice and cabbage leaves soaked in hot water. That was it, washed down with tea.

Before leaving Mozambique, I preached in a four-hour service at the main Methodist church in Maputo. I spoke about God being most real when life was most intense—something we had found to be deeply true in this war-torn land. Then we went to a settlement on the fringes of the city to visit another preacher who had been shot through the stomach in an attack on the area. We listened to his story, held hands, and prayed. I had little doubt that the faith we found in this pain-filled land would outlast the promises of Marxist utopianism. Whatever inspiration and encouragement we might have brought, it was the courage, resilience, and inextinguishable faith of the people that strengthened us. And well it might, because in our absence P. W. Botha had declared a state of emergency in South Africa and already some of my colleagues had been picked up in early morning swoops.

I was warned by phone that I might be on P. W. Botha's detention list and shouldn't leave the airport when I arrived in South Africa, so I decided to travel direct to London. I was already scheduled to be at the World Methodist Peace Conference there and simply arrived a little early, enabling me to speak out against what was happening at home untrammeled by emergency regulations. On arrival, I spoke on BBC, and gave a number of media interviews, saying that South Africa's rulers were "prisoners of their own immoral policies and reduced to the desperate measure of martial law." I described the ongoing exclusion of blacks as "the final foolishness, closing the door on hope" and urged the recall of Parliament, an end to the state of emergency, and the announcement of a national convention involving all recognized leaders to decide a new constitutional formula. "I say to Mr. Botha, 'You cannot defend a country indefinitely against its own citizens.'"

The Peace Conference was a first—a joint enterprise between the World Methodist Council's divisions of World Evangelism and Social and International Affairs, two wings of the council with very different emphases. The one tended to focus on individual faith-sharing and discipling, while the other was more issue-oriented. The conference reflected this dichotomy. I had been invited to preach at the closing service in Wesley's Chapel. For a full week, we had struggled with the issues of world peace, with some arguing that the only way was through changing people one by one and others convinced that only the transformation of social structures would bring peace. The thought of ascending John Wesley's pulpit was intimidating. What would he say on this occasion? Wesley would eschew each extreme because the genius of his theology was the way he married personal piety and social transformation. Those who clung to one or the other alone were betraying that crucial balance. I also believed that no matter how elite and highly educated the congregation might be, the grand old man would have made a call to commitment, so I decided to do the same. When I got to the end of my sermon, I said:

> Some of you here have been so busy with your personal spirituality that your hallelujahs have drowned out the cries of the poor and oppressed. You need to repent and ask God for a new commitment to social justice. Others have been so busy changing the world, protesting and picketing that you've forgotten how to pray. You need to repent and commit yourself to a new personal walk with Jesus. So, come together, kneel here and ask God to help you get your gospel together again.

And they came! Some forty clergy, professors, experts, analysts, believers, and skeptics came and knelt in a sign of contrition and a yearning for newness. I thought, "Well, Father John, that one worked. Thank you!"

My return to South Africa at the end of July was without incident except for the usual harassment at the airport.[6] I had let it be known that wherever I visited, I expected Methodists of all races to meet me together, but when we visited Cradock in the conservative Eastern Cape, a mixture of local intransigence and fear created a small crisis. In June, four anti-government activists from the black township outside the town suddenly disappeared. It emerged that they had been kidnapped by the Security Police, murdered, and their bodies burnt. Here we were, a month later, and the township was boiling; it was described by Alan Cowell of *The New York Times* as "a crucible of violence . . . in the manner of Northern Ireland or Beirut" and had been under massive military lock-down.[7] I felt that we should hold our gathering right there as a sign of solidarity with the people; I also wanted to visit the widows of those now known as the "Cradock Four." On the Sunday morning, we passed numerous armored vehicles perched on the hill above the township and drove down into its mean streets, where we saw a body partly covered by a piece of cardboard, still lying by the side of the road, a pathetic

---

6. In those years, every return from an international trip involved being held by authorities until all other passengers had gone, with elaborate searches of luggage and clothing and lengthy questioning about my travels.

7. Alan Cowell, "Defiance in South Africa," *New York Times*, April 14, 1985.

reminder of violence the night before. We were met at the Methodist church by the minister and his brave wife who took us into a church packed with black worshippers. The white Methodists of Cradock were conspicuous by their absence—except for one white couple sitting in the front row with their two small children. I was told that this family farmed in the nearby countryside and was known and unpopular among whites for their stand against racism. I was awed by their courage: not only had they made a stand in a one-horse white town where everybody knew everybody else, but they also came into the black township under the guns of the SADF for worship. We had church, and I tried to offer some hope and encouragement:

> This evil will end. Through the bravery of people like you: mothers, fathers, and specially you young men and women who refuse to cooperate any longer in your own oppression, you will be free. And when you are free, those white police and soldiers on the hill will learn that they can be free too—free from prejudice and hate. Until then you must know that God is with you in your pain.

But there was also work to do with the white Methodists. After worship, we drove back into Cradock to see why the whites had snubbed us. I asked the minister and a lay leader from the township to accompany us so they could see that there would be no inconsistencies in my message. The white Methodists had finished their service and—as if they were living on another planet—were holding a barbecue in the manse garden, which was where I found, or shall I say caught, them. Our arrival elicited first shock and then hostility. Their minister, who had done nothing to get his people to the official service in the township, was tongue-tied. I requested him, as politely as I could, to reassemble his people in the church. I heard grumbling and angry words, with some people storming off, but most of them filed sheepishly back into the sanctuary, expecting a dressing-down from the head of their church. I did express my sadness at their absence earlier, telling them just how gracious and brave the people were whom they had refused to meet. Then I said, "And it seems you didn't want to meet me. Perhaps you'd like to tell me why, or ask me any questions?" There was a surprised silence before one or two people spoke up with questions about some of the stories they had seen in the media about me. As I responded to more of them, there was a small thaw in the atmosphere, with nods in places replacing stony frowns. The ogre was more human than they thought. Then a middle-aged man stood up: "I am a policeman," he said.

"A real policeman, or a Security Policeman?" I asked.

He reddened and admitted he was the latter. "Welcome," I said. "I often have you guys in my services." He then proceeded to accuse me of being a stooge, aiding the "Communist Total Onslaught" on our country and peddling the Marxist line. I let him go on for a while, then I asked whether he had read the Obedience Charter. His look of puzzlement was enough. "You seem to be an expert on *The Communist Manifesto*," I said, "but you haven't read the charter that guides the Methodist Church. I have it with me. It expresses the collective mind of the most representative gathering of Methodists in our history. It is rooted firmly in Scripture and our Wesleyan convictions, and it defines what our church believes about the struggle in our land. So it's not me you have to decide about—it's the Obedience Charter. If you call yourself a Methodist, you will stand with it. If you cannot stand with it, there are other churches to join." That silenced him, and the meeting ended fairly soon after. We prayed, and the people went their way. I never received an apology from the minister for refusing to bring his people into the pain of the township to hear their president, nor for failure to educate his congregation about the Obedience Charter. Experiences like this confirm my view that apartheid could have ended years sooner were it not for cowards in our pulpits.

In August, church leaders met again with President P. W. Botha to confront him with a five-point call: repeal the pass laws, withdraw troops from the townships, end the state of emergency, release Nelson Mandela, and hold a national convention to write a new constitution. It was the first such meeting with him since 1980, and Botha had assembled his senior cabinet around the long oval table, with the nine of us parked at the bottom end. On his left sat the head of the National Intelligence Service with a pile of files in front of him. Each time one of us spoke, he would open a file and hand it to P. W., who would then alternate between perusing it and fixing the speaker with a malevolent stare—all this to intimidate. When it was Catholic Archbishop Denis Hurley's turn to speak, Botha launched a vicious attack on him: "I don't want to hear from you, Bishop Hurley," he thundered. "You openly support the communists. I am not listening to you." Botha went on to quote something Hurley had said recently that had particularly angered him, and then he simply bullied him into silence. Turning immediately to one of the black churchmen there—representing a much tamer denomination—P. W. turned on the charm: "Now Reverend X here is a real Christian; he cares about the upliftment of his people, not supporting revolutionaries." It was an ugly encounter, and we came out angry. Apart from agreeing to appoint a magistrate to investigate some of the security force atrocities we had reported, Botha had shifted not at all.

At the press conference afterward, Hurley said with good reason that "communication had been virtually impossible." I said it was clear from the meeting that "there are two clocks running in South Africa—one at five past midnight and one long before. We are trying to represent those for whom midnight has struck, where hopelessness and despair have welled over into rage." I didn't think there was any indication that Botha had heard us. "We can only hope that on reflection he will see," I said. That same day, presumably to neutralize any impact from our visit, Botha entertained two Dutch Reformed groups and right-wing US evangelical Jerry Falwell. Falwell came out full of praise for the regime, to which I later responded that Falwell's view was a disservice to justice: "He hasn't the slightest notion what is going on in the hearts and minds of the majority of people in this land."[8]

My dear friend Abel Hendricks, now bishop of the Cape Town area, was in the thick of the tumult on the Cape Flats, trying to keep the police in check and protecting "coloured" school kids as they rebelled. On August 29, when I heard that he and Methodist ministers Charles Villa-Vicencio and Alan Brews had been arrested together with Rev. Allan Boesak on a "Release Mandela" march, I flew to Cape Town and convened an emergency meeting of as many Methodist ministers and lay leaders as possible for that night while I visited the cells to try and make contact. I was refused permission to see them and was about to leave the cell block when somebody hailed me. It was the father of an old friend from my early days of ministry outside Cape Town. He had run the small police station there for many years and was a beloved figure in that part of the world. He told me he was excited because this was his last day in the police force; he had only five more minutes before retiring. "Well then," I pleaded, "maybe your last action can be a favor to your church: Can you get me in to see Bishop Abel Hendricks?" And he did. I couldn't see the others, but I did spend some time with Abel. He was not afraid for himself but deeply shocked at police actions over the past few days.

That night a large crowd came to the meeting in my old church in District Six. Charles Villa-Vicencio and Alan Brews arrived, having been released from custody. They spoke, explaining what they had done and why, and then I tried to put the day's events into the wider context of the insurrection and cruel repression spreading round the country. There was much anger, not always for the same reason: most were outraged that the police had dared to arrest their bishop, while some conservative white and "coloured" Methodists were angry that he had "got himself involved like this." Looking back, I know I failed somewhere that night. I came without a

---

8. "Storey Hits at Falwell," *Citizen*, August 20, 1985.

plan and gave too much weight to holding the church together. While many thanked me for coming so quickly and "shedding light on the situation," I was also accused of having failed Abel and the rest by not immediately leading the crowd out on another march to demand their release. A night march would of course have been foolish, giving security forces carte blanche in the darkness, but we should have done something more than vent.

A last major involvement before handing over the reins of the MCSA leadership was with the National Initiative for Reconciliation (NIR), another effort to try and shift the logjam in our country. NIR brought four hundred church leaders from forty-eight denominations to wrestle with the crisis in our land. I was deeply touched when aging anti-apartheid icon Alan Paton stood to read the words of Psalm 130: "Out of the depths have I cried unto you, Lord hear my cry." There he was, this man who was crying for the beloved country while I was a schoolboy, yet still believing, still standing for the goals we had come to seek together.[9] African Enterprise's Michael Cassidy laid down a marker by pointing us to the Exodus story: for the Hebrew slaves to cross the Jordan and arrive safely in the promised land, the priests who carried the ark of the covenant of the Lord had to lead the way, holding back the waters until the last of their people had passed over (Josh 3:13–17). "There is no hope for national reconciliation without the church first showing the way and paying the price," he said. Other speakers like Desmond Tutu spelled out that price. Reconciliation was not about "making nice"; it was about facing the truth about ourselves and our culpability—and changing our ways. It was at the NIR gathering that Tutu made his famous statement, "It is very hard for me to shake your hand when your foot is on my neck."

For me, there was another unexpected pilgrimage required in those days: forty-six pastors of the Dutch Reformed churches were attending rather tentatively, and I found myself in a daily small group with a few of them. As they shared their stories, I became conscious again of how deeply they resented English speakers like myself—to the extent that before addressing the black/white gulf they wanted first to talk about this. It came to me just how different South African history might have been if, after the Anglo-Boer War, my forbears had found the grace to ask forgiveness for the disastrous concentration camps where Boer women and children were crowded together in dangerously unhygienic conditions and where so many of them—as well as their black workers—died. I felt the need to make that apology to the group I was part of, and I hope that, coming

---

9. Paton's prophetic novel, *Cry, the Beloved Country*, had been published thirty-seven years before, just as the apartheid regime came to power.

from the leader of the largest English-speaking denomination, it made some difference for them.

The most dramatic outcome of the NIR gathering was the decision to bring South Africa to a halt on Wednesday, October 9. A "Pray-Away" was called—a day of prayer, fasting, and humiliation on which we invited the entire nation to stay home and go to their local churches to pray for transformation in our land. P. W. Botha was outraged at the prospect, and some unions growled about churches mimicking their strike tactics and not consulting them, but in the end the Pray-Away broke all records. Soweto at times looked like a ghost town, and it was estimated that 60 percent of its population participated. At CMM in Johannesburg, a steady stream of people came to pray throughout the day, and the service we held at lunch hour was strongly attended as even large corporations closed their doors for two hours. Cassidy wrote, "The most moving picture to me was the front-page headline and full-length picture of what they called 'the busiest road in South Africa,' from Soweto to the city. It was totally deserted except for one lone cyclist. The huge headline, surely the strangest in South Africa's history, came from the heart of Soweto and simply said, 'HEAR US, O LORD.'"[10]

I ended my year as the MCSA president, grateful that my final engagement had been one in which God's power to bridge the chasms of history and ideology had been affirmed in a small way for me. Having been battered throughout the year by an unbroken torrent of hostility from the racist right, as well as from time to time the slings and arrows of the hard left, it was good to lay this burden down. Reviewing my year of office before the Annual Conference, I noted that the call I had made twelve months before for an end to armed conflict and for the liberation movements and the regime to sit down and negotiate a new dispensation had been greeted by shock, but now "it has become the conventional wisdom among all sorts of people in politics, business and industry—all except in the Union Buildings."[11] I decried the breakdown in solidarity among those who opposed the regime: "We are in an era where the assassination of someone who thinks differently than yourself is almost as important as resisting the system and where the Church is seen as a rich prize to be co-opted by one or other wing of the struggle."[12] I was determined that the church not be hijacked.

---

10. Michael Cassidy, *The Passing Summer: A South African Pilgrimage in the Politics of Love* (London: Hodder & Stoughton, 1989), 302.

11. The Union Buildings in Pretoria is the seat of government in South Africa. Oddly, the Parliament is located in Cape Town, one thousand miles away, the result of a compromise in 1910 when different entities formed a Union.

12. Peter Storey, "Conference Hears of Year of Crisis," *Dimension* (October 1985), 1.

A bishop and his people: dancing outside CMM in 1985

I had begun my year of office pledged to be a "messenger of hope," and Elizabeth and I had sought to bring the gift of hope in the places we visited. In some of those places, I know that she and I had done so. In others I had failed, but we had both been the recipients of something very precious in return: the people we had met, especially among the "least of Jesus' brothers and sisters," had left an indelible mark upon us (Matt 25:31–46). The church may give us many reasons to be cynical, but in touching these lives, time and again we had found the real thing—Christ-like courage, rock-like endurance, humble faith, and love beyond understanding.

17

Stress Fractures

THE YEARS OF STRUGGLE, particularly from 1976 to 1990, were extraordinarily stressful, and some inner disharmonies were inevitable. Those of us leading the church's witness were not always of one mind. Labels like radical, liberal, moderate, conservative—and the relatively new "progressive"—were often too readily applied. I tried not to take them too seriously, because they have little meaning independent of context. To most whites, I was a dangerous radical, but the most driven ideologues saw their role as pushing leaders like me into even more aggressive positions or writing us off. We needed their impatience, but understandably, individuals and "gadfly" bodies unconstrained by large constituencies were freer to decide and act than the SACC member-denominations.

Another reason for occasional differences amongst us was our theological, cultural, and psychological dispositions. Calvinist churches, especially those breaking out of the Afrikaans Dutch Reformed family, were generally more pugnacious and militant than the English-speaking denominations. I decided that it was simply the nature of the beast. While traveling in Europe for the SACC, I had found the Netherlands churches to be the most self-righteous and shrill about apartheid, probably needing to compensate for the guilt they felt about their Afrikaner descendants in South Africa. Similarly, Afrikaners at home who rebelled against the apartheid-justifying Dutch Reformed family seemed to be longer on militancy than grace. Calvinism has a big dose of exclusivism in its DNA, and Afrikaans culture refers to something called *broedertwis*—"conflict between brothers." When both are in play the gloves are really off. I remember my first meeting with an Afrikaner minister who earned fame for moving with his family into a black township after becoming convinced of the wrongs of apartheid. He scolded some thirty black and white veterans of decades in the struggle as if we were neophytes. My feelings were mixed. When these Afrikaners change they certainly go all the way, I thought admiringly, but it's also a pity that the later they come to the struggle, the more they think they're the only ones here. Maybe his freshly opened eyes enabled him to see with the clarity of a convert the weaknesses of those of us who had trodden this path for many years, but I will not pretend that he didn't get up my nose.

One more factor needs to be added to the mix. Some of my ministerial counterparts were covert members of the ANC or PAC, and that did raise a question about whom they were speaking for.[1] I remember saying of one of them that "the politician in him always seemed to be a few steps ahead of the theologian," and sure enough, his political ambitions emerged openly later, only to be swatted aside by the party he thought owed him a top position. With few exceptions, clergy have made dismal party politicians, with little to show for it except a dented credibility. By contrast, people like Desmond Tutu retained their moral authority precisely because they eschewed such ambitions. I remember saying to P. W. Botha once, "Prime Minister, you should listen to what we are saying because we're the only people who come into your office who don't want your job." We need to be sure that is always true, which is why I believe that the church needs to keep some "prophetic distance" from political formations. This is not to be confused with avoidance of engagement: it is about being free to speak an uncompromising word into the situation—a word emanating from a theological, rather than an ideological, place. It is hard enough to discern God's word above the cacophony of our own cultural and ideological conditioning without being hitched to a party line, as well. A black past leader of the MCSA once summed me up this way: "Peter is not a party man: as a result of his struggle with the Gospel . . . his challenge to the church is not to sacrifice its independence . . . he has called passionately for the unbanning of the ANC and PAC while firmly objecting to the stance that puts people in the Nationalist camp beyond redemption."[2]

There is of course another theological position born largely out of Latin American liberation struggles. It invites the church into unashamed identification with political movements fighting for justice. The problem with that is writ large in South African history: the Dutch Reformed churches were so closely identified with the Afrikaner liberation struggle that it resulted in their becoming co-inventors and defenders of the apartheid project. It is one thing to obey God's call to identify with the oppressed and stand against the powers, but quite another to place the

---

1. Until 1990 the ANC, PAC, and SACP were banned and membership of them was illegal.

2. Mvume H. Dandala, interview with writer L. W. Keister, 1985.

church at the disposal of those seeking political power, no matter how God-pleasing their agenda might seem.

These tensions surfaced most prominently twice during 1985, the first being over the "Prayers for the Downfall of the Government" controversy. In 1984, Dr. Allan Boesak had called for "a day on which to pray for the downfall of the government." He went on to say, "If the rulers will not hear the cries of the people, if they will not change, if they continue to prevent justice, let us pray them out of existence. God will hear our cry."[3] An SACC-appointed work group later produced a document called *A Theological Rationale and a Call to Prayer for the End to Unjust Rule*. Without officially adopting it, the SACC Executive sent it as a study document to all regions, including the Western Province Council of Churches (WPCC). They jumped the gun by releasing it at a Cape Town press conference in May, claiming it had the SACC imprimatur. Boesak preferred to name it *Prayers for the Downfall of the Government*.

The row that raged for a while over the *Theological Rationale* and its *Call to Prayer* lay in a combination of factors. First, the premature release of the document was seen by some of us as a ploy to avoid a final vetting by the SACC and church leadership. Anglican Archbishop Philip Russell and I both protested that we were being asked to commend to thousands of churches a document that had not yet been adopted. The WPCC insisted erroneously that it *had* been adopted, but if their real intention was to impute a distinction between what they felt was their more "radical" position and that of the SACC Executive and church leaders, they got what they wanted. Second, countless prayers had been raised asking God to rid South Africa of its oppression, but this was the first theological statement seeking to justify the actual removal of those in government, praying that God *"may remove from his people the tyrannical structures of oppression and the present rulers in our country who persistently refuse to heed the cry for justice."* The Archbishop questioned whether he could support a call that essentially revised some of the prayers in the Anglican Prayer Book and said it was hardly honest for churches to make representations—even on behalf of the oppressed—to a government "when one is asking God to remove it from office."[4] I was as committed against P. W. Botha's regime as anyone else, but my Wesleyan doctrine of grace would not permit me to put them entirely beyond the pale of transformation by praying prayers that I said "limited the operation of that grace to one option only." God

---

3. Allan A. Boesak and Charles Villa-Vicencio, eds., *When Prayer Makes News* (Philadelphia: Westminster, 1986), 16.

4. Archbishop Philip Russell, Pastoral Letter to Be Read from All Pulpits on Sunday, June 16, 1985.

might well decide upon that option, but "it is not our business to limit him to it."[5] Desmond Tutu also distanced himself but did so privately "because of my loyalty to the SACC." He wanted to know why the call never named the sins of those in opposition groups.[6]

The media pounced eagerly on Boesak's provocative phrase. The controversy would not have lasted very long without the whiff of division in the air. Headlines trumpeted a "split" in the SACC. There was anger on both sides, with church leaders believing they and the SACC Executive had been blindsided by Allan Boesak's penchant for publicity, and his WPCC supporters feeling betrayed by our distancing ourselves from him. But there was no split. By the end of June, the SACC had met and cobbled together a statement that left most bruised egos—but much more importantly, the witness of the church—reasonably intact. It confirmed that the *Rationale* had never been adopted by the SACC and included an assurance that the Archbishop and I were in no way seeking to undermine unity in our statements. On that June 16, we all went to prayer in our thousands, and while the semantics of our prayers might have differed, their intention and intensity were the same. Things are always clearer from a distance, and looking back, I don't think any of us covered ourselves in glory. Both parties would have done better to talk to each other before addressing the nation. The misunderstandings of those days were unhelpful, and we needed a much deeper conversation about what was really happening behind the furor.

This tendency was even more marked when later in the year a group of anonymous theologians published a document called *Kairos—Challenge to the Church*.[7] The way it was released had ambush written all over it: on that day, CMM's primitive fax machine began to overwork and soon rolls of paper were snaking all over the carpet. My secretary was still trying to cut, collate, and staple them when a Catholic colleague walked in and told me that "a document is being released today that may be quite controversial. You should get ready for something of a media storm." With a little smile he then apologized for having "forgotten" to bring a copy with him and left. He was right about the storm. The most basic courtesy would have ensured that we could read and digest the content before its release, but I hadn't read the first page before the press was clamoring for a response. The anonymity of the authors added more unnecessary drama. Since when did Christian theologians make their witness hiding behind anonymity? Could that be

5. Peter Storey, President's Update sent to all Methodist leaders, June 14, 1985.

6. John Allen, *Rabble-Rouser for Peace: Authorised Biography of Desmond Tutu* (London: Random House, 2006), 331.

7. Known simply as "The Kairos Document," its full title was *Challenge to the Church: A Theological Comment on the Political Crisis in South Africa*.

called "witness"? Were they hoping to give the impression that all the authors were black Christians writing from the dust and struggle of Soweto when this was not the case?

Kairos named three theologies: "State Theology," justifying the *status quo* and represented mainly by the Dutch Reformed churches' close identification with the regime; "Church Theology," typified by the liberal multi-racial SACC churches such as my own, with their emphasis on calling for justice and reconciliation and nonviolence; and "Prophetic Theology," which they said, "analyses the conflict in society clearly, examines oppression and tyranny in the Christian tradition . . . states unequivocally that God sides with the oppressed and calls for participation in the struggle for liberation and a just society."[8] "Church Theology" and the multi-racial churches of the SACC were the main target and came in for a hammering. We were rightly accused of gaps between public profession and actual practice, but falsely accused of equating state aggression with insurgent response, which was nonsense. The churches had been fastidious in distinguishing between the primary violence of the state and the counter-violence of a violated people. We were told that our problem was that we elevated concepts like reconciliation and nonviolence into "absolute principles" without emphasizing justice—again untrue. Ignoring years of unequivocal opposition to the regime, *Kairos* scorned any belief in the value of talking to both sides of the struggle and accused us of being weak neutrals wanting to become a "third force" between oppressor and oppressed.

However, nothing was as neat and tidy, nor as black and white, as the sweeping generalizations *Kairos* presented. Attaching one theological typology to the "liberal multi-racial" churches was not very good analysis because no denomination was homogenous. The MCSA, for instance, was itself a site of ongoing struggle. There were Methodists of all the above types constantly engaging, disputing, learning, and painfully growing. What else had Obedience '81 been about? And when Moses went time and again to Pharaoh on behalf of the Hebrew slaves, did that mean he had become a neutral "third force"? Yes, we were guilty of often failing to act on our convictions, but *Kairos* insisted that our convictions themselves were wrong. We were told that if only we analyzed the context properly, we would see the futility of our approach.

In spite of many pungent and uncomfortable truths I agreed with, *Kairos* seemed to me to be driven more by political calculation than theological principle. Rebel Afrikaans theologian David Bosch called it "strategy posing

---

8. Bernard Spong and Cedric Mayson, *Come Celebrate! Twenty-Five Years of the South African Council of Churches 1968–1993* (Johannesburg: SACC, 1993), 121.

as theology."⁹ I was troubled by the ease with which the Jesus commitment to nonviolence and the New Testament emphasis on reconciliation were dismissed. So, what was *Kairos* after? Its closing "Challenge to Action" was no help: it ended with a whimper. There was little there that the churches were not already involved in doing to a greater or lesser degree. But when it hinted revealingly that the church's role was merely to "consult, co-ordinate and cooperate with 'the people's organizations,'" that raised questions as to whom the church of God was to take its instructions from. I concluded that the long-term aim of the document was to persuade readers that the regime was completely irredeemable and that any hope of achieving change by protest, economic, and other forms of pressure was long gone. If our churches could be persuaded of this, then the way would be opened for a more supportive stance toward the "armed struggle." That would be a coup for hawks in the liberation movements, whose military efforts had failed "by almost every yardstick" in twenty-four years of existence to achieve anything more than small, sporadic acts of "armed propaganda."¹⁰

Both Desmond Tutu and I declined to sign the document. He felt it falsely caricatured the witness of earlier church opponents of apartheid who had inspired his own witness. He also believed its theology of reconciliation was "less than Biblical and that the Church needed to continue to witness to reconciliation for all, at all costs, even death."¹¹ Being the son of one of the earlier witnesses *Kairos* scorned, I concurred. Also, as with the *Prayer* document, I would be denying a central tenet of my theology by concluding that anybody—*anybody*—was beyond redemption. His stance and mine were not popular; for some, in a struggle as intense and painful as the one we were in, to differ at all was treason. One was supposed to go along with documents like these, whatever one thought of them "for the sake of the cause." A clergy colleague of mine wrote a careful and compassionate critique of *Kairos* and was cruelly dismissed as a "supporter of the *status quo*," even though he was enduring a humiliating six-year sentence painting white lines on the streets of his town for refusing to go to war against his black compatriots. I warned that the document tended to replace "the blasphemy of a tyrannical state with the absolute rectitude of a people's struggle.... *Kairos* lays the foundations for a theology of resistance legitimizing the violent overthrow of a violent and tyrannical regime, but

9. Interview with the author at UNISA, Pretoria, 1990.

10. See "Conscripts to their Age—ANC Operational Strategy 1976-1986," Howard Barrell's DPhil thesis, quoted in Padraig O'Malley, *Shades of Difference: Mac Maharaj and the Struggle for South Africa* (New York: Viking, 2007), 202.

11. Quoted in H. Paul Santmire, "The Pathos of South African Theology," *Christian Century* 102, no. 33 (October 30, 1985), 965.

it may be that because of *Kairos'* poor understanding of the theology of non-violent resistance, others will take another way."[12]

Looking back, the irony of *Kairos* is that the incisive analysis it claimed was already behind the curve. While the churches were being urged to give up entirely on the apartheid regime, God was inspiring other options: by September 1984, Nelson Mandela had written from prison to the minister of justice inviting him to visit, thereby setting in motion the long, risky, and complicated set of negotiations that led ultimately to his release, the unbanning of the liberation movements by President F. W. de Klerk in February 1990, and the first democratic elections four years later. Mandela knew that the armed struggle had achieved little more than "armed propaganda" and was going nowhere. "I started *Umkhonto we Sizwe* (MK)," he said later, "but I never had any illusions that we could win a military victory; its purpose was to focus attention on the resistance movement."[13] Allister Sparks adds: "So, getting to see the government had always been a primary objective."[14] This was going to happen, not because of armed action by MK that had been singularly ineffective; it was happening because increasing numbers of black South Africans were refusing to cooperate in their own oppression, and more and more countries around the world were squeezing the regime economically and in other ways.

---

12. Peter Storey, "Kairos—A Response," Symposium on Kairos Document, Braamfontein, August 24, 1985.

13. Allister Sparks, *Tomorrow is Another Country: The Inside Story of South Africa's Road to Change* (Sandton: Struik, 1994), 26.

14. Sparks, *Tomorrow Is Another Country*, 26.

18

Winnie Crisis

LIKE MOST SOUTH AFRICANS, I was glued to my television set on April 14, 2018, as South Africa bade farewell to Winnie Madikizela-Mandela, freedom struggle hero in her own right and former spouse of Nelson Mandela. As I watched, I felt the sadness of having lost someone I had known personally and admired at her fearless best, but mixed in with that sense was anger because of my painful recollection of terrible events when she was at her worst. I was intimately involved in those events, so it was hard to watch one speaker after another ignore or aggressively deny the dark shadows that they still cast. By the time of her funeral, her life story was already being rewritten with every ounce of heroism recalled and every notorious deed airbrushed out. None involved on the day found the moral courage to also acknowledge her transgressions. Instead, her funeral was a state-sponsored half-truth.

Winnie's saga was a tragedy of Shakespearean proportions, which also inflicted deep injury on the ANC. I believe that the movement's failure to hold her accountable for her offenses in the late eighties and early nineties marked its first public slide from the moral high ground of the struggle. This woman who in her prime had stood for an unwavering, almost superhuman resistance to wrong, became a troubling liability. She often said, "I am the product of the masses of my people and also the product of my enemies," and it may well be that the wounds those enemies inflicted on her soul damaged her irreparably. My engagement with her certainly led to one of the most painful chapters in my life.

Elizabeth and I first met her in 1985 in a bleak reservation for blacks, where Winnie had languished under official banishment since 1977. Located 220 miles from Johannesburg, her new home might as well have been in a foreign land. The language spoken there was Sesotho, while Winnie was from the isiXhosa-speaking Eastern Cape. Winnie's roots, like Nelson's, were in the Methodist Church, and as leader of the denomination I wanted to bring her some encouragement.

Meeting Winnie Mandela in her place of banishment; the bishop of that area, Jack Scholtz, is on the right

Arriving in the township, we were joined by the local minister, who had made it possible for her to launch a center for preschool children in the church building. We drove up to House 802, just another dreary two-room matchbox house typical of black townships across the land. A Security Police vehicle was parked up the road, but we ignored its occupants and walked up the short path. Some flowers planted around the front door were a brave attempt at homemaking in the dust. Standing in the doorway with arms spread wide in welcome was a smiling Winnie Mandela. We exchanged greetings and went inside the small living room cum kitchen. Having become the first qualified black social worker in South Africa, and in spite of the language barriers, Winnie had lost no time making herself useful to the desperately poor people around her and had set up a small clinic with help from the MCSA. We compared notes about our different experiences visiting her husband on Robben Island, and she spoke of her work among the people. Then she and I went into the small adjoining bedroom where I told her of the call I planned to make at the coming Methodist conference for an immediate unbanning and return from exile of the liberation movements on the one hand, and a cessation of the ANC's armed struggle on the other. She was enthusiastic about the first and less so about the second. "This is an important call," she said. "It will encourage my husband and the movement, but it is too early to end the armed struggle." She nevertheless understood that my position was consistent with the church's emphasis on nonviolent forms of resistance. Before we left, we all prayed together and then each received one of her famous effusive embraces.

Winnie was strikingly beautiful. In addition to her intelligence and warmth, in her presence I had no problem understanding why a young Nelson Mandela had become smitten by this fiery woman—and why other men later became entangled with her. During her time in exile, reports of alcohol, drugs, and men had begun to surface, and I sensed that the layers of pain behind the smiling welcome were manifesting in damaging ways. By this time in her life, Winnie had been horribly abused both in and out of jail. Her times of imprisonment were hellish, with long periods of solitary confinement—sometimes completely naked—plus physical and mental torture. Back in Soweto, not a day passed without intrusive surveillance or worse: police dragging her out of bed in the small hours of the morning, demanding to search her bedroom. Her resistance was fierce, but the harassment was unrelenting. Despite all her courage, Winnie was becoming a damaged person. Throughout these years, the Methodist Church offered what support it could, and Mandela himself never failed to express his appreciation. When he wrote to me from prison that same year, he said, "This letter gives me an opportunity of thanking the Church, through you, for all that they have done for my family. Without that help Winnie's burdens would have been far more difficult to endure."[1] Sadly, however, no help was sufficient to prevent the emotional damage even then corroding her character.

A year after our visit and with typical defiance, Winnie broke her banning order and came home to Soweto. She took up residence with her daughter Zinzi in the house that she had shared with Nelson before his imprisonment. She literally dared the authorities to arrest her, but they were hesitant because her bold move coincided with the growing international momentum of the Release Mandela Campaign. All over the world, people were demanding that Nelson be set free, and in his absence Winnie, with her Evita-like magnetism, became the obvious face for the campaign. Her home was an essential stop for visiting dignitaries and diplomats, and she was showered with gifts and honors. Somebody coined the title "Mother of the Nation," and the African American community in the United States in particular elevated her to celebrity status. In their eyes, Winnie could do no

---

1. Handwritten letter from Nelson Mandela to the author, June 11, 1984.

wrong, and I would argue that this unqualified adulation added more damage to her psyche on top of all the horrors of police brutality.

Then, fatally, she surrounded herself with a shady group of tough youths nicknamed the Mandela United Football Club, who may have worn sweatsuits and sneakers but played little football. Instead, they became Winnie's enforcers, doing her bidding in Soweto with whatever brutality they thought necessary. Winnie carried no official position with the underground ANC cadres, but she set herself up as an alternative authority in the area, issuing orders and demanding obedience. Emma Gilbey describes how Mandela United began to almost imitate the behavior of the Security Police:

> Winnie's boys would burst into a house with much clamor and show of force, before compelling an intended victim into a vehicle and driving him off to a place of interrogation—Winnie's house. Once there, a mutated form of police questioning would occur, with verbal abuse, kicking, punching, whipping, beating and slapping. Instead of mock executions at gunpoint, victims would be hung from the ceiling; instead of being hooded or blindfolded, they would have plastic bags placed over their heads, and have their faces shoved in buckets of water. Instead of electric shocks, their flesh would be carved and as cited in one case, battery acid would be smeared into the wounds. And instead of being dangled out of the window by their ankles they would be thrown high up into the air and left to hit the floor—a practice known as "breakdown."[2]

Around these activities there was a curtain of silence. Proof of the fear inculcated by the Mandela United thugs was that although I moved in and out of Soweto regularly, I remained unaware of the growing crisis. I saw Winnie from time to time to arrange for international guests to meet with her clandestinely. On these occasions she was full of charm, and nothing appeared to be amiss. Visitors went away enthralled by her. It was only in July 1988, when news came that her house had been burned down, that I heard another narrative. I went to the site hoping to offer her some sympathy but found the charred ruin deserted. Over the road, an elderly man leaned on his gate watching me. I said, "This is so evil. The system never stops persecuting her." His reply was unexpected: "Bishop, this was not the system." He pointed up the road. "The boys from that school did it. This was done

---

2. Emma Gilbey, *The Lady: The Life and Times of Winnie Mandela* (London: Jonathan Cape, 1993), 159. Gilbey spent many hours with me and others when researching her book, and I believe it to be the most thorough and accurate reconstruction of the kidnap saga in print.

to punish her Football Team for raping one of the schoolgirls there." I was aghast, wanting deeply not to believe him. I drove to Winnie's office in the valley below, trying to process what I had just heard. As if to confirm the old man's words, I found the gate closed and guarded by a couple of surly youths who demanded aggressively to know what I wanted. I was irritated by their attitude. "I've come to minister to Mrs. Mandela," I said. "I am her bishop, and I don't have to answer to you." There were bullying undertones to the brief altercation that followed, but I was finally admitted and found Winnie in a mood of deep depression, staring into nowhere. She and daughter Zinzi sat in silence, while a wealthy African American friend hovered in the background, acting as if he was the authority in the household. I later learned that he was a North Carolina businessman who hoped to cash in on his ties with Winnie. She ultimately indicated without much conviction that "the system" had burned her house, but the conversation left me concerned that the neighbor may have been right.

After that, reports of other bullying actions by the Football Team began to surface, and I learned from the SACC general secretary that a "Crisis Committee" of anti-apartheid stalwarts had been formed to try and rein in their activities. Nelson Mandela himself had requested them to act. Meanwhile, Winnie moved into a much more commodious house in one of Soweto's upmarket areas. This was to become the site of the horrifying excesses that sucked me into the Mandela United violence.

Late in the night of January 7, 1989, Kenny Kgase, a twenty-nine-year-old man who had done some caretaking work at CMM, arrived at the church horribly bruised and terrified, saying that he had escaped from Winnie Mandela's house and pleading for protection. It transpired that twelve days previously, he and three others, Thabiso Mono (20), Pelo Mekgwe (20) and Stompie Seipei (14), had been forcibly abducted from the church mission house of Rev. Paul Verryn. The kidnappers were members of Mrs. Mandela's Football Team. Suddenly the most famous woman in the anti-apartheid struggle appeared to be involved in kidnapping and brutal assault.

I had appointed Verryn as the only white Methodist minister in Soweto because of his remarkable ability to relate across racial lines, his deep commitment to the black struggle, and his longstanding therapeutic work with people damaged by the apartheid system. He had credibility in the community, and I believed that he had the theological tools to interpret the gospel effectively in that context. Paul was not married and would have had the small mission house to himself had he not thrown it open as a sanctuary for fugitives from the apartheid system. Young men fleeing harassment, and others, coming out of detention, sought refuge with him, and so there were often as many as a score of them around the house. They would sleep wherever they could and, as was the case in thousands of Soweto homes, the idea of anybody, including Paul, having an entire bed to himself was unheard of. Members of the underground movement knew they could entrust to his care youths threatened or damaged by the "system." This was a risky ministry because, in the overheated political tensions of Soweto in the late eighties, the ruthless Security Police were not the only ones to fear; the merest whisper suggesting that one might harbor informers could lead to retribution. Youths coming out of detention were twice victimized, first by torture in the police cells and then by the understandable suspicion that they may have been "turned." Paul had practiced his ministry of sanctuary consistently for some years and seemed to be a master at treading the fine line required, but as is often the case with passionately committed people, he had little respect for anybody's authority except his own and was obstinate to a fault. Very quick to lay down the law with others, Paul was disinclined to take instructions himself.

In late October of 1988, he had reported to me that rumors were being spread in Soweto that he was sexually abusing youths under his care. Paul's sexuality was not an issue for me. To me, whether he was gay or straight was irrelevant, and later, in Winnie's trial, I clashed strongly with her advocate when he tried to make homosexuality an issue when cross-examining me. But Paul's stewardship as a minister toward vulnerable youths in his charge needed to be morally blameless and without hint of misconduct. I asked for an assurance that the rumors were false and, given my trust in his integrity, accepted his word on that score. I did, however, instruct Paul to enforce a couple of simple rules to protect himself. First, a line had to be drawn at the bedroom door; no matter how crowded the house, he was no longer to permit anyone to sleep in his bedroom, let alone his bed. In addition, a supervising committee was to be formed in his congregation to share the responsibility of care. Paul agreed, but unfortunately never implemented the first and most important instruction. What was seen by me to be a sensible safeguard for his reputation was probably dismissed by him as his bishop's ignorance of the pressures under which he and his charges lived. He was to pay a dreadful price for this disobedience.

During November 1988, there was some good news: Paul reported to me that a woman named Xolisa Falati, with her daughter, had sought shelter because her house had been burnt down. She was now providing a "maternal, stabilizing presence," he said. I was pleased to hear that discipline had improved, and with an adult woman in the house Verryn also felt better protected from rumor. Neither of us realized that Falati had been planted by Winnie. Two other newcomers into the manse at that time were Stompie Seipei and Katiza Cebekhulu. Katiza was a highly strung, very damaged youth on the run. Stompie was a thirteen-year-old legend hailing from a township sixty miles away called Tumahole. Because of his commitment to the struggle, he had become something of a mascot to militant activist organizations. I once found him in my office after a protest meeting at CMM. Looking at this child sitting on a chair with his feet not reaching the floor, I asked what he was doing there. I was told, "He's waiting for the Security Police to leave, so he can get out of the building." Laughingly I inquired what he had to fear. "He led the march," was the reply. In spite of his tender age, by the time Stompie entered Verryn's house, he had already been detained for a year and tortured. Some suspected that he had been turned.

The scene was now set for the drama that followed.

On the evening of December 23, 1988, while Paul Verryn was away, members of Mandela United suddenly burst into his house. Falati quickly pointed out Kenny, Thabiso, Pelo, and Stompie, and these four were grabbed and bundled into a waiting van. Katiza was also taken, but I am still unsure whether this was against his will. Led by a very nasty character named Jerry Richardson, the abductees were taken to a room behind Winnie Mandela's house where, according to Thabiso and Pelo's later account to me, and Kenny's evidence, they were confronted by Winnie herself. She accused them all of having sex with "the white priest," and Stompie was also accused of being an informer. Winnie began hitting them with her fists, then a whip, and then others, including Katiza, joined in. The vicious assaults continued until, in Pelo's words, "our eyes could not see for a week." He said they were told to accuse Verryn or be killed. During the mêlée, perhaps because of the "informer" charge, or because of his small size, Stompie was given the "breakdown" treatment—thrown up into the air three times and allowed to drop with a sickening thud to the concrete floor. According to one version of events, when the others were finally told by Jerry Richardson to go and clean up, Stompie's torment continued. In Emma Gilbey's reconstruction, after further assaults, Stompie confessed to having sold out four comrades in Tumahole, which would have sealed his fate.[3]

3. Gilbey, *The Lady*, 186.

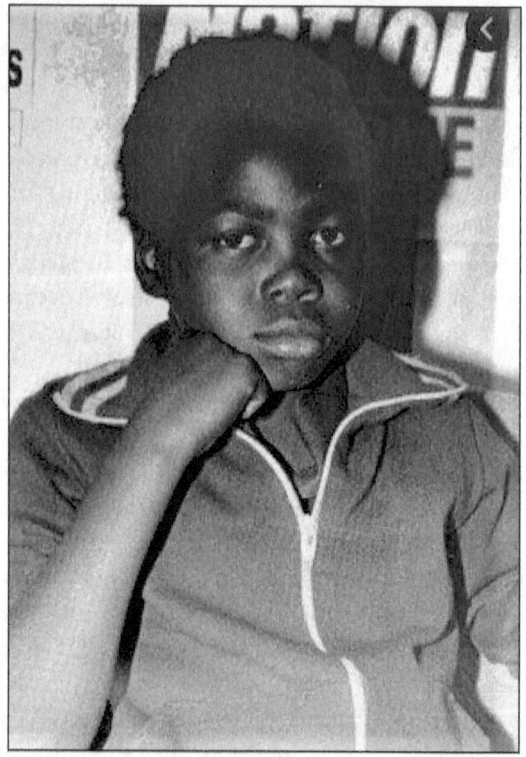

Tortured in Winnie's home and later murdered:
child activist Stompie Sepei

The prisoners were kept under careful watch for some days after being forced to mop up their blood in Winnie's backyard and the room where they had been assaulted. Sometime on January 1, 1989, Stompie was told to gather his things and go with Richardson. He was told he was going home. According to Katiza, by then he was "soft on one side of his head and couldn't see out of his eyes. He was also vomiting." We now know that Stompie's throat was cut later that night by Richardson and another thug named Slash and his body left in the veld.

Between the kidnapping and Kenny's escape, the three remaining prisoners were first held *incommunicado* in Winnie's premises, and then on January 3, they were taken by Richardson for what turned out to be a gruesome induction into the Mandela United team—an execution of a former Football Team member, Lerotodi Ikaneng. In the veld nearby, Thabiso, Pelo, and Kenny were forced to hold him down while Richardson and Slash cut his throat and stabbed him with a pair of garden shears. He was left for dead. After having apparently proved their loyalty, the three abductees were welcomed back at Winnie's house, given sweatsuits, and addressed as "comrades." Their faces and bodies were still horribly bruised, but they were now paired with other members of the club and given sentry duties. It was during sentry duty on the night of January 7 that Kenny found himself alone long enough to escape over the fence and run away to my church.

Paul Verryn learned of the abduction two days after it happened, but at first kept me out of the loop, seeking help from community leaders. Winnie initially denied that the youths were at her home, but when a prominent community leader arrived, she admitted they were there but refused him access.

To anybody in a relatively normal society, it might seem absurd that the police were not brought into the matter, but the Soweto of 1989 was not a normal society. The police were the enemy, their ubiquitous, abrasive presence a daily reminder of oppression. Involving them was out of the question. For all anyone knew, the Security Branch might themselves be involved in some way. If the matter was to be resolved, it would have to be done without them.[4]

Two days after Kenny arrived at CMM, Verryn finally briefed me on the crisis that was to occupy most of my waking hours for the next few months. I made immediate contact with the Crisis Committee, and we agreed to work in close collaboration. We were now dealing with a hostage situation, and before trying to untangle the roots of this saga, our first priorities were to ascertain Stompie's whereabouts and obtain the release of the remaining youths before they also "vanished." I was content to let the community leaders, who were better placed than I, do the direct negotiating. On January 12, during a visit by them to Winnie's home, Zinzi made the first admission that the youths were being held against their will, when she let slip that one of them—Kenny—had "escaped." What then had happened to Stompie? That day, three committee members were at last given brief access to the kidnap victims, who first claimed to be there voluntarily, despite the fresh wounds on their bodies. Katiza, finding himself alone with the committee, broke down and pleaded to be rescued. He said, "I'm going to die anyway, so I might as well tell the truth." He confessed that they had been told on pain of death to accuse Verryn of sexual abuse. Meanwhile, I informed Winnie's lawyer that the church was now monitoring the situation and would hold her accountable for the safety of the remaining youths and Stompie.

---

4. It turned out that the killer, Jerry Richardson, worked at times as an *agent provocateur* for the Security Police. Other Football Team members are suspected of having done the same.

The days following involved more visits to Winnie's house and further frustrating negotiations. I was concerned that we increase the pressure on her without her feeling completely cornered. I had a ghastly premonition that Stompie might already be dead and had to stifle my panic about the others. It seemed to me that there could be only two possible outcomes: either Winnie would release the youths, or if she panicked, they would vanish like Stompie. It would be easy for her to claim that they had crossed the border. Meanwhile, I had briefed the national leadership of my denomination, who were anxious that if the news got out that we were directly confronting Winnie, people with no knowledge of the facts could either misinterpret our actions politically or suspect a sex-abuse cover-up. The rest of the country would be astounded and enraged. I was left to handle the matter, but fortunately by this time I had access to a human rights lawyer whose advice at different moments in the crisis was invaluable.

Late on Friday 13, Nelson Mandela's lawyer, Ishmael Ayob, visited Winnie and threatened to take the matter to her husband. At the same time, he conveyed a message from ANC President Oliver Tambo in Lusaka requesting her to release the youths. The ANC in exile was by now alarmed about the implications of the "Mother of the Nation" kidnapping youths from a church sanctuary. When Winnie repeated her allegations of sexual harassment, Ayob proposed that he be allowed to take the youths to me so that they could repeat these charges. Winnie at first agreed and then changed her mind. Finally, she demanded I come to her house. This message only reached me a couple of hours before her deadline the next day and, after thinking it through, I demurred. So long as the youths were still in her house, they would not be free to tell the truth, and I had been unable to locate any Crisis Committee member to accompany me, something I deemed imperative if church and community were to work transparently with each other. In any case, when I tried to call Winnie to convey my decision, she was nowhere to be found.

Ayob did visit Nelson Mandela that same Saturday and returned with instructions to Winnie that she was to release the youths immediately.[5] She flatly refused. On Sunday, Ayob made another unsuccessful attempt. I sought guidance as to whether I could, in the name of the church, bring a writ of *habeas corpus* or failing that, an interdict preventing Winnie from harming the youths. It turned out that neither option would be open to me, partly because none of the Crisis Committee members who had actually seen the bruises and wounds was ready to give evidence against Winnie.

5. After eighteen years on Robben Island, Nelson Mandela had been moved first to Pollsmoor Prison in Cape Town, then finally to a house in the grounds of a prison near Paarl, fifty miles from Cape Town.

They were willing to be intermediaries, but I was discovering how deeply they all feared crossing her. In the end, it looked like it would be Winnie in one corner and the church in the other.

On January 15, I pulled Paul Verryn out of Soweto and sent him into hiding. I hated doing it because it could convey a wrong message, but by now there was convincing evidence that the Football Team was planning to kill him. Then I got a cryptic message from Ishmael Ayob: "They're coming out"—and they almost did. The youths were taken that night to Ayob's office, but escorts Richardson and Falati began to haggle. Ayob refused to take the youths unless their release was unconditional, and they were returned to captivity. This may be the reason why Ayob fell out of favor with Winnie and was suddenly replaced by another lawyer named Krish Naidoo.

By this time, it was decided to consult a much wider group of underground leaders about the impasse. A secret meeting of representatives of about sixty community organizations was being convened for the next evening.

When the actual release came, it was something of an anti-climax. A few hours before that meeting, I received a call telling me that the youths had been taken to Krish Naidoo's office. "There are four of them," I was told, "and one seems high on drugs." I quickly called community leaders to witness the handover and rushed to Naidoo's office. There we found Naidoo, Pelo, Thabiso, and Katiza sitting round the boardroom table with a scowling thuggish escort who gave his name as "Manois Maseko." It was my first meeting with any of them. Maseko immediately took a bullying stance. A long and heated discussion ensued in which he, backed by Naidoo, insisted that the youths were there to lay charges against Paul Verryn. I said I had not come to negotiate but to take them back into the care of the church and was not going to leave without them. I would listen carefully to any allegations they might make but would also be asking hard questions about how they came to leave the mission house in the first place. Pelo and Thabiso looked totally traumatized, with heavy facial bruises still visible, while the one introduced as Katiza was wild-eyed and jumpy. I told them of the meeting planned and indicated that any charges against Paul could be laid there. In the end, Pelo and Thabiso said they wanted to come with me, while Katiza refused and elected to stay with Naidoo. I had done all I could and decided to leave with Pelo and Thabiso while the going was good. The three of us left the office and then Maseko stepped into the elevator with us, and I could almost smell the two youths' fear. Once on the street, he muttered some threats and went off. Only then did one of them speak: "He is Richardson, he is the killer," said Pelo.

Once back at my office, I arranged food for the two youths. I indicated that they should hold their stories for the evening meeting—especially anything related to Paul Verryn—and also forbade contact with him. I didn't want to be accused of priming them in any way. Nevertheless, on the drive to the meeting, they broke their silence. They told me how badly they had been beaten, how they never ever wanted to go back to the Mandela house, and how worried they were about Stompie. They had been told to accuse Verryn or be killed. They had been assaulted by Mrs. Mandela herself, and Jerry Richardson was "the worst of them all." All I could say was, "You need to tell the truth tonight, do not be afraid—just tell the truth."

Getting to the meeting itself was a challenge. Fear of both the Security Police and the Football Team thugs made secrecy imperative, and we were directed to two false addresses before being sent to a small church hall. The room was filled with about 150 people, and the meeting was chaired by trusted community leaders. Some key clergy were there too, including Paul. Also present were about ten of the remaining residents in Verryn's mission house. The atmosphere was tense but controlled. After prayers and an introduction, a statement by the residents of the mission house about the abduction was read, followed by Pelo and Thabiso telling their stories. They had been taken to Mrs. Mandela's house against their will, beaten and whipped, first by her and then by the Football Team. There was shock when they showed their livid scars. In the middle of their evidence, a frisson of fear ran through the meeting when Krish Naidoo suddenly appeared, accompanied by Katiza and a Football Team member. There was a debate as to how security had been broken and whether it would be safe to continue, but in the end it was decided to go ahead, not permitting the newcomers to leave until the meeting was over. Pelo and Thabiso then told of Stompie's vicious treatment and how he had been taken away early in their detention.

When Katiza spoke, he admitted participating in the beatings. Asked whether he thought Stompie was dead, he answered, "Yes." He also alleged that Verryn had once "lain on top of him." Verryn was then asked to reply to this allegation and strongly denied it. Thabiso had made a similar allegation when interviewed in the Mandela house earlier. He was asked to confirm it but withdrew it unconditionally. "I was forced to say it," he said.

It was important for the credibility of the church that Paul's behavior be properly interrogated, so I addressed the meeting, calling for anyone with any evidence of inappropriate behavior on the part of our minister to come forward. I promised that if there was the slightest credible evidence the church would institute proceedings against Paul. No allegations were made, and instead a youth stood up and indicated that he had lived in the mission house since 1987, often sharing a bed with Verryn, and that no hint of any kind of misconduct had ever taken place. He asked the other nine residents present whether they supported his claim, and they all did. It was left for me to put the same question to the meeting at large. There was silence, followed by a unanimous motion of confidence in Verryn and a commitment to ensuring that he return safely to his workplace. Much relieved, I indicated that I was unwilling to proceed with any charges on the basis of just one allegation made by someone (Katiza) who had collaborated in the assaults. The meeting concluded that Winnie Mandela was using the allegations against Paul as a smokescreen to justify the kidnapping.

The most dramatic evidence of all came toward the end of the meeting, when Lerotodi Ikaneng, who had been left for dead by Richardson and Slash, entered the hall. He uncovered his throat, showing ghastly fresh stitches from ear to ear and told his own story of near death. He had managed to drag himself across the veld to get aid and had been in the hospital since then. Pelo and Thabiso, together with Kenny, had of course been forced to assist in killing him, and the two of them were deeply shocked, both relieved that he was alive, and terrified that they would be held accountable for his attempted murder. The crowd in the hall expressed horror and anger. Some demanded that we march immediately on Winnie's home in order to "deal with her," but cooler heads prevailed, and it was decided that a delegation would visit her the next day. However, the meeting did agree that she had lost the right to use the Mandela name and that the movement should distance itself from her.

I got home well after midnight, deeply thankful that a minister who I trusted had been cleared of suspicion and that at least the hostage phase of this nightmare was over. I had also been impressed by the thorough and scrupulously fair process I had just witnessed. The mystery of Stompie, however, remained, and a different ordeal, this time in the full glare of the public eye, had just begun.

19

Confronting Expediency

Unknown to us, Stompie had already been found. Just a few days after his murder and ten days before the hostages were released into my care, a passerby had stumbled upon a broken little body in a stretch of veld on the edge of Soweto. He notified the police, who delivered the body to the government morgue. It was to lie there unidentified until February 9.

Looking back, it is amazing that the entire drama had thus far escaped media exposure, but on Thursday, January 26, I was contacted by the *Weekly Mail* to tell me they were running a story about the abduction the next day and warning me that it included an attack by Mrs. Mandela on the Methodist Church. Reporters had been tiptoeing around the story for days, but none of their papers was going to risk getting out front of it—none, that is, until the *Weekly Mail* took the plunge.[1] I had no option: I gave a guarded statement and waited for the deluge, which was not long in coming. The next day, I was mobbed by news organizations desperate for further details. With Crisis Committee members refusing to go on record, I was fielding interviews with NBC, BBC, ABC, WTN, *The Guardian*, News of the World, Sky News—and more. The street in front of our home was jammed with TV vans, and I was wondering how many versions of my short statement there could possibly be. I had said simply that an abduction of youths had taken place at the hands of "Winnie's Football Club," that the Methodist Church, in consultation with community leaders, had been involved in confirming the youths' whereabouts and securing their release, that we were still concerned about a fourteen-year-old boy, that the perpetrators claimed they were protecting the youths from improper conduct by our minister, that community

---

1. The story was broken by *Weekly Mail* reporter Thandeka Gqubule, daughter of a prominent Methodist Church leader. Following Winnie's death, those attempting to sanitize the story falsely accused Thandeka and another journalist of being Security Branch spies.

leaders had investigated and found the allegations to be groundless, but notwithstanding this, that the minister concerned had requested an investigation by the Methodist Church to clear his name (Paul had indeed made this request to me after the community meeting). I concluded hoping that the "deeply felt resentment toward this group's physical attacks on people in Soweto can be channeled constructively to bring them to an end." I had been careful not to name Winnie as being directly involved, but that did not stop her from unleashing the first of a number of escalating attacks on the church, and when it became clear that the story was about to break, she had seen to it that Katiza was taken late that Thursday evening to a police station to lay charges of sexual misconduct against Verryn.

Much worse was to follow. That same Friday, Dr. Abu-Baker Asvat, a doctor reportedly called in earlier by Winnie to examine Stompie's terrible injuries, was shot dead in his office. This gentle community healer, beloved by the people of Soweto, had been visited by Jerry Richardson the day before, complaining of an illness. The doctor found no problem, making the purpose of Richardson's visit suspicious. Then, on the day the media storm broke, two youths pretending to be patients entered his office and shot him. A paltry fifty-one dollars was taken from his desk, and they escaped using an electronic button behind his desk to open his consulting room door—something they could not have known about unless someone had told them about it. This horrible act set two new narratives in motion: Winnie immediately hinted that the church was implicated, declaring that Asvat had been murdered because he was to be an expert witness in the sexual misconduct case. Community leaders dismissed this claim during a meeting I convened with them the next day. A second, much more plausible scenario, however, was that the one expert witness to Stompie's life-threatening condition after his dreadful beating had been silenced.

It was becoming worryingly clear to me that the Crisis Committee and I were diverging: their mandate might have been to rein in Winnie's excesses, but they would not speak against her, and they lacked urgency in the matter of Stompie's fate. I was shocked to discover that nobody had troubled to inform Stompie's mother of what we knew about her son, and unlike some of their courageous younger comrades, the committee members were acting with one ear cocked toward Lusaka, where the ANC in exile was extremely loath to see their fiery "Mother of the Nation" icon discredited. Ironically, another struggle hero was now involved: Asvat's nurse, who took the details of his killers, heard the fatal shot, and found his body, was Albertina Sisulu, spouse of Nelson Mandela's closest comrade, Walter. Many believed that if anyone deserved the title "Mother of the Nation," it was the strong, principled, modest Albertina, but she had none of Winnie's charisma.

On February 1, Paul Verryn and I left early for Parys and by 8:30 AM found ourselves squatting on a couple of packing-cases serving as chairs in the modest township shack where Mrs. Joyce Seipei lived. Nobody had told her anything about her son's disappearance, and it fell to me to break the news of his abduction and torture at the hands of Winnie and her gang. It would not be the first or last time during the struggle years that I had to bear such news to a mother, but there was something infinitely sad about the blank, unbelieving look that crept across her face as I spoke. I had to tell her that the outlook was grim and that she should expect the worst. When she finally spoke, it was to affirm her faith in God, "who had kept Stompie alive up till now." We prayed together and then left her in her pain.

I returned to another media clamor. Winnie had given a TV interview blasting the Methodist Church and now also the SACC for a "gigantic cover-up." Denying any abduction had taken place, she claimed that the Football Team had been dismantled long ago. Accusing Verryn of "sodomizing black children" and continuing with these activities with "the full knowledge of some of the top leaders of the church," she said he had a medical problem "which needs to be addressed by responsible leaders." She accused the SACC of covering the matter up to protect its overseas funding. Her allegations were becoming more bizarre each time she spoke. I made one more attempt to urge the Crisis Committee to rein her in. Beyers Naudé had rejoined the committee after an absence overseas and now seemed to be in charge. When we met late that night, he told me that Winnie had reneged on three meetings that week, and they had now given her an ultimatum to meet the committee and myself the next morning, or they would hand her fate back to the community. I questioned what they hoped to achieve. Naudé said that she would have to hand over the Football Team and its future to the Crisis Committee and agree to "negotiate a solution" with me; then we would all face the press together with "an agreed statement." I was shocked that somebody as wise as Beyers could believe—with murders piling up on each other—that there was anything left to "negotiate." He also showed me two statements from influential community organizations strongly backing Paul Verryn and the church and the decisions of the community meeting. *New Nation* and *The Weekly Mail* already had these statements, but the Crisis Committee was attempting to stop their publication "for the sake of not hurting negotiations with Mrs. Mandela." Listening to all of this, all I could see was the face of the stricken mother I had left earlier that day. I told Beyers that nothing would be achieved until I had answers to the questions about Stompie. He surprised me by saying that that was my problem. "We are not mandated to do the work of the church," he said. "That is up to you." My patience with the Crisis Committee was fraying. It seemed to me now that they were more concerned with damage control for the ANC than the brutal murder of a little boy.

The next morning, our lawyer and my Methodist Church superiors urged me to hang in a little longer, but I was dubious. I later learned that Beyers Naudé had held an off-the-record meeting with Winnie and Zinzi. I don't know what transpired, but when I met again with Beyers, I was told that Winnie and Krish Naidoo had asked that I be excluded from the planned meeting with them, now set for noon. I was not surprised and indeed a little relieved, requesting that the committee come to brief me immediately after, which they did. Naudé opened with another plea that the church and Crisis Committee "move forward in unity" for the sake of all concerned. He said that they had laid before Winnie all the evidence they had about the abduction, including the allegations made by the youths while still in custody. They briefed her fully on the community meeting that had cleared Verryn and censured her and told her that the church also had evidence that may or may not agree with theirs. Winnie in turn wanted me to know that she was willing now to "enter a wider discussion involving the committee, the church, the Mandela family, and possibly Ishmael Ayob." Instead of offering any explanation about Stompie, she said that "an ex-captain of the Football Club" had been arrested for his disappearance and other arrests were imminent, so she couldn't comment because the matter was now with the police. She confirmed that Katiza had laid a charge against Paul Verryn. After Krish Naidoo made a further appeal for unity, a member of the Crisis Committee made a poorly veiled threat. "The church ought to be careful not to go its own way," he warned, "because the church also has enemies." I felt my hackles rising. Earlier, he had been the most craven in refusing to help get a restraining order; now he had the cheek to issue warnings to God's church! I replied as calmly as I could that while I had always been committed to working together, the church would be guided by its conscience above any other consideration, and that we would not take kindly to threats. We left it that I would meet Winnie the following day to confront her with the evidence in the hands of the church. Once again I waited, and she failed to arrive.

The following days passed quietly, as if everyone was drawing breath. I was utterly drained but dragged myself to the Methodist Bishops' meetings, where the news came through that Stompie's body had been located after an anonymous call to the police. I rushed back to Johannesburg for a flurry of meetings. We were now definitely dealing with a murder, but before the implications could sink in, a new emergency arose. An underground leader called me with the terse message: "Football Team out on the hunt!" We knew what that meant. They had decided to go for broke, and anybody and everybody seen as a threat by Winnie's thugs could be in danger. We immediately rounded up the remaining youths at Verryn's mission house and moved them to a hideout in the country. We could not protect everyone, however, and during the night the Football Team targeted one of their enemies, firebombing a house and killing two family members, one of whom was a thirteen-year-old girl.

Things were now horribly out of hand. Winnie traveled to see Nelson in prison, and he banned her from talking to the media. Meanwhile, the Mass Democratic Movement had made a final decision to "distance" themselves from her. A hall at CMM was packed with journalists from all over the world as leaders of the MDM denounced the Football Team's "reign of terror" and bluntly accused Winnie of complicity in the abductions. They called for a "dignified distancing" from Mrs. Madikizela-Mandela, using her maiden name for the first time. I recall standing near them and saying to myself, "This is what moral courage looks like." I couldn't help comparing their sheer gutsiness with the cravenness of the Crisis Committee. When a reporter shouted the question, "Why has it taken you so long?" the painful answer from one of them said it all: "Because it was very, very difficult."

20

Soul Wounds

THE IDENTIFICATION OF STOMPIE Seipei finally brought the police fully into the picture. They now had a body, and Winnie's house had become a crime scene. Nevertheless, they were treading very warily. I couldn't help a wry smile at the politeness of a very senior officer of the Soweto Murder and Robbery Squad requesting to interview Pelo and Thabiso in connection with their abduction. I knew they were too terrified to return to Soweto, and I also knew all about police interrogations, so I agreed on condition "that it takes place outside of Soweto and that their lawyer and I can be with them." So it was that the day after the MDM press conference, I accompanied the youths to a police station where they made their statements. Three days later, two men appeared in court in connection with the Asvat murder, and four days later, Jerry Richardson and Football Team member John Sithole were charged with the abduction of four youths and the murder of Stompie Seipei. Winnie was left untouched.

The cracks between the ANC in exile and the MDM in South Africa were widening: Lusaka was urging that Winnie "not be shunned" while other MDM leaders stood firmly by their call to "distance" her.[1] As usual, she herself was way ahead of anyone in sowing new confusion. Speaking to *The Daily Telegraph*, she claimed that Stompie was not dead. "The body is not his. I am a victim of an orchestrated hate campaign by white churchmen." She charged that the SACC was plotting her downfall and "someone wants to destabilize the country to make my husband's release more difficult." Denouncing the MDM leadership, she alleged that the "black democratic movement is now infiltrated at the highest level." Then

---

1. The ANC leadership in exile under its President Oliver Tambo was located in Lusaka, Zambia. Underground communication with the Mass Democratic Movement was difficult and strategies sometimes diverged. Lusaka was anxious to retain Winnie's heroic profile, while MDM leaders on the ground had to deal with her waywardness, her murderous "Football Team," and growing anger against her in Soweto.

she repeated her charge that Abu-Baker Asvat had been shot because he held evidence of Paul Verryn's sexual assault. Arriving at my office one day during that week, I found the walls of the Central Methodist Mission daubed with slogans: "Kid Killer Winnie" read one, and another, "Storey pray for Winnie.'" It was becoming very difficult to keep things clear. I felt like I was spinning in a vortex of competing political agendas, and while I understood some of what was happening, I was determined not to be overwhelmed. The only thing that kept me sane was the remembrance of that little fellow sitting in my office not so long before, and the face of his mother. Winnie was not the victim—Stompie was.

Throughout this unfolding drama, one man endured a lonely anguish. Nelson Mandela could rely only on newspaper reports and fragmented messages. After I had gone public, I received a heartbreaking message from him, conveyed by Ayob: "Please ask Bishop Peter why he is doing this. Why can he not deal with Winnie pastorally as her Bishop?" I appreciated how pained and helpless Madiba must be feeling, but clearly he was not being given the full story.[2] I had already given Ishmael Ayob a full memorandum to give him, but he showed no sign of having received it, and I don't believe he had. It was desperately important to rectify this. By a perhaps providential coincidence, my Presiding Bishop Stanley Mogoba was due to visit Mandela in prison, so I prepared a note consisting of fourteen brief points—the evidence against Winnie and how and why the church had acted thus far. Mogoba undertook to put it into Madiba's hands. Essentially he needed to understand that we had only broken silence after Winnie had spoken to *The Weekly Mail*, that we had made superhuman efforts to get the youths out safely without a hue and cry, but that everything changed when Stompie was confirmed dead. Since then, Winnie had cast the blame far and wide, but the bottom line was that she was implicated in a capital crime, and the matter could no longer be contained.

This time Madiba got my message. After the meeting, Stanley Mogoba phoned and gave me a verbatim report. The pain-filled grace of Madiba's reply brought tears to my eyes:

> Mandela: "The fault is hers. My apology to the church, but why couldn't Bishop Peter have come closer to her instead of it being discussed in the press?"

Stanley Mogoba then offered my note and testified to the many attempts to meet her. He himself had been present on one of the days she failed to appear.

---

2. Nelson Mandela was widely known in South Africa by his clan name—Madiba.

Mandela: "I owe Peter an apology for what I've been thinking. It is an ugly situation."

Mogoba: "She is the one who has broken press silence."

Mandela: "Yes, I see."

Mogoba: "We are under great pressure from community and church for answers on the whole issue."

Mandela: "How would it be if I advise her to call a press conference—public apology—'I have done wrong, seek forgiveness and want to begin again?'"

Mogoba: "It has merits but may be too late."

Mandela: "I need to thank the church for all it has done over the years."[3]

It takes a great soul to bend to an apology under such circumstances, and I have always treasured that reply, but it worried me that even at this point, Madiba himself could still harbor hopes of the matter being dealt with by a press conference and an apology. We were way beyond that.

My response to Winnie's bizarre allegations in *The Daily Telegraph* was front page news, but I was getting ready for another sad journey to bury Stompie Seipei. Although the body had been identified by its fingerprints, Winnie continued to insist that Stompie was alive and now safely over the border. *City Press* stoked the rumor with a huge "Was it Stompie?" headline. The funeral the next day was attended by about two thousand people, far too many to fit into the sweltering church. The atmosphere was drenched in sweat and fear. There were rumors that Winnie and the Football Team would arrive to demand that the coffin be opened. I seemed to be the only one who knew that that was the last thing she would want to happen. As I delivered the eulogy, I tried to keep my eyes on Stompie's mother, stoic to the last but now with every spark of hope extinguished. I addressed her: "I'm so sorry, Mama," I said, "that I had to come into your home and tell you that your child, blood of your blood, flesh of your flesh, bone of your bone, was in all likelihood dead." I recalled watching her face and seeing in it the faces of too many mothers in South Africa. Today she might have the proud sorrow of a great funeral, but tomorrow she would be alone and her son would still be dead. Looking at the small coffin, I spoke to Stompie: "Your terrible and violent death was an unspeakable crime, and when I think of the way you died, I am deeply angry, but before your body was so brutally broken, your childhood was already dead. *South Africa killed your innocence*

---

3. From verbatim notes made by the author.

long ago. That is the greater infamy and deserves the deeper anger . . . in another land you might have been a choirboy, but South Africa made you a boy general. God forgive us."

Acutely aware of the anger in the crowd, I spoke against revenge. "If there are those who have come to stoke the fires of retaliation, you should go home because you do [Stompie] no honor." I said that the facts of his dying had probed beneath the surface of South Africa's pain and exposed the deeper wounds carved into an oppressed people's soul—"the erosion of conscience, the devaluing of human life, the reckless resort to violence and the evasion of truth." I said that the South Africa we were struggling for was one in which a mourning mother's pain and the life of a child should be infinitely more important than the loss of political face. Finally, I reminded the apartheid regime: "Long before his life was so brutally taken, Stompie Seipei was already willing to lay it down. And there are millions like him. If a fourteen-year-old child is willing to die for freedom, nothing will stop freedom coming. And, when that day comes, we will remember the Stompies and know they have had a part in fulfilling the Scriptures that declare, *a little child shall lead them.*"[4]

Two days later, Katiza joined those charged with Stompie's murder. I returned to the seemingly never-ending meetings trying to contain the crisis. By this time we were running out of ideas. At my last meeting with Ishmael Ayob, he had floated suggestions including a *mea culpa* speech by Winnie, admitting herself for psychiatric treatment, silencing her again, and moving her to Cape Town.

Matters were now in the hands of the police and the attorney general, and they were biding their time for reasons we only understood in early 1990, when State President de Klerk's bombshell announcement of Nelson Mandela's release swept everything else off the front pages. On February 11, the world stood still as Madiba strode to freedom, with Winnie beside him, her clenched fist triumphantly raised. For me, with millions of others, it was a moment to savor, but it was shadowed by the sight of Stompie's nemesis, still defiant, still not held to account, still acting as if the child's death, and many others linked with her Football Team, had not happened.

In May, I gave evidence in the trial of Jerry Richardson. He had been arraigned for the murder of Stompie and the attempted murder of Lerotodi Ikaneng, with various counts of kidnapping and assault. In the witness box, I related the long struggle to free the youths, and under cross-examination was asked only a couple of questions. Paul Verryn testified and was able for

---

4. Full text of this eulogy in Peter Storey, "I'm so Sorry, Mama," in *With God in the Crucible: Preaching Costly Discipleship* (Nashville: Abingdon, 2002), 121.

the first time publicly to deny the sexual abuse allegations. Kenny, Pelo, and Thabiso told their stories, implicating Winnie as well as Jerry, but Winnie herself declined to give evidence for Richardson and was not subpoenaed. Richardson protected her, denying that she had been in Soweto at the time of the kidnapping, and his defense team produced a Brandfort resident who testified that Winnie had been with her that weekend. Significantly, it was the first time in the eighteen months since the kidnapping that anyone—including Winnie—had suggested that she was absent from her home that night. In the end, Richardson was found guilty and sentenced to various periods of imprisonment for the kidnappings and assaults. For the murder of Stompie, he was sentenced to death.[5]

By September, the state took the leap and added Winnie's name to the others charged with the kidnappings and the events that followed. The trial began amidst a media frenzy in February 1991. Again, I had to give evidence and covered similar ground as in the Richardson trial. This time, however, there were differences: Winnie's defense counsel was the famous human rights lawyer George Bizos, who had defended Nelson Mandela and his colleagues decades ago in the Rivonia Trial and had built a formidable reputation. His strategy was to deflect attention from Winnie to Paul Verryn's sexuality. Journalists remarked that at times it appeared that Paul, not Winnie, was on trial. The other difference was that the drama was not limited to the courtroom. On the first day of full hearings, news came that Pelo, one of the key witnesses, had vanished after being fetched by "a senior ANC person" from Soweto. It was rumored that the ANC had spirited him across the border—but his disappearance spooked Thabiso and Kenny, who the judge had to threaten with imprisonment before they agreed to testify. When they did, Kenny had a torrid time, but when it came to the key events on the night of the kidnapping, he stood firm. Thabiso was unflappable and unshakeable on the key facts.

Now it was my turn. I had spent the night wrestling with why, through this tortuous train of events, I now had to mount the witness box to expose someone who had been my hero, who had suffered immeasurably, and whom millions idolized as a symbol of defiance and liberty. Yet she had become something else, denying not only liberty, but also life itself to some of her own people. I had tried so hard to ensure that when she was confronted, it would be by her own comrades, rather than one with the skin color of her oppressors. None of the Crisis Committee had been called, however, and when the crunch came, I, a white person, would stand in

---

5. Capital punishment was part of the South African legal system at the time, but in its very first ruling, the Constitutional Court of the new dispensation struck it down. Jerry Richardson was therefore not executed but died in prison in 2009.

what was still a white-dominated court, to help seal her fate. The Methodist Church had stood faithfully by her and her husband for all the years of their suffering, yet now the church, which had defended so many prisoners in the apartheid dock, would speak from the other side of the courtroom. It was a gut-wrenching position.

In the morning, my son Alan, who would himself go on trial just two months later for refusing to serve in the apartheid military, gave me a note to take with me. It read: *"Be strong in His love and don't lose sight of the vision God has given us that there is a butterfly in everyone—try to free the butterfly in Winnie, which only comes through love and the truth."* It was a poignant and important reminder of what my faith taught about every human being, and I think it helped me speak truth without letting my emotions about the whole saga cloud things.

When we got there, I saw Winnie standing with her legal team and found myself walking across the courtroom to greet her. I shook her hand and said how sorry I was that things had come to this. She seemed surprised, but we had no time to say more. I was sworn in and, according to Gilbey's record, was treated very differently than the earlier witnesses: "Storey was highly respected by all sides in court," she wrote, "the esteem in which he was held matched the deference with which he was treated."[6] But this did not mean that I had an easy ride. My evidence about the kidnapping and events following was detailed and fairly straightforward, but when George Bizos rose to cross-examine me, he ignored most of that and seemed concerned only to explore Paul Verryn's sexual proclivities in as much detail as possible. I objected to this focus, suggesting he had a homophobic agenda. Bizos appeared taken aback and vehemently denied my accusation, but I felt I had struck a small blow when he proceeded more cautiously after that. In his memoir, he recalls that the gay community and some editors accused his team of mounting a homophobic defense. He asks, "suppose Verryn had shared a bed with young women who had sought refuge in his house, what accusation would then have been made against us?"[7] That argument was specious and unworthy of a lawyer of his caliber. While the sharing of beds between siblings of the same sex in crowded homes was common in Soweto and therefore unremarkable in the mission house, no Soweto family, however crowded their home, would have countenanced bed-sharing between sexes. Therefore, why would Verryn? When the judge later vindicated Paul and ruled that there had been

---

6. Gilbey, *The Lady*, 261.
7. George Bizos, *Odyssey to Freedom* (Houghton: Random House, 2007), 494.

"a deliberate and protracted campaign" against him, I was gratified to have had some role in countering this part of it.

In the end, Winnie was found guilty of four counts of kidnapping and of being an accessory to the assaults. The judge slammed her "complete absence of compassion toward the victims of the assaults suffering in your own backyard, just outside your window." However, to the surprise of many, the judge accepted Winnie's alibi in spite of the fact that it took eighteen months before she mentioned it.[8]

At one level, I still feel deep sadness about the circumstances that placed me in that witness box and the dreadful harm the whole saga was doing to the freedom struggle, but at a moral level I have no regrets. With their reign of terror, Winnie and her thugs had become the very thing they claimed to abhor. The simple truth is that freedom won at the cost of destroying a fine person's character and killing a fourteen-year-old child is a stained freedom. Gilbey records: "the transformation provoked by Storey's appearance went beyond the manner in which he was addressed. As he stood ramrod straight, swearing his oath with authority and conviction, Storey appeared as *deus-ex-machina*, a soldier of God, restoring sanity and order to the proceedings."[9] If by that she means that I helped get closer to the moral heart of the matter, then I am grateful.

Of course, there were other voices. The government-funded *Citizen* accused us of "hiding a terrible evil" by keeping our "knowledge of the murder of Stompie" from the media and seeking to negotiate with Winnie for the release of the other youths, continuing, "if they had spoken up more forcefully at the time, the reign of terror ... might have been brought to a speedier end."[10] The truth is that we did not know Stompie's fate, but even if we had, an outcry in the media might have done just the opposite— the other youths may have been executed, too. Like most hostage dramas, we had to walk a fine line. I cannot claim that all the decisions I made in the midst of the whole messy business were right, but I am infinitely grateful that none cost anyone else their life. It turned out that Stompie was beyond help before I even knew of the abduction, but the rest of the kidnapped youths came out alive.

My final engagement with this saga happened at the Truth and Reconciliation Commission in 1997. The TRC held a special hearing on the

---

8. The witnesses who helped construct this "alibi" have all since retracted their statements. A Security Policeman named Daniel Bosman, who was in charge of tapping Winnie's Soweto telephone, has said that she was recorded speaking on it during the weekend of December 29–31, when she claimed to be in Brandfort.

9. Gilbey, *The Lady*, 261.

10. Martin Williams, *The Citizen*, November 29, 1997.

abductions and other gross human rights violations by Winnie's Football Team. Some of the hearing was behind closed doors—which I felt was a mistake—but Winnie herself demanded a public hearing as well, and I was asked to testify. By that time, I was teaching in the United States and had to return to Johannesburg. I arrived at the hearing jet-lagged and more emotionally vulnerable than I realized. I had never thought to seek counseling following the trauma of those days, and as I sat waiting for my turn to testify, suddenly it all became too much. I saw the lonely figure of Mrs. Joyce Seipei sitting against the wall, marginalized as always. I listened while various people I knew and respected tiptoed around the truth. I was shocked when a member of the Crisis Committee denied point blank something he had said directly to me. I was saddened to see even the redoubtable Albertina Sisulu taking refuge in forgetfulness rather than identify her own handwriting on the card that proved Winnie had visited Dr. Asvat's surgery when she claimed to be out of town. Earlier Sisulu had confidently identified her writing in a BBC television interview. I saw the imperious, seemingly impervious Winnie Madikizela-Mandela seated like royalty at the center of it all, dressed in full fashion. Then Paul Verryn had spoken movingly of his pain. He looked directly at Winnie:

> I have been profoundly, profoundly affected by some of the things that you have said about me, that have hurt me and cut me to the quick. I have had to struggle to come to some place of learning to forgive, even if you do not want forgiveness or even think that I deserve to offer that to you. I struggle to ... to find a way in which we can be reconciled—for the sake of this nation and for the people that I believe God loves so deeply.

His plea brought no response. Later I was to watch my friend and TRC Chairperson Desmond Tutu humiliate himself, begging Winnie to acknowledge some—any—responsibility for the terrible deeds that had been done. And in the middle of the packed hall I wept. Our third son, David, who had accompanied me, took my hand, and I think we managed my breakdown as quietly as possible.

I had kept a contemporaneous record during the hostage drama, which the police knew about but had never asked for.[11] For the first time I was able to go through it publicly. David Beresford of *The Mail & Guardian*

---

11. At the time of Winnie's death, retired Police General George Fivaz claimed to have reopened the investigation into Stompie's murder at the request of Sydney Mufamadi, Minister of Police in the new democratic administration, and that no connection between Winnie and the murder could be established. I was neither approached nor interviewed, and the evidence of many witnesses make nonsense of his claim.

described it as a "devastatingly detailed account" and said that I exposed Winnie "as a liar of terrifying ruthlessness."[12] It was not me, but the record that did that. When laid out as a daily diary, it *was* devastating. But I also felt it important once more to try and locate the horror of the abduction events in the wider tragedy of our land. Yes, Winnie was responsible and needed to be held accountable, but she was not the only one; the whole bloody saga of cruelty and pain that was apartheid, including the damage done with cold intent over many years to this woman was also present in the room. That is what the TRC was about. After lengthy questioning by lawyers representing Winnie and other interested parties, I asked to make a statement, because, I said, throughout the saga, the truth had been trimmed to prevailing political winds by politicians or suppressed because people feared for their lives. "I really believe that to dispel this suffocating fog of silence is very important for the future of our country."

I talked about four wounds these years had carved into people's souls— the erosion of conscience, the devaluing of human life, the evasion of truth, and the reckless resort to violence:

> The primary cancer may be, was, and will always be the apartheid oppression, but the secondary infection has touched many of apartheid's opponents and eroded their knowledge of good and evil. . . . A tragedy of life is that it is possible to become like that which you hate most and to be remade in the image of your oppressor. I have a feeling that this drama is an example of that. Unless this fact is recognized, then all the truth will not have been told. . . . The torture and murder of Stompie Seipei are important beyond the normal horror we should feel because . . . they may have been common-law crimes, but they are also about the ruthless abuse of power. Even given the latitude of a time of struggle, they resemble far too closely the abuses of apartheid itself.

I concluded by underlining the moral significance of it all by quoting theologian Walter Wink, who said, "It is not enough to become politically liberated, we must also become human."[13] I said, "This case is about recognizing the inhumanities which too many of us were capable of . . . and becoming human again."

---

12. David Beresford, "South Africa: More Questions Than Answers," *Mail & Guardian*, December 5, 1997.

13. Walter Wink, "We Have Met the Enemy: On Not Becoming What We Hate," *Sojourners* 15, no. 10 (November 1986), 15.

I kept silent about my disgust with some of the Crisis Committee's cowardly evidence but commended the MDM leaders who had the moral courage to take the stand they did. Then I turned to the matter of Paul Verryn, accusing the media for consistently associating his name with the words "sodomy" or "rape" in spite of the fact that the allegations against him had been thrown out by the community leadership and two judges. Everybody who had publicly accused him had, to my knowledge, withdrawn their allegations, except one. Looking at Winnie, I said, "It is my hope that before these hearings are ended, that last remaining accuser will withdraw her words and take back the accusations she has made against him."

She never did.

Her contribution to the hearings was a string of denials, but she did finally respond to Tutu's pleas with the grudging admission that "things went horribly wrong," and she was sorry. A reconciliation hug between Winnie and Mrs. Joyce Seipei followed: it was poor theater and unconvincing.

The next day, I gratefully settled into my seat for the long flight back to the tranquility of a university campus far, far away from South Africa's tormented story and the sad flotsam it kept washing up from the wreck we had made of our past.

When the Truth Commission's findings were announced, it found Winnie "politically and morally accountable for the gross violations of human rights committed by the Mandela United Football Club" and that "the abductions from Verryn's house had taken place on her instructions."[14] She was present during the assaults on the youths and "initiated and participated in the assaults." It also found that Winnie had "deliberately and maliciously slandered [Paul] Verryn in an attempt to divert attention away from herself and the associates of her household." The finding about Stompie was less clear, although the commission accepted the corroborative testimony that placed her at the scene and implicated her in the assaults. It stated that "in all probability she was aware of his condition," and this "compounded her complicity" by failing to get the necessary medical help for him. It also noted that he was last seen alive at her home and that she "was responsible for his abduction and was negligent in that she failed to act responsibly in taking the necessary action required to avert his death." Despite the fact that it made these strong findings, I felt that these hearings were a low point in the commission's life.

---

14. *Truth and Reconciliation Commission of South Africa Report* (Cape Town: Juta, 1998), 2:568–81.

21

Thin Orange Line

THE NATIONAL PEACE ACCORD (NPA) was the best kept secret of South Africa's transition to democracy. The "miracle" could never have happened without it, but it has gone deliberately unacknowledged by politicians of all stripes, and historians have given it nothing like the weight it deserves. We owe more than we will ever know to the "thin orange line" of peacekeepers who demonstrated a degree of bravery and selfless patriotism that demands our esteem and gratitude.[1] It is fashionable these days for people who were hardly out of diapers in the 1990s to smear the transition as a "sell-out." They have absolutely no idea how desperately near we were to conflagration and how close they came to growing up in a blitzed wasteland. The National Peace Accord was a major reason why they didn't.

I had often wondered how we would know when our adversaries had run out of road and what we would do with that moment. President De Klerk's famous speech on February 2, 1990, is usually regarded as the marker, but for me and thousands of others it happened four months earlier in Cape Town when Archbishop Desmond Tutu, Allan Boesak, and the city's courageous new mayor led thirty thousand citizens in a peaceful march to City Hall. Only a week previously, there had been chaos in those same streets when police used a high-powered water cannon firing purple dye to disperse demonstrators—leading them to amend the Freedom Charter's *"The people shall govern,"* to *"The Purple shall Govern!"* This time everything was different.

Two days later, we took to the streets in Johannesburg. After a service in St. Mary's Cathedral, I and a number of faith leaders set out for Security Police headquarters two and a half miles away. Most of the one

---

1. Peace Monitors wore an orange vest with two superimposed doves on the front. The original design had one dove but at the last minute it was learned that a single dove was apparently a bad omen in Zulu culture.

thousand people who had worshipped with us followed. The march had been banned, so we waited for the inevitable clash with the riot police, but they never appeared. We picked up pace, and as we marched, instead of the expected police attack, onlookers began to join us. They left the sidewalks and swelled our ranks. Now there were two thousand, and then five. Halfway along the route, still no police action, and the crowd had grown to twenty thousand. Then, trotting breathlessly alongside us was a little grey man typical of the civil servants of the apartheid regime. He was waving a piece of paper, begging one of us to take it. We were not going to unlink our arms—so we asked him what it was. He told us it was permission from the chief magistrate to hold the march. We looked at each other in amazement and then glee, telling him to keep his piece of paper. We knew that we'd won. When we got to Security Police headquarters, we walked right into the lion's den and delivered our protest.

March of the 25,000 on September 15, 1989: approaching Security Police Headquarters; the marshall in the foreground with the headband is our student activist son, David (Credit: ANA Pictures/*The Star*)

"O God, you and your people have done a beautiful thing today!"—Leading the crowd in prayer opposite Security Police headquarters

Then two other leaders and I climbed onto a roof and looked down at this amazing crowd of around twenty-five thousand people standing in silence, stunned at their achievement. They stretched a couple of city blocks and then out of sight around the corner. I was handed a bullhorn, and I asked the crowd to sit down in the street and then led them in prayer: "O God, you and your people have done a beautiful thing today!" As the first words of the prayer reached them, without being asked, they began to repeat it aloud. Phrase by phrase, the words of thanks to God and the cry for a new South Africa were picked up and carried through the gathering—like a sacred wave—until all had joined in. It was a mystical and unforgettable moment. Then I spotted my son David below me. He was one of the marshals for the march and was mouthing something urgently. I finally got his message and called everyone to their feet to sing *Nkosi Sikelel' iAfrika.*

Later I wrote: "It was as if the people of Johannesburg were coming out of a long, dark shadow—as if this momentary throwing off of oppression was a foretaste of the future everybody longs for." But it was even more than that: together with the great march in Cape Town it was the end, the last protest march under apartheid.

Nine days after De Klerk's speech, like millions of others, I watched Nelson Mandela's triumphant walk from prison with a sense of unreality and wonder. The new day we had prayed and worked for was beginning to dawn. But not long before, I remember warning my synod that "both possibility and peril" lay ahead. Yes, we could finally say that a majority of white

South Africans knew in their hearts that the days of white supremacy were over, but some would retreat into a "fanatical bravado" typified by white extremist groups; nor should we underestimate the destructive power of "the shadowy security establishment." I warned that "the worst of the cruelties may still be ahead."[2] And they were. We were entering South Africa's most murderous years, not only because of the violent rearguard actions of white racists. Most of the killing that lay ahead was by black political formations, notably Buthelezi's Inkatha and Mandela's ANC.[3] They had sniffed power, and their contestation let loose a flood of violence. Having had some experience mediating between such groups, I was not surprised to see the "solidarity of the oppressed" begin to unravel, but I doubt that many of us had any idea how vicious the ensuing war—aided and abetted by the "security establishment"—would be. More than fourteen thousand men, women, and children would be killed between 1990 and Freedom Day in 1994. As horrible acts of murder and destruction spread, government and political leaders seemed either helpless or unwilling to stem the violence.

That was when civil society stepped in, and a remarkable alliance was born. Religious and business leaders, trade unions, human rights lawyers, and other deeply concerned citizens came together to intervene. Many of the lawyers we worked with had paid a heavy price since student days for their commitment to democracy. The business leaders knew that war and chaos could only torpedo the economy. Church leaders were determined that all these years of costly witness and painful struggle by ordinary people would not be squandered by reckless and ambitious politicians. After tense shuttle diplomacy, this alliance dragged the politicians kicking and screaming into one room, and said, "Enough already! You're not going to leave here until you agree to compete in a way more appropriate for the birth of a democracy." The result was the National Peace Accord (NPA). The NPA laid down codes of conduct covering all of the signatories as well as the police and security forces.[4] It was a unique construct: because the police and military were so mistrusted, the government was outsourcing the task of keeping the peace, inserting between them and the population a parallel organization

2. Peter Storey, Bishop's Address to the Annual Synod of the Central District, MCSA, June 1990.

3. Mandela's African National Congress tended to be a "broad church" of all ethnic groups, including many "urbanized" Zulus, although its most significant leaders were Xhosas. Inkatha was tribal, claiming to represent the five million Zulus in South Africa, and led by Chief Mangosutho Buthelelzi, who was determined never to accept ANC rule.

4. The thirty-three page accord was signed on September 14, 1991, by all the parties except the white right wing, the PAC, and the Azanian People's Organization (AZAPO) and was established by Parliament in the National Peace Institutions Act.

run by church and business people and the best of civil society, with the other parties agreeing to abide by the NPA's rules. National, regional, and local peace committees were to hold police and the political formations accountable. It was going to be a tough job. In October, I addressed a mixed bag of politicos about the hypocrisies that they would need to be rid of: "How can you say, 'I believe in peace' while still using hit squads to assassinate black activists?" I asked. "How can you say, 'I believe in peace' and demand to carry 'traditional' weapons? How can you say, 'I believe in peace' and insist on arming 'defence committees?' How can you say, 'I believe in peace' and shout 'one settler, one bullet'?"[5]

Putting the necessary structures in place often meant bringing to the table people who were literally shooting at each other by night. The task of NPA Local Peace Committees (LPCs) was described in the Accord as: *"creating trust and reconciliation between grassroots community leadership of organisations including the Police and Defence Force"* and *"settling disputes causing public violence by negotiating with the parties concerned."*[6] This was a massive ask. While the setting up of these committees in most places prevented violence from taking hold, the story was very different where it was already endemic. There, NPA mediators and monitors risked their lives daily in the cross fire of heavily armed antagonists. One of the key persons trying to set up LPCs in Soweto was Elizabeth's boss, the director of the Independent Mediation Service of South Africa (IMSSA). She was his PA and they would drive deep into Soweto to wait in some church hall or other—often in an atmosphere thick with fear—for representatives of the warring groups to turn up, sometimes having to do so three or four times before succeeding. Given such levels of suspicion and the fact that nothing quite like this had been tried anywhere in the world before, it took months to put the Regional Peace Committees (RPCs) and LPCs in place. During this time the violence continued to escalate, and the media were quick to write the NPA off as a failure. In the end, they would be proved wrong.

The only people with the credibility to chair these bodies were trusted human rights lawyers, business leaders, and church people, ironically most of them white. It was a new experience for those of us involved. I found myself co-chairing the RPC overseeing Johannesburg and Soweto with a retired Democratic Party MP and businessman as my partner. Our area was one of the most volatile in the country. Chairing a committee of all political parties, including those who were fighting each other, as well

---

5. Peter Storey, "Addressing white security forces, Inkatha, ANC, and PAC," Seminar on Violence, Yeoville, October 29, 1991.

6. National Peace Accord, 7.4.8.2, 7.3.8.4.

as the SADF and police, was like herding wildcats. To get them to begin to listen to each other took months. I had my own lesson in the complexities of peacemaking when we went away for a weekend of "team building" and found myself in a small group with a colonel of the Security Police whose task had been to harass me for years. He had seen to the death threats my children used to hear when they answered the telephone, the strange-looking objects left on our front doorstep at night, and other intimidating actions. Now I had to sit in the same group with him and actually *listen* to him. I found that very difficult, and it helped me understand a little of the depth of mistrust and memory that especially our black compatriots had to overcome. I told him that "making nice" would not work between us; actions alone would count. We agreed that trust might come later. Meanwhile, there was a job to be done.

Staff appointments for the RPC team took an eternity, with every single one having to be "by consensus"—which meant getting every party to accept each name. The effort was worthwhile, however, and slowly an outstanding multi-racial, multi-party team emerged. Together they recruited and trained thousands of peace monitors—many of them unemployed black youngsters. These youths had known nothing but violence from the apartheid system and became increasingly excited to learn that there were non-violent ways of resolving conflict. Once trained, they went out unarmed into places of dreadful strife, intervening and often placing themselves between warring groups. They, not the politicians, were the real workers of South Africa's "miracle." COSATU member Alfred Woodington was an example.[7] In a standoff between angry ANC demonstrators and a police detachment whose tense commander had already ordered them to aim their weapons, Alfred approached him across the dividing no man's land armed with nothing but the orange Peace Accord vest with its two doves across his chest. As he approached he repeated quietly, "Do not fire. It's okay. I know these people, and I can calm them." And he did, preventing yet another massacre. Encounters like that were not uncommon.

The violence in our area was in townships where single-sex hostels housed Xhosa and Zulu migrant laborers, now being pressured to take sides. In some hostels, both groups had lived together for years but were now killing each other at the slightest provocation, each group trying to expel the other. Hostels housing mainly Zulu Inkatha Freedom Party (IFP) supporters were often located in ANC-supporting townships, and they became armed fortresses from which these men would sally forth bringing death to nearby homes or be attacked in turn by armed youths of the ANC

---

7. Congress of SA Trade Unions, allied to the ANC.

"Self Defence Units." One such situation was in Alexandra township. The IFP had infiltrated battle-hardened fighters and weapons into the hostels, and people walking in streets nearby became targets of snipers.[8] The local population had organized themselves, too. It was during one crisis between the two groups that I was called to try and mediate. Our key NPA volunteer there was Rev. Liz Carmichael, a quiet Anglican priest of prodigious stubbornness and courage. I found myself back in Alex Stadium where thousands of people had gathered fearing that an Inkatha attack was imminent. Some were arguing for a preemptive strike. We pleaded with them to hold off while we tried to make contact with the Inkatha commanders, which meant braving the dreaded hostels.

Armed men grudgingly allowed us through the barbed wire perimeter, and we asked to meet with their senior *indunas*.[9] I wondered how these patriarchal Zulus would respond to a woman, but Liz was undeterred. This was her NPA area, and she was going to see it through. We were taken down a maze of passages deep into the dark bowels of the massive building. More armed men. Filth was everywhere, and one wondered how human beings could live in these conditions. Finally, we found the commanders and were able to speak with them. I remember telling them that there were thousands of people at the stadium, convinced that the IFP was about to unleash their fighters, and there was great danger that they would strike out of fear of being attacked. I had experienced Inkatha's aggressiveness on a number of occasions so had little trust in them, but Peace Accord business required strict impartiality, and I thought I could detect, not so much aggression, as fear. These hard men seemed to be convinced that the crowd in the stadium was arming to attack and overwhelm *them*—and were asking why they should not strike first. We assured them that their fears were unfounded that day; their men could stand down. Then, hoping we had been convincing enough, we threaded our way out into the daylight and back to the stadium. There we conveyed the news that if people returned to their homes, no attack would happen. We knew that if we were wrong, people would die undefended that day, but we were not wrong. I came away utterly drained and with two thoughts: the first was how life or death hung daily by such slender threads; the second was sheer awe for the courage of Liz the priest who had no need to be there at all, except for her allegiance to the one who said, "How blest are the peacemakers" (Matt 5:9).

---

8. These Inkatha fighters were being trained at secret camps by SADF special forces. In some of the worst massacres, there were consistent reports of "whites with blackened faces" among the killers.

9. Chieftans.

The brutality of the internecine violence seemed to have no limits. Our monitors saw things no human being should have to look upon: dismembered and gouged bodies, dazed people crawling on the ground searching for an amputated body part, disembowelled infants, a taxi-load of dead, and they sometimes came back at the end of the day with glazed eyes, ashen and silent. Some asked me to write a prayer they could pray before setting out or refer to in stressful moments, and I did:

> A Peace Monitor's Prayer
> God of the nations and of all people,
> I ask that today you will be with me
> in the work that I must do.
> Let my heart be open and my mind clear,
> In my attitudes keep me fair,
> In my decisions make me wise,
> In my actions hold me impartial.
> If I encounter danger, give me courage,
> Under pressure keep me steady,
> Help me to treat each person
> as equally important to you.
> Hear my prayer that today
> not one of your children
> will die or suffer injury
> and that peace may prevail.
> Amen.

The Swedish government had sent a team of specialized trauma counselors to help monitors who were breaking under the strain. They were a great gift to us for many months, and there were many tears when they went home.

The "thin orange line" was sometimes stretched to the breaking point, and I instructed churches in my episcopal area to release their clergy for at least one day a week for "peacemaking or peacekeeping" work. Not all complied, but those colleagues and lay people who did were magnificent and could look back on those dangerous days knowing that they helped to birth the new South Africa.

Another dramatic encounter I was involved in happened in Kagiso township on September 16, 1990, and was not so much an NPA exercise as something of a "Methodist miracle." It was my second visit in a few days. Earlier, I had come with Bishop Desmond Tutu and his successor at SACC, Rev. Frank Chikane to these same dusty streets, under a pall of smoke from still-burning houses. Zulu hostel-dwellers had swarmed out of their hostels on a killing and burning spree, leaving scores of houses destroyed and many people dead. Wherever we went, crowds pressed us with stories of the horror they had endured. "Don't speak peace to us!" they shouted. "Give us guns or go away!" Now it was Sunday, and I was back in Kagiso accompanied by a group of courageous clergy. We had come to express solidarity with the victims of the raid. Our Methodist church was packed, and during the singing and crying we laid hands on grieving mothers who had lost loved ones and prayed for them.

Then came the sermon from the bishop—one of the many times when words threatened to fail me. But as I sought to console these people, my mind kept being invaded by a vision of the hostel where the violence had come from. I have seldom felt such a clear sense of being led. Did God not care also for those lonely migrant men? Was it not unscrupulous politicians who had preyed on their frustrations and fears and whipped them up into doing this? I began to speak about them: their lonely and desperate circumstances, far from their wives and children, often despised by the more educated and settled families around them. As I spoke, I sensed a response and, most remarkably, even some of the bereaved mothers were nodding as if their pain gave them an extra measure of empathy. Next, almost not believing my own words, I told the congregation that God needed someone to reach out to those hostel-dwellers to start building a bridge of healing between them and the people of Kagiso—and that I felt impelled to do that now. Announcing a hymn, I invited whoever felt similarly called to come with me. God would go with us, I said, then headed for the door.

Some seventy people joined me. We marched the mile or so singing the hymns of the faith, hoping they would signal our peaceful intentions. I was also grateful for the identifying cassocks and gowns of my fellow clergy and the bright red blouses worn by the Methodist women's movement. As we approached the fortified hostel, our hearts were in our mouths. Armed men patrolled the rooftops, and gun muzzles were visible in darkened, broken windows. Once in those gates there would be no easy way out.

But we sang our way through the gates and into the compound—surrounded now on all sides by hostel buildings and sullen armed men. Their leaders listened incredulously as we explained our desire for peace and reconciliation, asking their forgiveness for the years of marginalization they had suffered at the hands of the local people. The need for peace, the importance of families, both here and far away, the danger of being dehumanized by political agendas—these were the things we shared. Everything I said had to be interpreted into *isiZulu*, a slowing down process that may have helped in the danger-laden atmosphere: each phrase had two chances of being understood. And we spoke of God, the God of their ancestors and ours, who wished all of us to live in peace.

It didn't happen quickly or all at once, but after a time, the atmosphere began to subtly change. Weapons began to fall to sides and hands began to reach out to each other. Slowly the tense standoff gave way to something different. Voices began to lift in song, heads bowed in prayer. Fear and hate had given way to compassion and consequently a slender bridge had been built back into the hearts of these violent men, making a chance for future peace.

Driving home that day, I couldn't believe what had just happened. I was overwhelmed by awe at what God was capable of drawing out of us poor, fragile, and frightened creatures.

Such dramatic moments were few. In most cases, we had to think beyond peace as a *concept* and embrace it instead as a tough *process* involving painstaking steps: opening lines of communication, building trust, developing a problem-solving culture, agreeing on codes of conduct, and committing to being held accountable to those codes. Holding the peace committees together was a superhuman task. Initially tirades and walkouts were common, but over a period of two years, the stubborn impartiality of NPA staff, mediators, and monitors slowly began to win through. Antagonists began to recognize the humanity in one another, trust deepened, and grudgingly relationships began to be established between enemies. We were experiencing at close hand the birth pangs of a new South Africa.

In April 1993, Chris Hani, the most charismatic young leader of the black liberation struggle, was assassinated by a white man. The country teetered on a knife's edge as two million angry people marched in cities all around South Africa. As many as 200,000 of them came to his funeral in Johannesburg's 100,000-seat Soccer City Stadium. The burial was to be in a "white" suburb fourteen miles away. Clashes between angry ANC mourners and both whites and Inkatha supporters seemed inevitable. At the last moment, the ANC leadership recognized that they couldn't handle it and asked the Peace Accord to organize the logistics. Our RPC swung into action, holding at least twenty-one meetings with different parties in a matter of hours, arranging food for the thousands gathering in and around the stadium the night before, and organizing hundreds of buses to get them from there to the graveside afterward. We set up a Joint Operational Center (JOC), bringing leaders of all political, police, and military formations into one room.[10] The police agreed to keep some distance away from all activity

---

10. The JOC was manned by senior decision-makers from each party so that decisions could be made immediately without having to refer them. As sometimes happened in these surreal days, the person who the ANC appointed to the JOC found himself working with a Security Branch officer who had once tortured him in prison.

unless called in by the JOC, leaving the job to them and their monitors. That day, when a racial bloodbath could have erupted, fewer than twenty people were killed in the whole of South Africa. Tragic as those deaths were, the NPA and its peace committees had proved their worth.

Ahead lay the sternest challenge of all—South Africa's first democratic election. In our region, we would be monitoring as many as forty political meetings each night. Would the thin orange line hold?

22

Taking on the Guns

LATE IN 1993, I was sitting in our lounge in Johannesburg. Alan was on vacation from seminary, and he walked in saying, "I saw something on CNN about a hand-in of guns in Chicago. Why can't we do something like that here?" He had already written some thoughts down by way of a proposal, and I don't remember much discussion because the idea seemed to speak for itself. We were both involved in the National Peace Accord. The land was awash with guns, and political violence was still at horrifying levels—in our region, nearly four thousand people were killed in 1993 alone. What if, in addition to all that the Peace Accord was doing, there was a campaign inviting people to hand in their guns before the first democratic elections in April 1994? So began the story of "Gun Free South Africa," something many still think was my most quixotic, naïve, and foolish quest. Yet few memories bring me more satisfaction and gratitude.

Earlier I had set up a "Religious Bodies Sub-Committee" of our RPC to recruit and train peace-workers from churches, synagogues, mosques, and temples and to explore the unique role faith communities might play in making peace. Many fine faith leaders joined it, and eight of them now sat on the RPC itself. We organized peace-building workshops, created guides for preachers to use in their pulpits, and committed to recruit and train a thousand of the five thousand peace monitors our RPC needed for the coming election.

It was to this body in 1994 that I spelled out the vision of a Gun Free Election Campaign, proposing a two-week amnesty a couple of weeks before polling day for people to hand in firearms. The idea was initially met with incredulity and skepticism. One member pointed out that my suggested starting date of April 1 was appropriate for such a foolhardy quest—and given the timeframe, I soon found out that he was right about the date. But I persisted: "Guns are the symbol of all our fears; they now dominate life in South Africa," I said. Whether guns were used to wreak political violence on left or right, were stockpiled by fearful whites, or were at the heart of the massive spike in crime, the campaign would be a statement by the unarmed majority in this country that they refused to be held hostage and were determined to ensure peaceful elections. Why could we not do it? Slowly the group began to come around, and when I put it to the full RPC and promised them that the religious bodies would drive it, they gave it a somewhat bemused blessing.

At the request of the police, the idea soon expanded to a national hand-in, but when I lobbied a prominent ANC leader, he was adamant that he would never hand in "my Kalashnikov," nor would any ANC cadres, until after the elections. Power needed to be transferred first, and once that happened, he would be willing "to lead the march to hand in our AK-47s" himself. He unknowingly did us a favor because much as a Gun Free Election was to be desired, we soon found that we needed more time to organize the hand-in. Consequently, December 16, 1994, was chosen instead. One of the most divisive public holidays in the past dispensation and now named Reconciliation Day, it was appropriate for our purpose.[1]

How I was going to manage all of this, I was not quite sure. The months leading to the April elections had thrown up a pile of demanding responsibilities. In addition to my normal duties as a bishop responsible for one hundred clergy and some three hundred congregations, I was involved in a number of key processes. One was preparing for the five-hundred-strong World Council of Churches Central Committee coming to South Africa for the first time. Another was piloting a massive two-year process called "Journey to a New Land," designed to reshape and position the MCSA for the advent of democracy. Then I was still chairing most RPC meetings, which were becoming more frequent and tense as the election approached, as well as the very first Police/Community Relations Committee in South Africa.[2] I was also chairing the inter-church committee designing the great Thanksgiving service to be held in a Soweto stadium the day before Nelson Mandela was expected to be inaugurated as president. Ironically, the SABC now felt that I had an important word for the country because I found

---

1. Reconciliation Day was formerly known as The Day of the Covenant, a remembrance of the Boer victory over a Zulu army at Blood River in KwaZulu-Natal on December 16, 1838. Gatherings on that date had been occasions to whip up Afrikaner Nationalism and sense of manifest destiny.

2. Now regarded as commonplace, the idea of South African police officers sitting down with community members could not have been more foreign in 1993, but with the help of the humble but unstoppable activist Phiroshaw Camay and David Storey and an inter-party committee we were making slow progress, creating a template for Police-Community relations across the land.

myself being called to broadcast special messages every time new crises arose in relation to the countrywide violence.

It was a full plate.

In a statement released near the hand-in date, I said that GFSA had three main goals. The first was to open a debate South Africa had never had: on the culture of guns. This certainly happened—an early surprise was the wakening of a gun lobby that we didn't know existed. After I addressed a meeting in Durban, two white men identified themselves as from the South African Gunowners' Association (SAGA) and soon afterward an article appeared in *Man Magnum* magazine slamming my presentation and warning members that GFSA was determined to take their guns. From then on, SAGA never stopped attacking the hand-in project. Its followers sent a steady stream of letters to newspapers. Apart from the debate about whether civilian access to firearms made a society safer or more dangerous, gun owners were outraged that we were calling for licensed as well as unlicensed weapons to be handed in. We decided this because as many as 15,500 licensed firearms were being lost through theft or carelessness every month, most often ending up in the hands of criminals. Also, until recently only white South Africans had been permitted to own firearms; a focus on unlicensed weapons only would look like GFSA was discriminating against blacks. SAGA's regular attacks made sure that the issue of guns was seldom out of the media. They say there is no such thing as bad publicity.

Our second goal was to educate children to the dangers of guns. At GFSA's launch on November 3, an eight-year-old became the first child to hand in his precious toy gun, and this element of the campaign ballooned beyond all our expectations. Many of us were kept busy attending hand-ins at schools and youth clubs. It was especially moving to stand in a dusty Soweto school campus and see children handing in even the wood or wire "guns" they had fashioned for themselves. In some cases, we were able to give books in exchange, but most brought their toys in a spirit of real sacrifice. Thousands were handed in, and the toy gun phase climaxed on December 14, when a national store chain crushed their entire stock of "realistic" guns under a steamroller outside Johannesburg's city hall. I have since met some of those kids—now men and women—who say that the hand-in formed their thinking about guns for life.

The third goal was to "reduce the number of guns in circulation through the voluntary hand-in on Reconciliation Day." This was obviously the biggest challenge. In August, a small multi-faith delegation went to our new president to seek his endorsement: Would he let us issue a certificate of appreciation signed by him to each person handing in a gun? It was the first time I had visited Madiba in his new offices and was surprised to find the portraits of former prime ministers and presidents lining the anteroom where we waited. The new justice minister was present, and I asked him, "What are these guys still doing here?" He looked at the pictures and said, "Well Peter, they are our history," and then added with a smile, "and believe me, they *are* history!"

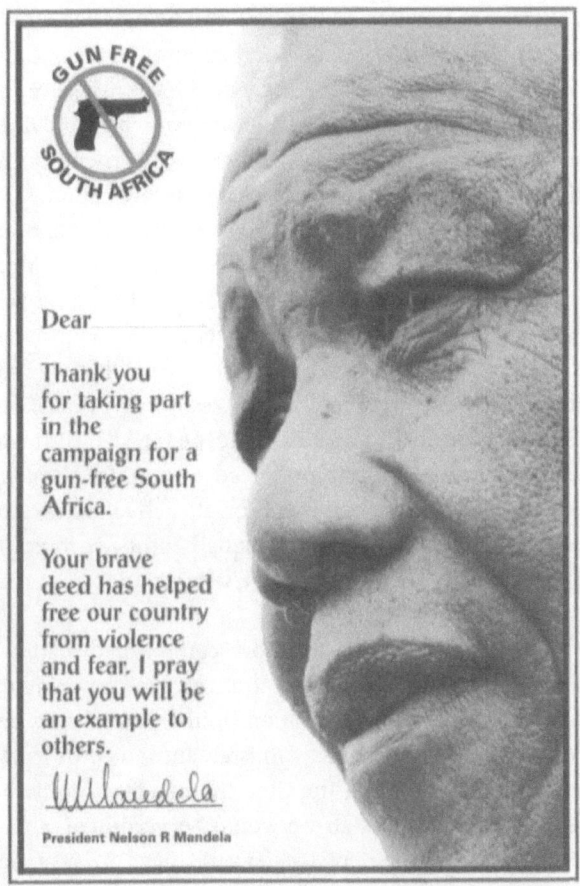

Mandela lends his weight to the campaign

When President Mandela came in, he looked tired and was wearing a comfy old pair of slippers. Listening to our presentation, he examined the documentation we had given him, and though our group covered the Christian, Jewish, and Muslim faiths, typically he wanted to know whether the Dutch Reformed Church was among our supporters. I replied that we had not had much luck with them. In the end we got his backing. He said the campaign was both "timely and necessary" and told us not to give up on the Afrikaans churches. Right away, we put in orders for the all-important certificates carrying his face and magic signature, with the words: "Your brave deed has helped free our country from violence and fear. I pray you will be an example to others."

We kept up a barrage of press releases, TV, and radio contributions, all aimed at persuading people that their trust in firearms was misplaced. "There is a difference between feeling safe and being safe," we would say. "Many more people have been robbed of their guns and worse, killed with their own weapons, than have successfully defended themselves against an intruder." Eighty percent of our population was not armed and did not want to live in an armed camp. There was still time to reverse our growing gun culture and help turn the tide toward a safe and secure nation.

Fundraising was tough. Some large corporations that showed enthusiasm in the beginning took fright when the campaign became controversial. We were promised free advertising by SABCTV and went ahead preparing a week of hard-hitting TV adverts to take us to hand-in day, but permission was suddenly withdrawn. We learned that the chairperson of the Public Interest Advertising Committee was part of SAGA and had waited until we had made the ad and then torpedoed us. Ultimately sixty-five corporate donors and trusts produced just under $175,000, while others donated office space, equipment, or attractive prizes. Apart from receiving the "Mandela Certificate," persons handing in firearms would be entered in a drawing with a $30,000 first prize and about thirty other smaller cash and in-kind prizes.

Getting the amnesty was a far more complicated matter. Without amnesty, the police would be obliged to arrest anyone bringing an unlicensed firearm to one of our reception points. Long hours spent with police lawyers, the relevant cabinet minister, and our own legal advisers brought no satisfaction, and all the time the hand-in date was drawing closer. Twenty-four hours was all we would be permitted, and it turned out that to achieve it Parliament itself would need to suspend the relevant laws. The problem was that Parliament was about to adjourn for its December break, and in the end it took a late-night phone call to the formidable speaker of the house to secure a commitment to get it done on the final day of business. The safety and security minister was at last able to announce a "twenty-four-hour indemnity" beginning midnight, December 15. We were cutting things very close.

Alfred Woodington hands in his AK-47 in the CMM Chapel on the first Reconciliation Day, 1994

At 8:30 AM on December 16, we held a special interfaith "hand-in service" in the CMM Chapel focusing on what we hoped would happen all around the nation. Leaders of different faith communities stood behind the altar to witness one of the peace-monitor heroes of pre-election days come forward with an AK-47 rifle and two grenades, weaponry he had kept hidden for many months in case he would have to resort to them. He had called me the night before, confessing to a deep struggle because he realized that the act of handing them over would also mean parting with his trust in the use of force, and he still found that difficult. It was therefore very moving to see him approach and to take his assault weapon and lay it on the altar. Some other people also came forward, and then the service was over and the waiting began. I found the inactivity hard to bear.

The results at the end of the day were not good.

By any ordinary measure the hand-in had failed. The enormous efforts we had made over the past months to move our nation in a new direction yielded a paltry 327 guns plus 6,800 rounds of ammunition and 200 other bits of lethal weaponry. I couldn't believe that in the whole nation, so few people had responded, and for a while I was gutted. Around me, others seemed less downcast, reminding me that "every gun taken out of circulation represents possible lives saved," and that this was "only the beginning," but it was a hard moment. The next day the *Star* carried an honest headline: "Millions Hanging on to Their Guns," but rather kindly told readers that I was unperturbed, reminding them of my earlier words: "Even if no guns come in today the campaign has already succeeded in its first objective—it has opened a debate on the growing gun culture in our land."[3]

I needed more reassurance than that, and it came in an odd way. The day after the hand-in, I received an anonymous call from an Afrikaans-speaking man saying that he was "tired of killing people," and asking me to come alone to a certain place where I would find "something I wanted." I asked why he hadn't made use of the amnesty, and he said he had been thinking about it but was only finally persuaded by the *Star*'s picture of "that guy giving you his AK." By then, the deadline had passed. Given the venom my leadership of the campaign had stirred up, especially among white males, the whole idea was risky, but something in his voice convinced me. I confess I watched the remote pick-up area for quite a time before approaching it, but it turned out that he had been true to his word. I found an SADF automatic rifle with a large supply of ammunition, plus a haversack full of hand-grenades. Very gingerly, I brought the dangerous load home and started telephone negotiations with the police about handing it in without being arrested myself. However disappointing the results overall, this was a powerful reminder that every weapon handed in could be the difference between someone's life or death.

From this inauspicious beginning, a movement was born. Gun Free South Africa has consistently punched well above its weight and won the respect of government. It has gone on to lobby successfully for "Gun Free Zones," a rejection of gun ownership rights in South Africa's new constitution, and gun control legislation that has reduced the number of firearms in circulation.[4] After the Firearms Control Act of 2000 was passed, compelling evidence emerged of a reduction in gun deaths based on figures from South Africa's four largest cities over the period from 2001 to 2004. In Cape Town, for instance, the firearm homicide rate almost halved: from 34.1 to 18.7 per 100,000.[5]

Was the campaign quixotic? Maybe, but for some reason that has never been a worry to me: it is the early days in a long journey, and we are not the first to tackle what seem to be impossible odds. The fact that cigarette

---

3. Susan Thomas, "Millions Hanging on to Their Guns," *Star*, December 17, 1994.

4. The gun lobby, assisted by America's National Rifle Association, fought hard to have a "Second Amendment-type" right inserted in the new democratic Constitution. GFSA opposed this and prevailed. Firearm ownership remains a privilege, not a right, and subject to stringent tests and conditions.

5. It has unfortunately spiked again recently, due to hundreds of guns collected in more recent hand-ins being sold to criminal gangs by a corrupt senior police officer who is now in prison.

smoking is now universally frowned upon as a public health hazard is due to more than five decades of determined campaigning against a powerful addiction and massive vested interests. Trust in violence is also addictive, and I have faith that in time the deadly relationship between people and firearms will be seen for the public health issue that it is.

23

Days of Grace

"Welcome to South Africa's day of grace!"

The words of a BBC anchor as dawn breaks over the Union Buildings in Pretoria are wonderfully appropriate. It is Tuesday, May 10, 1994, and we are about to witness our first democratically elected president take the oath of office. Getting our scarred nation to this place has required more than the usual supply of grace—perhaps the "grace upon grace" that Scripture speaks of.[1] The road has been arduous and deadly. South Africans, especially black South Africans, have come through hell to celebrate this moment.

Watching the event unfold on my TV screen, I see the leaders of the nations, the great and the good—and the not so good—assembling to be part of history. But they are not uppermost in my mind today. Instead, I am seeing flashbacks from the recent past, some horrifying and others awe-inspiring. They are mainly about ordinary people enduring excruciating horror or doing extraordinary things.

I think back to the atrocities I had seen two years before, where an Inkatha *impi* slaughtered forty-five children, women, and men in an orgy of killing.[2] I recall traveling to meet with survivors in a community hall and not being able to finish what I wanted to say. I broke down because there were no words for pain as deep as theirs—only tears.

I think of how terrifyingly slender was the thread holding us back from disaster after this massacre when Mandela's anger drove him out of negotiations, and how some church leaders shuttled back and forth across the land, sitting first with him, then President De Klerk, then Buthelezi and then doing it all over again. The future of forty million people was literally

---

1. John 1:16: "Out of his full store we have all received grace upon grace, for while the Law was given through Moses, grace and truth came through Jesus Christ."

2. Known as the Boiphetong massacre, it was perpetrated on June 17, 1992, and brought about the breakdown of talks between the ANC and the government.

in the hands of these three proud men. I marvel at how, in spite of the centrifugal forces tearing at them, each grudgingly came to accept that he was bound to the others by the mysterious alchemy of our nation's history—and perhaps, at this critical time, by a greater Providence.

I picture Chris Hani dead in his own blood and how the voice of a stricken Nelson Mandela came across the airwaves, slowly, harshly enunciating his people's shock and anger at the white man who had done this. Then, with the inspiration of a soul acutely tuned to the greater good, he spoke of the white Afrikaner woman whose vigilance ensured the perpetrator's arrest: a brief speech that saved the nation from disintegrating into chaos.

I think of 26,000 peace monitors nationwide, more than 90 percent of them black youth from volatile townships, going out day and night to form that thin orange line separating enemies, listening, calming, reasoning, and most times bringing a measure of peace. Alongside them I saw the faces of our international friends, public policing experts from Scotland Yard, trauma counselors from Sweden, United Nations monitors. I saw Elizabeth meticulously compiling the database of our six thousand regional peace monitors so we could contact them at any time—and trying to memorize some of their names so as to pray for them and our son David as he and others literally put their bodies between warring antagonists in dusty townships.

What other country anywhere, I ask myself, would virtually outsource its security to lawyers, churches, the business community, and township kids at the most dangerous moment in its history?

I remember the bomb that detonated two streets away from CMM just before the election, killing nine people, one of whom was on her way to our morning worship. Ninety-two people were maimed and injured. I remember how other bombs exploded in and around Johannesburg that week, killing and dismembering people as white extremists made their final cowardly effort to stave off the democracy they feared. And I remember the last massive explosion at Johannesburg's international airport on election day itself.

But I also recall the many Afrikaners, most of them once staunch supporters of the regime, who in these last years wanted to be part of something different. One was the Security Branch colonel I have written about earlier. I was once his target, but he never let us down. Others were civil servants. We were far apart in so many ways yet were finding each other around the shared challenge of bringing South Africa through to this moment.

I see in my mind's eye an elderly Zulu hostel-dweller who in the midst of a season of gruesome killings openly approached the gates of an enemy hostel. Convinced by the Rev. Mvume Dandala's Hostel Peace Initiative, this dignified migrant worker stood before his foes asking to see their leaders.³ He came with a request and a question: "My request is that if you kill me now, you will let my body go home to Zululand for burial." Then the question: "How many more of us have to die before the killing ends?" The guards at the gate were struck by his quiet courage. They took him in to their leaders, and the beginning of a new reconciliation between these tribal groups was born.

And now we are here at South Africa's "Day of Grace."

Early on April 27, Elizabeth and I had gone to the nearest polling station to vote. The sight that greeted us was deeply moving. Black people lining up for the first time with whites and knowing that when they went into the booth to make their X, their votes would have equal weight. Nearly a quarter century later, nobody bats an eyelid at the thought, *but you had to be there!*

Later in Soweto, armed with a newfangled cell phone and with bright orange Peace Monitor stickers on my car, I drove from one station to another, marveling at the miles-long queues of people waiting to do something they had never done in their lives. Soweto was quieter than I had ever known it. As I drove by, people waved happily at my Peace Car, and I remembered the not-so-distant past of burning buildings, tear gas, and rock-strewn streets, growling armored vehicles and roving bands of armed youths. All was now quiet. At one voting station deep in Soweto, the UN observer there grinned widely as I arrived and said, "I from Nepal," reminding me of just how many people around the world cared about our freedom. He could hardly speak English, yet he was getting on wonderfully with the Independent Electoral Commission (IEC) staff, monitors, and voters, and enjoying himself immensely. Everywhere I got the impression that our international guests had a sense of the immensity of these days, not only for South Africa, but also for the human project.

Only one ugly incident marred an otherwise miraculous first day. Driving with another monitor, I came across one of our Peace Cars stopped alongside a minibus with a large Peace Accord sticker on it. The car doors were open and so was the sliding door of the minibus. There were a number of men inside it, and one of our peace monitors was standing as if carved of stone, facing into the van. As we arrived, I caught a glimpse of guns pointing at him, then the sliding door was slammed shut and the minibus roared off.

---

3. Rev. Mvume Dandala was my successor at CMM and its first black superintendent minister. He came from the Eastern Cape, but because he had once served a church in KwaZulu-Natal, he was uniquely placed to be a bridge between his own Xhosa people and Zulu culture and concerns. Mvume's Hostel Peace Initiative was one of the unsung peacemaking triumphs of the early nineties. I recall watching a soccer match with him, the players being hostel-dwellers who had been killing each other just months before.

When our monitor got his voice back, he said that we had saved his life: "Those were Inkatha guys from Nancefield Hostel; they had a whole lot of guns on the floor, and they were forcing me to get in." It was worrying that a vehicle with peace stickers was being used for running guns into the hostel, but I thought better of giving chase and reported it in instead.

Conferring with Peace Accord monitors in Soweto during the first democratic election in April 1994

The drama wasn't over, however. Having fallen into a deep sleep, I received a call around midnight from Piet Coleyn, the director-general of Home Affairs. He was an old-guard civil servant and would normally have been in charge of the whites-only elections of the past. Now his department had to render logistical assistance to the new IEC. He was extremely stressed and put a surprising question to me: "Bishop, can you assemble five hundred church people at the Civic Center by 4 PM tomorrow?" He said that he had come out of a stormy meeting of the political parties at the IEC headquarters. There had been serious altercations between party representatives over real or perceived irregularities at counting stations and mistrust of IEC impartiality. The parties were demanding that there be another layer of "outsider monitors." The problem was that they couldn't agree on whom they could trust to do the job. "Then I had an inspiration," he said. "I asked them if they would trust the churches, and they all agreed. So can you help us? It could save the election." I immediately woke other church leaders, and we set in motion an all-night telephone chain to our clergy who in turn called their lay people. The plan was to get as many as possible to Johannesburg's Civic Center the next day.

That Thursday morning in Soweto, the voting remained peaceful. At some point, I stopped at the memorial where Hector Pieterson had been the first youth shot in the youth uprising on June 16, 1976, and two men recognized me. Full of smiles, one shouted, "Hello, Bishop! We have the vote now, Father! You can die now, your work is done!" I think I knew what he meant, but still . . .

The Civic Center was an unfortunate choice of venue given its location on a sort of island with rush-hour traffic roaring around it, but amazingly, not five hundred, but nine hundred people had arrived. They were crowded around the entrance to our venue, but a big padlock prevented entry. Fuming, I called Coleyn, who apologized and told me that the parties were still locked in negotiations. Could I bring the people back the next day—Friday—at 4 PM? I couldn't believe my ears. Here I was with nine hundred people, some of whom had traveled long distances. How would they react? With nothing but a bullhorn, and competing with the traffic noise, I tried to explain the situation: "I apologize for the inconvenience," I shouted, "but everyone at IEC is stretched to the limit. They still need us to save the election—just not today." The Rhema Bible Church in the suburbs would make a far less problematic venue, and I asked the crowd if they could gather again there the next day. With remarkable goodwill, they agreed. I said a prayer and reminded them: "We can be the difference as to whether this election succeeds or fails."

That night, again near 12 PM, the phone rang. Piet's voice was cracking with anxiety and fatigue. He was sorry about the disaster at the Civic Center, but it was important now that we get our people to the Rhema church by 9 AM rather than 4 PM. Once more the telephone chain was set in motion, and I tried to sleep, wondering how many would arrive. I needn't have worried: next morning a staggering 1,200 people waited expectantly in Rhema's megachurch sanctuary to hear what was required of them. After a further agonizing wait of two and a half hours, Coleyn and his team arrived. Following a couple of hours' training, the IEC expected our people to leave for 720 destinations immediately without having given much thought to the logistics involved, so a group of church leaders took over the entire operation. Calling in travel agents, they deployed over 1,100 people to polling stations across the country. Some went by car, others by air, and most arrived at their destinations the next day. Many slept in their cars for two or three nights, some in the clothes they had worn to the briefing. We received reports that the presence of the church had added credibility to the process while providing much needed assistance to exhausted election officials.[4]

The intervention was crucial to getting the election back on track. I was also proud of the contribution religious bodies had made to a peaceful election by putting one thousand peace monitors into the field, and of the Peace Accord as a whole: "We had 6,000 monitors in this region alone," I said, "Their highly visible presence was a powerful assurance to people that voting would be safe."[5]

And so to the Union Buildings and our day of grace.

Nothing could have prepared me for the waves of emotion now rolling over me. A kaleidoscope of sights, sounds, and experiences coming too rapidly to process: our brand new multi-hued national flag flying at every mast, and my heart feeling pride for the first time. Listening to the rich accents of the Chief Rabbi reading Isaiah's magnificent words:

> For a small moment I have forsaken thee . . . in a little anger I turned my face from thee for a moment . . . in righteousness shalt thou be established; thou shalt be far from oppression . . . and from terror . . . violence shall no more be heard in the land, nor ruin and devastation within thy borders.

and:

> Though the mountains shall depart and the hills be removed . . . never . . . shall the covenant of my peace be removed from thee.[6]

In the crowds on the lawns below, joy overflows, and South Africans of all races are baptized into a new spirit of oneness. A centuries-long yearning has at last been unleashed. A white man on crutches, struggling as they sink into the soft lawn, is lifted up by the mainly black crowd and passed over their heads to the front. White policemen smile and join in the dancing, and the roar rising from the packed masses when they hear Mandela's words echo those of God's prophet:

> Never, never, and never again shall it be that this beautiful land will again experience the oppression of one by another and suffer the indignity of being the skunk of the world.[7]

---

4. "Churches Mount Election Rescue," Wits Vaal Peace Secretariat Press Release, May 3, 1994.
5. "Churches Mount Election Rescue."
6. Portions of Isa 54:7–10 (Chief Rabbi's translation).
7. Nelson Mandela, "Inaugural Speech," Pretoria, May 10, 1994.

I go to my kitchen window with tears streaming down my face and look out toward a church on a nearby hill. It stands on the edge of what was once the vibrant black ghetto called Sophiatown. The racists who ejected its people back in the fifties renamed it *Triomf*. I remember that its priest was ejected, too. He wrote one of the early books damning apartheid, called *Naught for Your Comfort*.[8] All must have seemed lost then, but it was not: unknowingly, Fr. Trevor Huddleston had nurtured one of the champions of justice who was to help reshape South Africa. For eighteen months, he had faithfully visited an altar boy named Desmond Mpilo Tutu confined in a tuberculosis sanatorium. Young Desmond never forgot that care and the Christian compassion that inspired it. Looking up at the church on the hill, I am glad that the ageing Huddleston is back in South Africa for this season of grace, and wonder if he has any real comprehension of how powerfully that youth brought comfort—in the real meaning of the word, *strengthening*—to the millions of oppressed people now set free. "Thank you, God, thank you!" I say, over and over again.

The days following Mandela's swearing in were magical. In July, having taken up residence in the Presidency in Pretoria, he threw a banquet—not just any banquet, but one with a biblical touch. He invited those he called "veterans of the struggle" who had made some stand against apartheid in the fifties and sixties. When we drove up the winding drive for the first time in our lives, Elizabeth and I couldn't suppress our laughter because parked on the pristine grass of ex-President De Klerk's golfing greens were now rows of dusty buses from rural South Africa. From now on, those rutted greens would present a significant putting challenge! True to his character, Mandela had invited unsung and unrecognized stalwarts from all over the land. So many people had stood up to apartheid where it was most dangerous, in rural towns and farmlands far away from the media attention that could sometimes ameliorate the harshness of the "system." We sat near a man who was a Methodist and an ex-MK cadre. He had been interrogated and tortured for a year before spending twenty-two years on Robben Island. Now he was sixty-five years old, and this was the first official recognition of his sacrifice. Rather too lightly, I said, "So you're a 'graduate' of the island?" He replied, "No. That would make it sound too easy." Then he thought for a while and said, "But yes, I am a graduate; on Robben Island I learned to forgive."

When President Mandela got up to speak, he took a moment to upbraid us: "When you sang the National Anthem, you mumbled through the second

---

8. Trevor Huddleston, *Naught for Your Comfort* (London: Collins, 1956).

part,"[9] he scolded. "We are one nation now. Make sure you learn *Die Stem* for next time." His next few sentences took my breath away. "You honor me because of your presence," he said. "Please know that I am here only because of you." Then he continued: "I have invited you so you can see for yourself the place where the evil deeds of the past were planned." A rumble of anger rolled through the audience. Then he said, "I have also invited you here so that by your noble spirits, you can cleanse this place." All around us there was a collective intake of breath. You could see the straightening of old shoulders as this remarkable man who had sacrificed so much humbly affirmed *their* dignity and *their* sacrifice. It was a golden moment.

In September that year, President Mandela was to be our guest of honor at the MCSA Annual Conference, and I was touched and not a little nervous when I got a call from his office asking me to write his speech. I sweated long and hard on the draft, but knowing that he was at his best when he removed his spectacles and went off text, I left spaces for him to do so, and I think he enjoyed that. It needed to be a warm speech made amongst friends, and began: "To visit you is a personal homecoming, because of the role this great Church has played in my own life . . ." He delivered the speech much as I had written it but made one significant change: wherever I had spoken of the role of the churches, he spoke of "faith communities" instead, showing once more his desire always to include. I admit that I had written one paragraph as a kind of litmus test of his position on church/state relations, but he never hesitated, saying firmly, "All governments, no matter how democratic, need constructive criticism and advice from those who live close to the people and who listen for the voice of God. I ask you therefore to continue to play your prophetic role, always seeking to hold this nation and all its leaders to the highest standards of integrity and service."

---

9. The post-1994 National Anthem of South Africa is an amalgam of *Nkosi Sikelel' iAfrika* and *Die Stem*, anthem of the previous order.

The first Freedom Day, April 27, 1995: presenting a memento
made from melted-down guns to President Mandela

Days of grace continued under the benevolent and deeply human influence of Mandela. On April 27, 1995, our first officially marked Freedom Day, Elizabeth and I were at the Union Buildings for the ceremony. Somewhere in the program, I was to present Madiba with a small sculpture made out of melted-down guns from the hand-in. A couple of hundred "VIPs" jostled for the front seats facing the podium. It was easier to take seats in the back row of the platform, with the crowded lawns behind us. When the president arrived, he took one look at the set-up and said he would prefer that the podium be moved to the rear edge of the platform so that he could see the people on the lawns below. The result was that everyone had to turn their seats around, leaving the most pushy VIPs now in the back row and Elizabeth and I by sheer luck right next to him. Suddenly the last were first, the first last. As he sat down with a smile and polite handshake, I wanted to laugh out loud. As if it were the most natural thing in the world, this amazing man had just gotten us all to act out one of the more uncomfortable parables of Jesus (see Matt 20:16). I wished I could preach that kind of sermon, but you needed to go to prison for twenty-seven years to do so.

24

Search for Healing

NOW THAT WE WERE the world's newest democracy, one further task faced our weary nation. Forty years of apartheid cast a long dark shadow over all of us, and the challenge was how to exorcize the demons of our cruel and divided past. Many of those who had suffered demanded Nuremburg-type retribution for the architects and perpetrators of apartheid's ghastly atrocities, while the apparatchiks of the past regime predictably urged the nation to simply "forgive and forget." Getting this wrong could easily have driven the country back into strife or even led to a coup.[1]

Two high-profile court cases demonstrated to the "prosecute and punish" camp just how difficult it would be to secure convictions even of the most prominent perpetrators.[2] In any case, our wounded country needed all its resources to build newness rather than spend decades chasing the chimera of retribution. On the other hand, the call to forget by members of the previous regime was an outrageous presumption. We did not want to emulate the denialism of the American South. There, the slave-owning past lay buried but never gone, and we saw how it continued to seep to the surface of US society like toxic waste, poisoning the present and future. We wanted to leave no room for denial, no contested history.

Instead, our new nation determined to steer a course between the twin reefs of "prosecute and punish" and "forgive and forget," courageously asking a new question: Is it possible to both *remember* and *forgive*? It was South Africa's willingness to attempt that much tougher task that gave birth to the Truth and Reconciliation Commission (TRC). With its motto, "Without

---

[1]. Both the SADF and the police remained under white command, and armed right-wing extremists still threatened to "take back our land."

[2]. Lengthy prosecutions of both a former SADF chief and "Dr. Death" (the SADF medical officer who headed the biochemical unit accused of producing poisons for political assassinations) failed, partly because the regime had shredded millions of incriminating documents before the democratic government came to power.

truth, no peace, without forgiveness, no future," the TRC would be uniquely designed to enable victims to tell the stories of their pain and perpetrators to disclose their evil deeds. Provision would be made for reparation and rehabilitation for victims. Perpetrators could be granted amnesty provided they met stringent conditions.[3] Above all, it was hoped that beyond these two possibilities, there might be another: the opportunity for reconciliation. An additional element surprised the world and made South Africa's TRC like no other: it took the huge moral step of acknowledging that no matter how noble their cause, those in the liberation struggle who had committed gross human rights violations or atrocities would also need to seek amnesty and their victims be heard. Even though there was no moral equivalence between the inhumanities of apartheid and the struggle for a more human South Africa, as the new Justice Minister put it, "We would never want to see ourselves condoning human rights violations simply because they were committed by freedom fighters."[4]

Much would depend, of course, on the character and caliber of those chosen to adjudicate this search for truth and reconciliation, and in late 1995, I learned that President Mandela had appointed me to the panel that would select the TRC Commissioners. Our task was to deliver a list of twenty-five names to the president from which he would appoint up to seventeen commissioners. Those chosen would shoulder the awesome responsibility of bearing the pain of apartheid's victims, deciding the fate of its villains, and delivering the truth about the struggle years.

The selection panel consisted of four political party representatives and four others from civil society and the churches. The act required truth commissioners to: "Be of moral integrity with a commitment to human rights, reconciliation and the disclosure of truth; not a high-profile member of a political party; be able to make impartial judgments; and should not be an applicant for amnesty." Any South African could nominate candidates, and we were each given a pile of files containing details of the 299 nominations. Wading through them, I was appalled by some of the names: How could people so compromised have the cheek to let their names go forward? After a couple more meetings, in which the politicians sparred with each other inconclusively, I felt we needed to get honest, so I sent round a memo making it clear that I could not recommend anyone who by their action or inaction had implemented, or collaborated with, apartheid. To me that was a moral absurdity. Nor would I vote for anyone involved in the violent

---

3. Contrary to widespread claims by TRC detractors, only 849 of the 7,111 applications for amnesty were granted.

4. Dullah Omar, "Speech in Parliament," May 17, 1995, quoted in Alex Boraine, *A Country Unmasked* (Oxford: Oxford University Press, 2000), 69.

dimension of the anti-apartheid struggle, nor anyone—black or white—who in the bad years had been concerned simply with advancing an academic or professional career without engaging with the moral and political struggles of the day. "For people who ignored the pain of apartheid to think they can adjudicate on others' suffering is a terrible arrogance," I wrote. I wanted to ask them all: "Did you suffer?" or at least show me where you used the skills and position you gained on behalf of the oppressed. There was also the issue of *memory*: "Many nominees were babes in arms when some of the worst evils were perpetrated, but now put themselves forward as 'experts.' I can't see how they could possibly empathize with victims or understand the impersonal forces which drove some of the evil-doers." Finally, I was uncomfortable with the degree of self-promotion among many nominees. "Those who promote themselves in order to get onto the Commission will use the hearings for the same purpose," I said. The TRC was not about them; it was about those who endured suffering and those who bore guilt. In my voting, I would be looking for some humility and selflessness.

Having delivered my soul, I wondered how on earth we would achieve consensus. After we had each narrowed our preferences down to forty names, we could begin to decide who should be interviewed. The interviews were held in public and were variously absorbing, boring, and troubling. We were struck by just how many South Africans had amazing stories to tell and how rich were the people-resources of our land. Equally, there were still some who seemed to think that long lists of academic achievements somehow qualified them for the task. One professor seemed surprised to be asked whether he had ever been a member of the Afrikaner *Broederbond*, wondering why that was relevant.[5] We also needed to probe uncomfortably into the sensitivities of some who had endured long spells of detention and torture. When we invited one prominent candidate to speak about his experience, it was clear that his wounds were still too fresh. Listening for months to multiple stories of similar suffering might undo him.

I began to appreciate how shrewdly the panel had been designed. The politicians had instructions from their principals to push certain names, but more often than not, they were checkmating each other. When they failed to get a candidate favoring their faction, they realized that the next best thing was someone who would at least be fair and impartial. That was when those of us who were non-party appointees could suggest names more widely

---

5. The *Afrikaner Broederbond* or "Band of Afrikaner Brothers" was a secret society of politicians, academics, church leaders, and other elite Afrikaners who were the intellectual driving force behind the apartheid regime's policies. They were also the gatekeepers: no Afrikaner came into political leadership unless first approved by the Broederbond.

acceptable to all. Another development that impressed me was how attitudes to certain high-profile candidates changed. Some panelists were meeting people like Bishop Desmond Tutu face-to-face for the first time in their lives, rather than the caricatures they had known in the media, and were frank about how these encounters affected their thinking. Toward the end, we all had a fairly good idea of who would have made the most outstanding "first team," but considerations of race, gender, region, profession, and language made compromises inevitable. When we finally reached consensus and sat back in weary relief, one member said, "Hey, guys, I hope you won't ever tell my party who I voted for. It wouldn't go well for me!"

I am an unabashed champion of the TRC process. I followed it, participated in it, defended it in my newspaper column, and have spoken about it in every corner of the world.[6] It may not have been perfect, but I believe it to have been the most magnanimous and healing process any nation has devised for dealing with a shameful past. The awe with which it is regarded internationally is unquestioned, yet the fashion in today's South Africa is for mostly young black South Africans who never lived through those days to deride it as a "soft option" that let off the main perpetrators—the whites—far too cheaply. I hope its critics will think again, or at least tell us what they would have offered in its place. When Mandela took office, the most powerful military in Africa and a massive police force were still under white control. The agreement to transfer political power peacefully was an almost miraculous achievement, but without the offer of magnanimity in return for truth, it could not have happened. Thousands more would have died.

The TRC has also been criticized for being "religious," but in our context, that was not inappropriate. South Africa may rightly be a secular state, but South Africans in the main are not secular people. I mean no disrespect for the law when I say that some wrongs are just too big for law to handle. The travail of our history did more than produce punishable brutalities: it lacerated our souls and corroded our humanity, so the model we needed was one of grace. It is significant that in the most searing TRC hearings when victims broke down while telling their stories, the audience sang hymns—not struggle songs—to help them through. Those who brought their pain to the TRC were looking for more than a verdict or even reparation: they wanted healing, and this may be why it was more appropriate for Desmond Tutu, a priest with a pastor's heart, rather than a judge, to lead the commission.

---

6. I authored a regular op-ed column called *Faith and Life* for the *Sunday Independent* newspaper.

Of course, no one can force repentance on anyone else, but the TRC did the next best thing—it created a kind of "sacred space" in which contrition, if expressed, would find hospitality rather than rejection. It was up to perpetrators to decide whether they would use the gift of that space to begin the healing of their guilt or simply follow the letter of the law to escape prison. I saw both. When hearings contained expressions of deep contrition and when—amazingly—someone would say, "It is not easy, but I must forgive," the whole nation breathed in the new life set free by those words. Victims who found the magnanimity to forgive—and Desmond Tutu reminds us that more often than not they did—seemed to enlarge the heart of the nation itself. We were witnessing a new kind of South Africa being born.

On the other hand, it was galling to listen to a portly mustachioed ex-general reciting his misdeeds—including the shooting of women and children in a cross-border raid—in a toneless, almost defiant monotone while the families of some of the dead sat just a few yards away, pain etched into their faces. He didn't once meet their eyes as they heard the details of their loved ones' deaths for the first time, and with such lack of shame one was tempted to ask, "What's the point?" Yet, even in those circumstances I sensed *something* happening. As he recited his cruelties, this man who once struck fear into others began to look more and more *ordinary* and *banal*; he seemed to shrink and become *little* before our eyes. When the hearing ended without any *rapprochement*, the family got up and walked past him and one of them said it all: "*Suka Wena!*" ("Get lost!"). The hoped-for confession and forgiveness may not have occurred, but now he was known; he would no longer haunt their nightmares and was feared no more. The importance of that new freedom cannot not be overestimated.

Of course, the TRC had some design faults. A bad mistake was to grant immediate amnesty to perpetrators who met the required criteria, while leaving the victims' reparations and rehabilitation to a slow-moving Parliament increasingly distracted by other priorities.[7] Another failure is that it should have gone deeper into our society. I believe that TRC-type hearings should have been carried through to every town and village and every township in the land. Only the churches could have facilitated such local hearings. They had the trust of the people as well as the infrastructure to ensure it happened in every one of those places, but we were very tired.

---

7. Once Thabo Mbeki became president, I feared that reparations and rehabilitation for victims of apartheid would take a back seat. He was an ex-exile, and I had found little interest among returned exiles in the suffering of their "internal" compatriots during their absence. They still perpetuate the myth that it was primarily their work outside the country that had brought about the end of apartheid. The failure to follow through with the TRC's recommendations in this regard is a moral disgrace.

It is sad that we failed to use this remarkable instrument of healing and reconciliation in an ongoing process. A damning criticism lies with the government for being slow to prosecute perpetrators who were refused amnesty, as well as those who failed to come before the Commission. The supreme sadness, however, is not about the TRC, but about those South Africans who should have taken it most seriously. Instead of attending the hearings and in spite of the searing daily TV and radio reports, most whites turned their backs on the TRC and the challenges it posed for their own lives. I am ashamed that they did, and if we whites are feeling marginalized now, it is perhaps a deserved consequence of that apathy and denial. The truth is that contrary to today's conventional wisdom, the TRC never failed South Africa. It was white South Africans, a weary church, and a distracted Parliament that failed the Truth Commission.

In the summer of 1998, I was called back from the USA once more, this time to give evidence against ex-President Botha himself. Botha had spurned coming before the Truth Commission, claiming that he had nothing to confess and that Afrikaners "asked forgiveness of nobody but their God," thus laying himself open to a criminal charge. My evidence was needed to show that the 1988 bombing of Khotso House was a gross human rights violation because of the people it injured and may have killed. Botha's minister of police and his top police general had already told the TRC that the SACC headquarters had been bombed on his orders, but the TRC legal team had also called the regime's most infamous assassin, Colonel Eugene de Kock, to clinch their case.

Just before testifying, I had a happy reunion with Desmond, and we shared the sense of wonder at how the wheel had turned since those bruising encounters with Botha in the 1980s. The prophetic warnings of those years, often made at the end of hope's limits with nothing but the promise of a just God to lean on, had come true. This once all-powerful ruler, called the "Big Crocodile" by fearful cabinet ministers, was now "the accused," standing in the dock before a black magistrate. He, more than any other apartheid ruler, had tried to crush the witness of the church, first with the Eloff Commission, and later with the destructive violence of a massive bomb. Now he would have to sit and listen to the consequences of his actions.

In court, I found myself sitting right next to the man whose nickname was "Prime Evil." Colonel Eugene de Kock had been brought from jail where he was serving 212 years and two life sentences for over 100 state-sponsored murders. The frightening thing about him was how ordinary he looked with his nerdish thick-lensed spectacles; he was anything but the image of a ruthless assassin. P. W. Botha, large and still intimidating, occupied the dock just a few yards away. When my turn in the witness box came, I testified to the horror, the incredible destruction, the bloodied victims of the explosion, and the miracle that nobody had been killed. I called it the most violent act of terrorism by the apartheid state against the church of God. Then "Prime Evil" described how he and his team planted and detonated the bomb. He was clear that the orders to "destroy Khotso House so it could never be used again" came from Botha himself. De Kock was scathing about the "cowardly" politicians who ordered men like him to do their dirty work. Desmond Tutu testified to the extraordinary lengths the TRC had gone to in trying to make it as painless as possible for P. W. to come before them. He ended his evidence with an appeal, saying that P. W.'s government had caused "deep, deep anguish and pain and suffering" to many people. "If Mr. Botha was able to say: 'I am sorry that the policies of my government caused you pain.' Just that . . . that would be a tremendous thing and I appeal to him." Defiant to the last, Botha made no response.

There was a lighter moment. At 3:30 PM that day, both prosecution and defense suddenly indicated to the magistrate that they needed a little more preparation. Court was adjourned, and everyone made a hasty exit. The real reason was that an important rugby match was about to start in a nearby stadium. I was walking to my car when Desmond's chauffeur-driven Merc stopped next to me: "Jump in, Petros!" he shouted. "We're going to watch the rugby." And we did. The two of us sat in the cramped VIP stand—Desmond the only black person in sight—surrounded by burly Afrikaners. They greeted us politely enough when we arrived, but as they cheered on their local heroes, I had little doubt whom they supported in the other match going on in the magistrate's court down the road. That night I emailed Elizabeth: "Only in South Africa could we be in court one moment with an ex-State President, the world's worst killer, and a Nobel Laureate and then go off to watch rugby with a bunch of Afrikaners who could not be more polite when the Arch comes in!" I have no recollection of who won the rugby match.

Botha was found guilty and sentenced to a fine of two thousand dollars or twelve months' imprisonment, plus a further twelve months, suspended for five years. However, a higher court later upheld an appeal based on a small legal technicality, and Botha escaped punishment.[8] Before the verdict, I had written to friends that it really didn't matter because enough of the truth about his deeds had now emerged. However, I was discovering how deeply my feelings were affected by encounters like this. To the many friends who had been praying for this trip, I wrote, "I went up to the old man, greeted him with a handshake, gave evidence against him and then

---

8. Alex Boraine has the full story of what led up to Botha's subpoena and of the trial and aftermath. Boraine, *A Country Unmasked*, 188–220.

sat very near him for three days. There is no desire for retribution, but the experience did bring back the intense feelings of those days. They are quite indescribable and destructive to one's well-being and emotional health. Sleep has been hard to come by since."

I was not alone in this. The truth is that there were few unwounded souls in South Africa. Desmond Tutu called his fellow TRC Commissioners "wounded healers" who shared a costly privilege.[9] For the rest of us who paid attention, the memories stirred by the TRC hearings may have been hard to bear, but that is how it should be with difficult truths: such truths are the only path to newness and true healing. We will never know how many people from different sides of the struggle found healing because of the TRC. Nor can we know what might have happened to our future without a TRC at all. What we can be sure of is that never before in human history has any broken society been so willing to trust the healing of its past to something beyond the law and its retribution, something essentially *spiritual* at its heart. As the Apostle Paul said of the Spirit's work long ago, "There is no law dealing with such things as these" (Gal 5:23).

---

9. Desmond Mpilo Tutu, "Foreword," in vol. 1, *Truth and Reconciliation Commission of South Africa Report* (Cape Town: CTP Book Printers, 1998), 1–23.

25

America the Vulnerable

IN MID-1997, I RETIRED as bishop.[1] Leadership needed to pass to a younger generation, and Elizabeth wisely said, "We can think about something new." American friends had seen what the wear and tear of the "bad years" had done to us both and wanted to help with healing. They invited us for an eighteen-month stay in the USA, with me teaching at two seminaries and pastoring a large United Methodist Church (UMC) congregation.[2] While we were there, I was offered a professorship at Duke University Divinity School in North Carolina, and this stretched our sojourn in the United States to nine happy years.

Elizabeth and I enjoyed America. I had traveled there many times since 1966 to preach, teach, and engage in anti-apartheid work, and she had sometimes accompanied me. Now, in addition to teaching at Duke, I found myself speaking all over the US, visiting some 140 cities. There was enormous interest in the recent South African "miracle," but I found my listeners equally curious about my take on the state of their nation. They sensed that any critique I might have would be coming from a friend.

---

1. A bishop in the MCSA episcopacy is a function, not a status. Bishops are elected by those they serve and face reelection at regular intervals. The title "bishop" is relinquished when the term ends.

2. I am deeply grateful to Asbury Seminary, the Methodist Theological School in Ohio, Calvary UMC in Nashville, and Duke University Divinity School for their hospitality to Elizabeth and me.

Preaching at a United Methodist Annual Conference in Ohio

Most were unaware of the startling parallels between our histories. The first European settlers in North America and the Cape of Good Hope arrived within a few decades of each other, to be met by cautious hospitality from the indigenous inhabitants. Both settler groups presumed the superiority of their culture and religion, confident in their sense of "manifest destiny" and using the Bible to justify their presence as "Christianizing" influences. Both soon fell into conflict with indigenous peoples over land and divergent understandings of ownership, with settlers trekking inland in covered wagons and dispossessing the inhabitants mainly by trickery or force. Both used slaves from other lands for labor and resisted their liberation, and both fought bloody civil wars among themselves about the right to their "way of life" and the future of the indigenous people and slaves among them.[3] Both emerged as modern industrial nations, dominating neighboring economies and cultivating powerful spheres of influence.

Of course there were differences in demographics and scale: South Africa's whites never numbered more than 22 percent of the population, while in the US, conquest, disease, and repeated waves of white immigration reduced Native Americans and the African American slave descendants to minorities.[4] Politically, South Africans dominated a subcontinent, but America

---

3. Slaves in the Cape of Good Hope were mainly Muslims brought from the Dutch East Indies, now Indonesia. They totalled around seventy-one thousand compared with the nearly four million West Africans brought to America. They were set free by Britain in 1834.

4. That was in 1904. Today whites constitute less than 10 percent of South Africa's

came to dominate a world, which meant that whatever happened in the US was seldom a domestic matter only: the old truism still held that "when a president sneezes in the White House someone on the other side of the world catches a cold." I urged my listeners to remember it.

I spoke of Elizabeth's and my wonderment at contemporary American society. We observed how hard people worked and the way life was ordered around kids and sport and pets and summer camps and weight loss and school outings and fitness and TV and little league and big cars and obsessive wellness and buckets of sentiment and truckloads of patriotism and so many *commodities*, so that it seemed that nothing was not for sale. Outsiders looking in might not be sure quite what to make of it all, but there was no doubt that America was a force of nature on our planet.

American religion fascinated us too, with every weird and wonderful version on show. The amount of primitive fundamentalism was staggering for such an advanced society, and there was a whole genre of preachers whose TV programs were platforms for undisguised extortion. Yet, beyond the antics of televangelist hucksters, we found across the nation a deep pool of genuine piety and faithful discipleship, and there were American churches where I heard some of the best preaching in my life. We also found friends in Christ as close and precious as any we had ever known. I had questions, of course, like, "How come more US Christians go to church on Mother's Day than Good Friday?" And coming from a Methodism that banned the national flag from its sanctuaries, I wondered what Jesus, murdered by the Roman state, would think about having to tolerate Caesar's banner a few yards from the pulpit in his Father's house. To what extent had American Christianity been co-opted?

---

population. In the US, people of color are expected to be in the majority by 2040. Hispanic Americans will by then be the largest group of "non-white" Americans, with African Americans expected to be between 13 and 20 percent of the population.

Distinguished Professor: with Elizabeth at Duke University
Divinity School in North Carolina

A Shameful Geography

"No country has a monopoly on racism," I used to say, "but you and I share a particularly shameful geography: we come from racism's two favorite places—apartheid South Africa and the American South." In both places, racism was more than prejudice, more than crude notions of white supremacy. It had become *systemic,* so deeply ingrained and such a powerful driver of our cultures, that it was intrinsic to the social fabric itself. Beyond simply practicing race discrimination, many of the systems by which we lived and worked *depended on it in order to function.* Every sphere of life—the economy, politics, the criminal justice system, education, health and welfare, the shape of our cities and social life, the practice of religion—everything bore the marks of a prejudiced history and was still tainted with it.

When practices become systemic, they bypass the conscience, giving their practitioners a free pass. At the height of apartheid's cruelty, foreign tourists visiting my church would regale me with stories of the beauty of my land and the hospitality of our people. "We don't know what the fuss is about," they would say, "we've stayed on Afrikaner farms and seen how they treat their black workers. They seem to be kind to them." My response was: "That may be true, but you see, whites can afford to be kind in our personal encounters with blacks *because we let our institutions do our sinning for us.*" Blacks could never live next door to us, attend school with us, compete or even train for the same jobs, earn commensurate salaries, or marry our children. There were laws for all those things. Our prime minister could tell the world that apartheid was simply a policy of "good neighborliness"—all the while using the draconian powers of a police state to ensure that the "neighbors" he spoke of were kept firmly in their place.

Furthermore, systemic racism is far more difficult to uproot than we realize, lingering long after the laws have gone. Jim Crow and legalized apartheid may be things of the past, but their legacy of alienation still festers in society's structures and in its soul. The apartheid laws of South Africa were struck down two decades ago, but every city stubbornly remains a "tale of two cities." Spatial apartheid, carefully designed to separate, still rules, still divides, still discriminates. The same is true for American cities sixty years after Dr. King marched for justice.

This is why the self-serving white objections to the Black Lives Matter (BLM) protests that swept the US in 2020 simply served to underline why BLM had to happen: of course, "all lives matter," but after denying that truth for 350 years, whites do not sound convincing raising it now. Desmond Tutu often said about us whites that "the only person you can't wake up is the one who is pretending to be asleep." There is hope however: in addition to the scale and largely nonviolent character of the BLM demonstrations, young whites seemed to "get" what systemic racism is about and joined the struggle to root it out.[5] Perhaps at last there is a generation in the dominant culture who want to listen, learn, and act.

I also warned my hearers about the dangers of nationalism and exceptionalism. Most of us love our homeland, but something happens to people fed on a diet of perpetual self-adulation. The consequence of being told *ad nauseum* that ours "is the greatest nation in the world" is that people tend to believe it, losing touch with our national frailties. Then, when our "greatest nation" lets us down or fails to play to our self-image, disillusionment is rapid, and the resultant cracks can be exploited.

---

5. In spite of efforts by the Trump administration to paint the BLM demonstrations as "destroying our cities," the number of violent incidents compared to the nationwide scale of the protests was miniscule. See Harmeet Kaur, "About 93% of racial justice protests in the US have been peaceful, a new report finds," *CNN*, September 4, 2020, https://www.cnn.com/2020/09/04/us/blm-protests-peaceful-report-trnd/index.html.

The Populist Virus

The first two decades of the twenty-first century have not been kind to liberal democracies. Even before the crash of 2008 and before COVID-19 cast its fearful infection across the world, another disease was eating away at them from within. Right-wing populism—the "re-fracturing" of humanity—has taken hold in many countries, reversing the advances in world comity achieved so painfully since World War II. All societies have an ugly *alter ego* of extremist politicians and hate-mongers, but they have tended to be confined to the margins, tolerated and largely ignored. Social compacts and democratic institutions, designed to order the nation's discourse more or less fairly and in a civil manner, have served to hold them in check.

All that changed at the turn of this century when post-truth relativism and social media found each other. A cultural trend absent of any ethical constraints and a technology without conscience conspired to gift extremism with the loudest megaphone the world has ever seen. Suddenly there were no rules, and the new freedom to invent one's own "alternative truths" and realities was weaponized by a worldwide web with the power to spread anybody's hatreds into everybody's home. It was soon clear that regardless of all the good it promised, cyberspace was much more readily captured and dominated by the loudest, crudest, most hate-filled voices. Racism, nativism, xenophobia, and separatism were right out there with all the other "isms" clamoring to spread their poisons, and they found fertile ground in the USA, especially among white people fearful of change.

A moment that exposed how dangerous this had become in the US was January 20, 2009, when a talented, beautiful, and admired black family took up residence in the White House, claiming it for the first time as the house of *all* the people. For many of us, it was as if Americans had demonstrated at last that they could look beyond race and skin color to talent and character. Yet, in the very moment that hundreds of thousands joyfully thronged the Mall to hear Barack Obama take the oath of office, something sinister was stirring. It turned out that a significant slice of America was *enraged*. It was as if this black family had committed trespass by entering that house, ignoring the "right of admission reserved" signs that had stood so long over its door. A large swathe of conservative opinion-makers and white Americans simply refused to accept a first family that didn't look like them—it *wasn't right*. Black Americans, after all, were surely not *really* Americans?

There is a direct line between these developments and Trumpism. The confluence between post-truth cynicism, the internet's moral vacuum, and white fear of losing control over American identity opened a space for someone like him to emerge. His shrewd use of social media to outflank traditional channels of communication and engage directly with masses of uneasy and troubled Americans did the rest. *"No Twitter, no Trump"* might be overstating it, but his use of that platform will forever be identified with his populist presidency. It is also unlikely that the flood of support for him among white voters would have been so strong had that black family not dared to occupy the White House.

America is learning the hard way how dangerous it is to tolerate the intolerant. The Trump years made any resolution of the nation's racial and economic injustices much more difficult and dangerous. We know not to have too high expectations of politicians, but Trump's ignorance of his own nation and the wider world was matched only by the arrogance with which he treated both. His contempt for all human beings except himself made him incapable of any relationship that didn't serve his ambitions. His inability to empathize with others' suffering meant that whatever the number of COVID deaths, he has yet to show any sign of being moved. Whether in his governing, money-making, or philandering, men and women were there to be used, then cast aside. He played the quintessential schoolyard bully who cannot be liked and therefore must be feared. Dominance was all. When leaders begin appearing on flood-lit balconies to bask Mussolini-like in the adulation of their followers, those of us with long enough memories said, "Beware America: down that road lies fascism."

The fact that President Trump and his corrupt family dynasty were unseated by the 2020 election does not end this danger. Seventy-four million voters supported his brand of right-wing populism, many of them with cult-like devotion and seemingly untroubled at being pawns of his authoritarian ambitions. The Biden administration now in place has the enormous task of restoring truth and dignity to the nation's leadership, as well as taming a murderous pandemic that Trump allowed to run amok and rescuing the economy from maybe its worst calamity ever. It will have to do so in the shadow cast by the events of January 6, 2021, when a beaten bully lashed out and incited his followers to march on the nation's Capitol and "show strength."

The attack that followed had an eerily almost identical forerunner in South Africa in 1993. During the multi-party negotiations led by Nelson Mandela and the regime's leader, F. W. de Klerk, three thousand neo-Nazis and other white racists, many of them armed, outraged by the possibility of a multi-racial, human rights-based democracy emerging from the talks, overran the police cordon and smashed an armored vehicle through the doors of the negotiation venue. They poured in behind it, and for two tense hours, while delegates and staff took cover in meeting rooms, they marauded through the building, trashing it, urinating on furniture, and searching for Mandela and de Klerk, talking of killing the former as a "terrorist" and the latter as a "traitor." The event made clear how razor-thin the line was between a peaceful transition to democracy and utter disaster. After the attackers finally departed, escorted by hastily reinforced police units, the multi-party delegates immediately reconvened and soundly denounced the "rape of a lawful and legitimate negotiating process." With new urgency, it resolved "to accelerate the process of negotiations so as to bring about a democratic constitution for South Africa that will ensure peace, prosperity and protection for all."[6] The good news is that in spite of this attack and a further attempted right-wing coup, South Africans of all races rallied against extremism and continued to propel their country into freedom.[7]

The shameful scenes in the Capitol on January 6, 2021, are now burned into America's consciousness and should be more than enough to give it pause. Like the outrage in South Africa nearly thirty years ago, the assault on the Capitol cracked "America the Beautiful" wide open and revealed it to be much more "America the Vulnerable." It offers the American people opportunity to step back from the precipice and to reflect on how close they came to disaster.

But will they?

---

6. "Resolution of Condemnation and Outrage at the Violent Attack on Negotiating Process accepted by the Negotiating Council on Friday 25 June 1993," para. 3, 4, 5.2.

7. The similarities between these two historical events are further seen in the police's response to the rioters. Regarding the South African attack, "Mr. Mandela asserted tonight that the police would have fired their guns if the protesters had been black, but Government officials defended the restraint, saying that if the police had challenged the heavily armed invaders they might have started a bloodbath." Bill Keller, "White Separatists Storm South African Negotiations," *New York Times*, June 26, 1993, https://www.nytimes.com/1993/06/26/world/white-separatists-storm-south-african-negotiations.html.

26

A Church the World Might Take Seriously

IN THIS DANGEROUS AND surreal time, I have listened for the witness of the American church, but the silence has been deafening. By "church," I do not mean right-wing evangelicals whose Faustian bargain with candidate Trump promised him religious "cover" so long as he met their political demands. As Jesus might have said, "They have their reward already" (Matt 6:2, 5). Nor do I mean those who have grown their megachurches by marketing a "prosperity-friendly" Jesus and a challenge-free gospel. They too have their highly visible rewards in grand mansions and private jets. Both give Jesus a bad press, and their silence would be a relief.

Nor do I mean the isolated voices of courageous preachers like Dr. William Barber who seem to stand almost alone in the pulpits of the land and whom I salute for their prophetic bravery.

The silence I cannot understand is that of the "mainline" churches—churches with theologies forged on the anvil of centuries of witness in all sorts of testing contexts. Why have these seasoned churches retreated so cravenly from the public square, leaving the field to religious apologists for the powers? Do they feel that they "did their bit" in the Civil Rights era? Have they settled into comfortable irrelevancy? Is pastoring these days simply caring for the personal needs of their congregants and managing a shrinking franchise for their denominational leadership?

How will history judge the United Methodists for literally tearing themselves apart in a family fight about human sexuality, yet maintaining a resolute silence while a hate-mongering president set a whole nation against itself?[1] Could they not look up from their own navels long enough to see what a real moral crisis looked like?

---

1. At time of writing the UMC's SEXIT debate appears to be nearing its tragic denouement making a nonsense of the word "United" in its name and its "Open Doors and Open Hearts" brand. The question arises as to whether a church denomination

Back in 2003, when I queried the absence of any prophetic response to the disastrous road the Bush-Cheney administration chose after 9/11, I found UMC pastors cowed by feelings of irrelevancy on one hand and fear of losing members and money on the other. I was told that "we no longer have the influence we used to have," or "half of my congregation would up and leave if I spoke out." Where did this thinking come from? The notion that you can be a faithful preacher without some members "following no more" is un-Jesus-like (John 6:66; 12:42; Gal 1:10). With regard to lost influence, since when did the biblical prophets check their "influencer index" before speaking out? Ezekiel was told that "whether they listen or fail to listen—for they are a rebellious people—they will know that a prophet has been among them" (Ezek 2:3–5 NIV). Our task is to tell the truth—no more and no less—and to leave the "influencing" to God. Faithful witness can be costly, but at least the price paid might be proof that the world is taking the church seriously. I think of, say, the Central Methodist Mission in Sydney, Australia, under outspoken preacher Rev. Alan Walker, where the prime minister was known to ask each Monday, "What did Walker say yesterday?" Or the SACC in South Africa, whose witness the Botha regime tried to silence first with an intimidating tribunal and then a bomb—in each case failing to do so.

I long for America's "mainline" churches to find their public voice again, to break free from the paralysis of their corporatized structures and the terror of membership loss. Fear is a disempowering pulpit companion: it is a visceral, not a theological, thing. The casting out of fear, on the other hand, is profoundly theological. It happens when we love God's people and God's world with the love of Christ so passionately that we refuse to spare them the truths—no matter how painful—that can save them. That kind of love drives out fear (1 John 4:18 NIV).

How then may our churches recover the authority and courage required for faithful public witness? Quite simply, the most important gift a faithful church can give the world is to be different from it,[2] which is why:

- Churches become faithful witnesses *when they know who they are*. What we bring to the interface with our world is not a different set of propositions so much as a *different citizenship* and the radically different perspective it produces. I don't know how many times I had to remind my church members that we hold a dual citizenship: "I have two identity documents: one declares me a South African citizen by

---

deciding that the only way to resolve its divisions is to split apart can offer any healing word to a divided nation.

2. Which is deeply related to what it means to be *holy*, "set apart."

birth, but the second declares me a citizen of God's kin-dom by baptism. Following Jesus is about deciding which of those citizenships will have first claim on my life."[3] The American church must hear this too and choose. I recall visiting with a Sunday school class in Florida a couple of months before another US election. The pastor told me that it was his "brightest" class and that I was in for a good discussion. I gave a brief introduction on the theology of church and state, then sat back astounded as Republicans and Democrats in the class tore into one another. Soon I asked to be excused: "I'm leaving," I said, "I could have got all that on Fox or CNN, or any number of office watercooler discussions." Not once in the twenty minutes had I heard the name of Jesus, nor any attempt to bring his mind and spirit to bear on the issues they were discussing. Here was a reputedly strong church whose leading laity were incapable of thinking *theologically* about a subject as important as the future direction of their nation. Like much of their wider denomination, they suffered from a "balance of payments deficit," importing their thinking and opinions from the prevailing culture, rather than exporting the mind of Christ into that culture. Their birth certificates clearly had more influence on them than their baptism. These were *American* Christians, not *Christian* Americans.

- Churches also become faithful witnesses when they *learn a new geography*. We should engage the world like people returning from another land where the rules are not the same and people live differently with each other. In that land, we have seen the "peaceable kin-dom" that invites a transformed way of being human and of life together. Returning home, we see our own land with new eyes. Because of the contours of that other place—let's call it "New Jerusalem"—our *status quos* now stand out in troubling contrast, and we can no longer let them be. A new order—what Jesus called the Reign of God—must break in on our world, or we are lost. The prayer for that reign to "come on earth as in heaven" becomes our *raison d'etre*. We have visited God's future for our world and must speak urgently about it, embracing and embodying it, whatever the cost. That is what I saw happening at CMM in Johannesburg in the seventies and eighties: looking out at the glorious racial and cultural diversity of my congregation, hard won at the cost of so many white members, I would say inwardly, "Thank you God, your future for South Africa is already present in this place." We preachers are called to be the ambassadors of God's tomorrow, inviting people

---

3. The use of "kin" instead of "king" is a non-sexist preference to the word "kingdom" and a reminder that in Christ we are a family, not a hierarchy.

to explore it today and to live by its values, in defiance of the pain and brokenness of the now.

Such important geography!

Reclaiming the Public Square

Armed with these understandings we will claim our place in the public square. The prophetic tradition reminds us that the church is called not only to pastor wounded souls, but also to minister to the character of the nation. When "truth stumbles in the public square," often betrayed by politicians who see no further than the next election, it falls to the prophetic church to speak the truths about justice and compassion that matter most to God (Isa 59:14 GNT). Our presence may be questioned and even threatened by the powers but cannot be surrendered. Any notion that the first amendment of the US Constitution serves to "keep the church out of politics" is false. In God's economy, the tasks given church and state are different, but that neither quarantines the church nor immunizes the state. Far from limiting the church's right to address the powers, separation of church and state simply enables us to do so with more integrity because we should be unentangled from those powers.

However, the public square must first be *re*-claimed because it has been captured. Where it was once populated by prophetic giants speaking biblical truth to power on behalf of those Jesus called "the least," today there is a different breed: "court prophets" who legitimize the rich, the excluders, and the exploiters by giving them a religious face. They have no hesitation in playing the power game themselves and must therefore be properly named and denounced. The far evangelical right has become little more than a brazen political lobby: its sordid deals with Caesar and slavish support of Trumpian white nationalism disqualify it from speaking for Christ.

All of which underlines how important it is that the church's public witness be theologically, rather than ideologically, driven. Authentic Christian commitment to social justice is primarily relational: it is not born out of some cold political ideology but from gazing into the face of Christ and seeing there his suffering love for humanity. We are not called to be liberal or conservative, left-wing or right-wing people, but Jesus-imitators, reminding our hearers that because of him we can no longer accept that "the way things are is the way things ought to be." That is why the church cannot permit itself to be sucked into any party. Its moral power must arise from its disinterest in political power. When the SACC leadership confronted State President

Botha and his cabinet, we said to him, "Mr. President, you should listen to what we're saying because we're the only people coming into this office who don't want your job." We also told him that he should believe us "because we are present on the ground in places you don't even know exist." Churches located with the least and lowest speak with an authority that cannot be earned in any other way because they speak from Jesus' home address.

Discerning God's Concerns

If the American church was to be liberated from obsession with its survival and rediscover its true identity, its "home country," and its public voice, what might be some of the important issues addressed by this newly prophetic Body of Christ? It seems to me that there are at least five priorities with which every congregation ought to be wrestling—each one a gospel imperative crucial to the survival of humanity:

- *The first is the issue of wealth, poverty, and good news to the poor.* America's spiritual survival and its ultimate security depend on how it relates to the poor of the earth. Nothing blinds as effectively as riches, which may be why the only character whom Jesus honors with a *name* in any of his parables is Lazarus, the beggar at the rich man's gate (Luke 16:19–31). A prophetic church will take economics as seriously as Jesus did. It will do Bible study around his teaching about the "least of his brothers and sisters," asking, "What is Jesus saying to our nation about being rich when people are poor?" It will swat away the emotive "socialist" labels that predator capitalists use to intimidate any who seek true economic justice. It will lift up gospel economics as the plumbline measuring all of today's systems, especially those that permit a tiny percentage of obscenely rich people to control the world's wealth, manipulating the political policies that keep poor people poor. It will challenge our addiction to reckless growth and encourage all who are working to replace greed-skewed economic systems with ones that bring life. Until the lesson of Zaccheus (Luke 19:1–10)—that salvation comes to our houses only by sharing with the poor—is heeded, those living in the American bubble of plenty will continue to be alienated from the rest of humankind. Until money-obsessed churches themselves begin to live this biblical truth, they will not be able to proclaim it. As long as the church relies on the very systems it should be denouncing as antithetical to gospel economics, it will be silenced, settling for charity rather than justice. Its soul can only be truly redeemed if it finds authentic ways of reconnecting with the poor. At a dinner some time before I joined the Duke Divinity School faculty, I recall Duke's well-known theologian Dr. Stanley Hauerwas asking me in his point-blank way what the problem was with the American church. "You're too rich," I said, "Is that all?" he asked. "That's everything," I replied.

- *The second great issue is that of flag and altar.* During apartheid, South African Methodists banned the national flag from our churches because it represented a pariah racist regime. When we hoisted a beautiful new flag proclaiming our freedom in 1994, most people assumed that the ban would be lifted, but it stayed. They wondered why. "Our new flag bears none of the stains of the old one," they said. "Just wait," we replied. Sure enough, a quarter century into the life of our new democracy and our flag has already gathered plenty of grubby marks. But the reason for banning a nation's flag from places of worship goes deeper than the deeds of a particular regime: it lies in the essential nature of both church and state and the relationship between them. American Christianity, intentionally or not, often gives the impression that flag and altar exist in a reinforcing relationship, implying a mutuality between the gospel and the "national interest." Outside observers have even questioned whether for many citizens the US "is now perceived as a divine project" and "no longer a nation but a religion."[4] A rule of history—and surely of sound theology—is that Caesar will always be Caesar, and God will always be God. Some Caesars may be more just and humane than others, but their DNA remains the same and will at some point likely place them in contention with God. A prophetic church will do serious theological work about church and state. Instead of worrying about the word "God" being replaced in the Pledge of Allegiance, Christian Americans will be much more concerned about the Pledge of Allegiance replacing God in their lives. They will seek the appropriate "prophetic distance" to ensure that the church is not co-opted by the state. They will be clear that offering Caesar absolute loyalty is not patriotism, but idolatry. They will model the true patriotism that loves country enough to hold it accountable to God's demands for justice and compassionate fair-dealing, calling out its leaders when they stray from those priorities. We are not being kind to our congregations, our political leaders, or the nation when we avoid this issue.

4. George Monbiot, "America is a religion," *Guardian*, July 28, 2003, https://www.theguardian.com/world/2003/jul/29/usa.comment.

- *The third issue is that of violence and peacemaking.* We need to reclaim God's world from what Walter Wink calls "the myth of redemptive violence."[5] It is easier to live with the idea of war and even to believe it has redemptive possibilities when the real thing always happens to other people in lands far away. Only a tiny fraction of Americans today have known war up close.[6] Apart from the horrific attack on September 11, 2001, it is 155 years since any part of the US mainland experienced the utter horror and carnage war brings, which may be why nowhere in the world today is the myth of redemptive violence so uncritically promoted as in the US. A prophetic church will do serious Bible study about why Jesus named peacemakers, not warmakers, the children of God. It will repudiate the belief that you can save people by killing them, redeem a nation by destroying it, or bomb some other country into democracy. It will rightly question whether the allocation of fifty-five cents in every US tax dollar to the military is not a carefully cultivated idolatry, prizing the warrior culture above the health, educational, and economic needs of America's people. It will ask why this trust in might when the majority of US military ventures—even apparent "victories"—have failed to achieve their declared goals, leaving brokenness, chaos, and immense suffering behind them. It will study the growing body of evidence about how nonviolent campaigns and interventions by the peacemakers of the world have succeeded far more often than those based on military might.[7] It will help its members explore nonviolent direct action. A prophetic church will also engage honestly with the history of mob violence and interpersonal violence in American culture. Mob violence between 1607 and 2001, most of it by "native whites" who have rioted "in some way and at some time against every minority group in America," has caused an average of more than five thousand deaths and serious injuries per year for 395 years.[8] If those numbers

---

5. Wink, *The Powers That Be*, 42–62.

6. A 2020 census document indicates that roughly 7 percent of American citizens have served in the military but only a tiny fraction of those were involved in actual combat operations. See https://www.census.gov/content/dam/Census/library/publications/2020/demo/acs-43.pdf.

7. A study of 323 violent and nonviolent resistance campaigns between 1900 and 2006 showed that nonviolent campaigns are successful 53 percent of the time, while violent ones only succeed 26 percent of the time. Darian Woods, "The Magic Number Behind Protests," *NPR*, June 25, 2019, https://www.npr.org/sections/money/2019/06/25/735536434/the-magic-number-behind-protests. See also Erica Chenoweth and Maria J. Stephan, *Why Civil Resistance Works: The Strategic Logic of Nonviolent Conflict* (New York: Columbia University Press, 2011).

8. MIT Historian Robert Fogelson, *Violence as Protest: A Study of Riots and Ghettos*,

horrify, they do not compare with the deaths wrought by "individual interpersonal violence." In the twentieth century, more Americans were killed by other Americans than died in all that century's wars, including World Wars I and II.[9] A prophetic church will question whether the overweening culture of gun ownership is an idolatry of force over faith. In all of society, the followers of Jesus should surely be those working hardest to make violence extinct.

- *The fourth issue is that of inclusion and exclusion.* A prophetic church will confess its collusion over the centuries with the human addiction to division, "othering" different groups of people sometimes to the extent of destroying their lives. At the close of a seminar I led in a downtown UMC church in Michigan, the Lansing Gay Men's Choir was to sing for us, but their performance was held up for a while. The choir leader explained: "At the last minute two of our singers found that they were too traumatized to cross the threshold of this sanctuary. Coming here brought back all the hurt and rejection they had experienced at the hands of the church." By commission or omission the church has excluded not only people of different sexual orientation and gender identities but variously foreigners, refugees, people of other denominations or faiths, those it has decided are "unsaved," and the poor. Above all it has subjugated women and shared in the oppression of people of color. To justify each exclusion and make its prejudices respectable, the church has preferred to fixate on selective biblical proof texts rather than the wide, welcoming sweep of God's redemptive project in Scripture and the determined inclusiveness of Jesus' ministry. Prophetic churches will major in the ministries of hospitality, sanctuary, and reconciliation, joining Jesus in his insistence on journeying to "the other side." They will align themselves with the Holy Spirit who in the Book of Acts demolishes one excluding wall after another because "God has no favorites" (Acts 10:34—11:18). They will seek to be sensitive as the Spirit continues to probe with relentless hospitality those places in the church's life where prejudice continues to pose as religiosity. A prophetic church will seek forgiveness from those in its midst whom it has hurt and rejected as well as encourage greater openness to cultures and nations around the world who have suffered centuries of "othering" at the hands of the powerful "Christian" West. Its message to the excluders will be: "it is better to open your arms in joyful welcome to the 'other' now than to have them pried open sooner or later by the Holy Spirit."

---

quoted by Ira Leonard, "It's the American Way: Violence is the engine of US History. Why can't we talk about it?," *Hartford Advocate*, March 20, 2003.

9. Leonard, "It's the American Way," *Hartford Advocate*, March 20, 2003.

- *The fifth issue is that of seeking the forgiveness and restoration of creation.* It is hard to find language to describe the shameless plundering of the natural world by its human occupants, but even harder to explain our slowness to recognize what we have done. The planet is in deep pain because of us and may not recover. A prophetic church will repent of its past blindness and complicity in this respect. It will affirm that people, plants, and animals, and earth and sea and sky are bound together in a God-given covenant of interdependency, and that humankind has broken that covenant with almost fatal consequences not only for ourselves but also for all living things. It will denounce absurd "Bible teachings" that because the "end times are near," sustainability doesn't matter and unlimited exploitation of the earth's resources is just fine. A prophetic church will educate its people in the true biblical stewardship of our fragile home. It will expose and confront corporate despoilers of our shared planet while seeking to ensure that where the church itself has responsibility for land and properties, it will model sensitive care of creation. A prophetic church will make clear that none of the other pressing issues facing church and world have any hope of resolution unless the present destruction of the planet can be reversed.

What would happen if denominations invited their thousands of congregations to put aside much of their incessant, program-driven, member-entertaining busy-ness to involve their people—children, seniors, and everyone in between—in a commitment to spend maybe two full years doing Bible Study, praying, researching, robustly conversing, honestly confronting, humbly learning, and praying some more, around each of these five priority areas? What if real redemptive actions at local, regional, and national levels were to flow from this process? I believe it would transform every participating congregation forever. With each congregation becoming an informed center of gospel-shaped action, I have no doubt that the surrounding community would be impacted.

Unsurprisingly, I could see the actions flowing from this process adopting a shape the reader has come to expect by now. Congregations would:

- *Proclaim* God's lifegiving intention for these priorities, fearlessly naming the ways and places where that intention is being betrayed, *teaching* people to think theologically about them, so that their consequent actions are formed and informed by the mind and example of Jesus;
- *Bind up the broken* by following Jesus to the places where love leads: where the wounds inflicted by the world's domination, exploitation, and "othering" are felt most sharply, to bind the wounds of those sinned against by the powers, and stand with them in their struggle for justice;

- *Embody* in their life together the Jesus vision of hospitality and inclusion, seeking to be "visual aids" demonstrating how true community looks and feels, where burden-sharing is real and true *koinonia* brings lifegiving renewal;
- *Work* humbly with all—of all faiths or no faith—who "do the will of the Father" by seeking nonviolent, Christ-like ways to transform, or, if necessary, replace the forces that have disfigured God's good purposes, bringing God's justice and compassionate fair dealing to each of these areas.

These ways of being prophetic also transform worship. Worship is of course the beating heart of the church, but often one wonders what it has had to beat about. Worship should be where we come hungry and thirsty, crying out to be recentered in who God is and who we are, in deep need to be fed and mended for our work in the world, but it is too often a polite weekly ritual where the faithful come to re-establish their credentials with God, or simply to be comforted and uplifted. Comfort and uplift may be a necessary part of helping us make it through the week, but my experience has been that the more insistently a congregation engages with the issues closest to God's heart—like those above—the more focused and real its worship becomes. In such congregations, when God's people come bruised and depleted from engaging the powers and serving the least, their need to be fed is almost palpable, and it is in the encounter between costly ministry and God's grace that newness happens and the Spirit comes. We offer our work in the world and are met with a resurrecting, restoring, and redirecting Word, sending us forth alive, in-Spirited, and joyful again to "serve the Lord" wherever God is found.

And here's the thing: the reason why I am so confident that such an enterprise as I have suggested would transform every participating congregation forever is because none of the five priorities I mention above is about the church. Rather, each is about the world that God so loves. *That is the transforming shift.* For too long God has looked upon our ecclesiastical doings and asked, "When are you going to get that it's not about you? When will you get that my church is only the church when it is engaging and serving my world?"

And at last, we may hear God saying, "Church, I think you've got it—you could be a church that the world takes seriously."

27

Postscript: Loss and Gratitude

Loss

IN 2006, ELIZABETH AND I came home to South Africa. On our return, the MCSA gave me a final task to help transform the training of our ministry. Clergy formation was something I had become passionate about, and I was asked to head up a twelve-million-dollar project establishing a new residential seminary in KwaZulu Natal. I gathered a team, and we threw ourselves into designing, funding, and building a place that would seek to "form transforming ministers for church and nation." We finished the new campus in three years and named it Seth Mokitimi Methodist Seminary, commemorating the first black presiding bishop of the MCSA, whose life had modeled the kind of transforming ministry we hoped our seminarians would emulate.[1] It was good to be part of honoring his legacy and making my contribution toward the future of our church. I remained involved until the end of 2012, first as chairperson of the governing council and then as interim seminary president. There are now over one hundred seminarians in residence, with many more students enrolled in the seminary's distance-learning program.

---

1. As impoverished children, Seth Mokitimi and his brother attended school on alternate days because they had only one school uniform and set of books between them. He became a brilliant student and after ordination was chaplain at Healdtown College where Nelson Mandela fell under his influence. Later he was responsible for clergy formation and, in defiance of the regime's threats to confiscate the church's property in "white" areas if they chose a black leader, the MCSA elected him Presiding Bishop in 1963.

Seth Mokitimi Methodist Seminary campus

In the precious two years following, Elizabeth and I spent time together traveling internationally and within our beautiful land or simply enjoying our little cottage high above Cape Town's sparkling False Bay. In 2013, we spent seven carefree weeks in Washington, DC, where I preached and taught at Mount Vernon Place UMC just a few blocks from the White House. On the Fourth of July, Elizabeth got to see her heartthrob Neil Diamond perform live on the lawns of the Capitol.

In 2014, she began to be troubled by small *petit mal* seizures. We made a nostalgic road trip to the Eastern Cape, spending a reflective day in the tiny village of Salem where her forbears and mine had settled after landing through the surf on Africa's shores on the very same day in 1820. In the little Methodist Chapel they built soon after, we quietly gave thanks for all that had flowed from the sturdy faith those simple Wesleyan people had bequeathed to us. We also gave thanks for the widespread missionary and educational endeavors that flowed from there. Fallible those preachers and educators may have been, but because of them millions of black voices rise in Christian worship across South Africa today. Both Nelson Mandela and Robert Sobukwe were impacted by their spiritual descendants, and one of history's ironies is that a faith spread initially under the shadow of empire contained within it the seeds of colonialism's demise.

On the last day of 2014, we shared a quiet fifty-fourth anniversary, looking forward to the new year. Less than a month later, in the early hours of January 26, 2015, Elizabeth suffered a massive stroke, immobilizing her left side. We sped her to the hospital, and during that day nearby family were able to be with her. In spite of speech difficulties, she was also able to have precious phone time with those in Johannesburg. The last visitors that night were Gilbert and Jane, our friends from District Six days, and Gilbert led an evening prayer. Elizabeth was serene and beautiful, her smile all-embracing, her eyes bright. Around 9:30 PM, I left with a smiling "Goodnight" and promised that we would see each other in the morning.

Death came with a heart attack at 5:10 AM. By the time I got there the hospital had laid her gently in a private room, and because it took time for family from far away to gather, we were with her for most of the hours of that day. She lay utterly serene as we took turns to spend time with her, to grieve and pray and breathe our own thanks to her for her life of self-giving. I left her at about 5 PM.

It was a hard leaving.

Messages came from all over the world. This woman who always said she felt most comfortable in one-on-one relationships had reached a multitude. Most of them wanted to tell of some transforming encounter with her.

Under the shadow of Cape Town's mountain, a great congregation gathered in the stone church where her family had worshipped for generations, where she was baptized, where she met Jesus, where we first met and later married, and where we bade farewell to all four of our parents. It was a place soaked in generations of prayer and worship, and God had used it well to form us, nourish our souls, and tie us together. Elizabeth's simple pine coffin with its rope handles spoke of her simplicity of heart, the single pink rose laid upon it told our love, and a glorious free arrangement of her favorite flowers—roses, daisies, and roadside cosmos among them—declared the joyful freedom she had sought and discovered in Christ and shared with so many people.

Alan did the costly work of praying us into the service. A visibly frail Desmond Tutu said beautiful things of his friend and former assistant, and Jane and our sons each paid tribute. Eldest grandchild Simone spoke for Jessica, Frances, Sarah, Adrienne, and Scott. Then the liturgy took us to the inevitable parting:

> O God, all that you have given us is yours.
> As first you gave Elizabeth to us,
> so now we give Elizabeth back to you.
> Receive her into the arms of your mercy.

We had known each other for sixty-two years and been married for fifty-four of them. Carving a life after such loss is not easy, but our sons and the special people in their lives are good people who care well. When there is much to be thankful for, gratitude brings a balm that slowly overwhelms one's sorrow. None of us knows what happens after death, but I do know this: our lives in all their totality—from birth to death and beyond—are held in loving hands. I have never needed more than that.

Much, much later, when the time seemed right, I took Elizabeth's ashes to Knysna, the beautiful estuary town some three hundred miles from our home. That is where we two first fell in love. Whenever we holidayed there on Leisure Isle, Elizabeth used to take her morning coffee to a bench that looked out across the lagoon toward the Knysna Heads. It was her special, sacred spot. Now, just below it, in the warm embrace of a January evening, David and I waded out into the water, and I quietly released her ashes into the ebbing tide, to be borne out through the Heads into the ocean beyond.

Gratitude

Looking back on the sixty years since I began my active ministry, I cannot think of a more privileged time and place to have been alive, nor will I ever cease to be grateful for being permitted to play a tiny part in the story of my nation's long and painful road to freedom. I said in a sermon once, "If you want to know whether God is alive, don't go to the places of comfort and ease; inquire rather in those places where the fires of testing burn most fiercely," and I have found that to be deeply true. When I arrived to serve my first church in 1960, our land was a prison. The horror of the Sharpeville massacre had turned the future toward confrontation, tumult, and war. When I discharged my last duty fifty-three years later, it was in a South Africa free and finding peace. The cost of the years between was immense, not least for the person called to lead us to freedom: Nelson Mandela allowed his pain to be transformed into a gift, leading us in a way that made all of us want to be better human beings. Much has gone wrong since, but for a brief, glorious epoch we showed the world what a "rainbow nation" with that kind of spirit could look like. Only those privileged to have lived in *both* South Africas can testify to the almost intoxicating difference between them.

I am even more grateful to have spent my life serving this amazing community called "church." There really isn't anything quite like it. I'm tough on it because I love it so. The church told me where my primary citizenship lay. It introduced me to Jesus of Nazareth, nurtured my spirituality, helped me want to be different, and put me in places where I could be of some use. However, I do know this: there is the church of Jesus and there is this other thing that we keep trying to organize as if it belonged to us. The first is a community of hope, love, and justice that excites and challenges; the second is something of a boring institution obsessed more with survival than purpose.

I am also grateful for the Wesleyan heritage that shaped my discipleship. I believe that it has much to give to a needful world. At its simplest, it is about three priorities: introducing us to the life-changing, disturbing love of Jesus of Galilee, declaring what kind of world God wants, and birthing the kind of transformed people whose lives and actions make such a world possible. It sounds clear enough, but I know that given half a chance we Christians lose the plot and slip comfortably into a cozy, irrelevant pietism. That is why I am grateful for the anti-apartheid struggle. It galvanized us and called us out into relevance. It was because we forgot about ourselves for a while that our contribution had significance. I venture to believe that Jesus continues to implore us to focus first on "setting your mind on God's kin-dom and God's justice above all else" (Matt 6:33).

Maybe that is why for most of 2017 I found myself in yet another struggle, this time within my church. The MCSA had dismissed a lesbian minister from our clergy ranks because she dared to marry the person she loved instead of hiding in a secret partnership. Many of us saw the church's action as loveless and unjust—an apartheid based not on skin color but sexual orientation—with the church now the oppressor. She asked me to represent her in the last of a long series of hearings of her case. It was a painful privilege to do so. In the end, we failed to move the MCSA to a more enlightened position, which was very hurtful to her and others like her in our ranks and all who love them. I wrote to *New Dimension:* "The church we love will one day look back on its treatment of this remarkable woman and apologize with sorrow and contrition."[2] It will.

And so the struggle continues, not only for the hearts and minds of men and women, but also in religious and national institutions. Always it is about bringing our individual or corporate consciences into conformity with God's dream of a world of compassion and justice. The single lifespan given to each of us is our one chance to play a bit part in God's long love story with the world. If we hold back for fear that our effort will make no difference, we rob God. Playing our part offers no guarantees, nor will we have the last word, but—

---

2. Peter Storey, "Letter," *New Dimension,* July 2017.

You say the little efforts that I make
will do no good: they never will prevail
to tip the hovering scale
where justice hangs in balance.
I don't think
I ever thought they would.
But I am prejudiced beyond debate
in favor of my right to choose which side
shall feel the stubborn ounces of my weight.[3]

3. Bonaro Wilkinson Overstreet, "Stubborn Ounces (To One Who Doubts the Worth of Doing Anything if You Can't Do Everything)," in *Hands Laid Upon the Wind: Poems* (New York: Norton, 1955), 15.

www.ingramcontent.com/pod-product-compliance
Lightning Source LLC
Chambersburg PA
CBHW022002220426
43663CB00007B/924